FOREWORD

The reference to 'a little m' in the subtitle of this book may seem strange. It comes from the way in which the Church Missionary Society at one time indicated whether or not their male missionaries were married. A small *m* was simply added to the name to show a wife was present as well! And so, the missionary wives began to refer to themselves as the 'little m's'.

I am glad to say that the CMS long ago abandoned this usage. Now both spouses are named fully and both are regarded equally as missionaries working with the Society.

But in any case Marjory Stanway was never a small appendage to her husband. She is a person of grace and intelligence, who entered fully into the life of missionary service in Africa and into Christian ministry in every place where she has lived. And if it is true that a good secretary can triple the boss's output, it is a fact that Marjory made possible and enhanced enormously the ministry of Alf Stanway, whether in Africa, Australia or the USA.

Bishop Alfred Stanway was a remarkable Christian leader. His work continues to bear fruit across the world. The recent publication of his book, *Prayer: A Personal Testimony* (Acorn Press, 1991) is enabling a new generation to get to the heart of his ministry. The hallmark of his life was confidence in God and the standards he set were based on the character of God as revealed in Jesus Christ.

Although not intended as a full biography, Marjory has set about to write a personal memoir of her husband. We can be very grateful that she has done so and I have great pleasure in commending these recollections. They will illuminate the life and work of a great Christian of our time. Both Alf and Marjory would simply want this story to be an encouragement to others to get on with the practical task of living the Christian life. I am sure it will do that.

John Wilson
Bishop of the Southern Region
Anglican Diocese of Melbourne

ACKNOWLEDGEMENTS

My sincere thanks and appreciation are due to Miss Margaret McKechnie for not only typing the manuscript, but for her helpful assistance with research.

I also thank sincerely Sir Marcus Loane for valuable comments and advice, and the Reverend Kevin Engel and Bishop John Wilson who have given considerable help with the manuscript. Canon David Hewetson has given valuable editorial assistance which I appreciate very much, and my thanks too to Mrs Judith Savage for typing the manuscript onto computer disk and for editorial work.

Marjory Stanway
Melbourne 1991

ALFRED STANWAY

The recollections of a 'little m'.

by MARJORY STANWAY

ACORN PRESS

Published by Acorn Press Ltd A.C.N. 008 549 540 Canberra
Office: PO Box 103   Orders: PO Box 282
        Wanniassa   Brunswick East
        ACT 2903   Vic 3057
                                     Tel (03) 387 2675
                                     FAX (03) 387 5099

National Library of Australia
Cataloguing-in-Publication Data

Stanway, Marjory, 1915– .
    Alfred Stanway, the recollections of a 'little m'.

ISBN 0 908284 11 X.

1. Stanway, Alfred, 1908–1989. 2. Stanway, Marjory, 1915– . 3.
Missionaries — Africa — Tanzania — Biography. 4. Church of England
— Bishops — Biography. 5. Church of England — Missions — Africa —
Tanzania. 6. Bishops — Australia — Biography. I. Title.

266.36092

Cover Design: Gavin Van Langenberg.
Typesetting: Bookset, North Melbourne.
Printed by: Shortrun Books, Mitcham.
Map by: Ian Heyward, Canberra.

TO
MARCUS LOANE
WHOSE STEADFAST AND
ENDURING FRIENDSHIP
ENRICHED ALF'S LIFE

Alfred Stanway and Alpha Mohamed preaching in the Cathedral at Dodoma.
(Photograph by Ian Knight)

CONTENTS

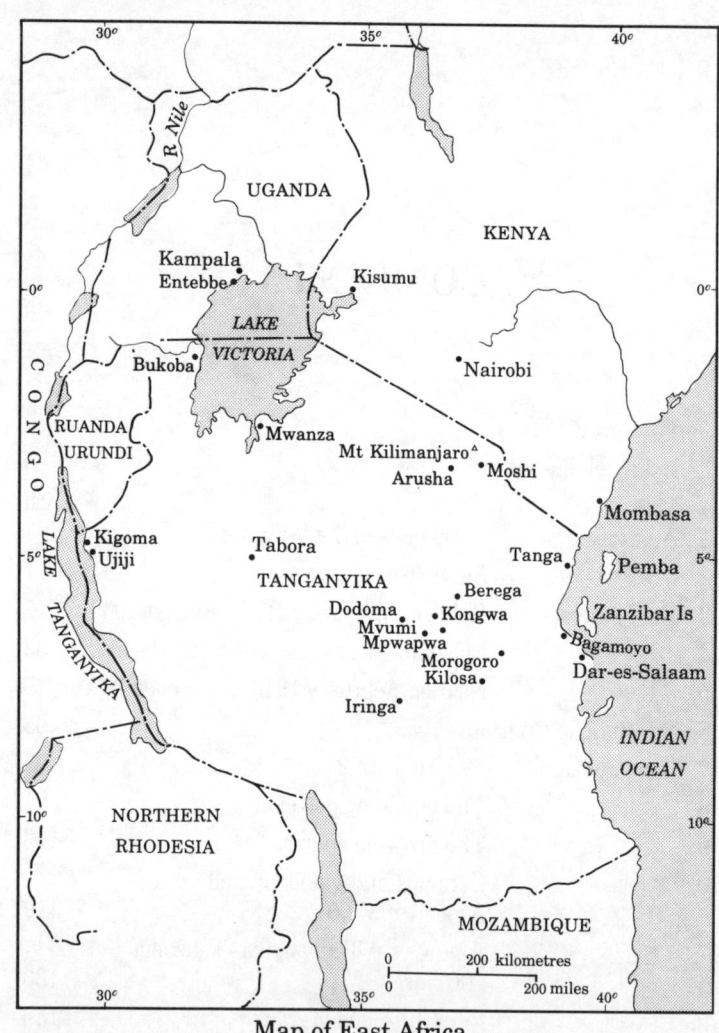

Map of East Africa
(with principal places of interest during the Stanways' ministry
1937 - 1971)

CHAPTER 1

EARLY DAYS IN THE WIMMERA

This is a book about Alf. It is not a biography. It is an attempt to depict Alf as I knew him from our fifty years together. It speaks of his ideas, his sayings, his achievements, all issuing from his dedication to do God's will, which was the dominating factor of his everyday life.

The Stanway forebears came to Australia in the 1850s from England. They were Cornish people from Truro and Falmouth. They settled on the south-east coast of South Australia at Millicent and were engaged in different occupations.

Alf's mother's people were Dawsons. (Bishop Arthur, formerly of Grafton, discovered that he and Alf were 'kinsmen': their great-grandfathers were Dawson brothers who came to Australia on the same ship.) They took up land at Robe on the south-east coast of South Australia. They were, and are to this day, sheep farmers on the same property. Alf's mother's brother, Robert, worked with the CSIRO in investigating the copper and cobalt deficiencies in the soil which affected the sheep's health. His mother, Rosa, was baptised, confirmed and married in the little Anglican church at Robe. Their marriage was recorded in the Millicent Times newspaper on Saturday, 5th May 1900. It says:

A Robe correspondent wrote on April 30th, 'This morning at St Peter's Church, Robe, Mr Alfred Stanway, third son of Mr Jas. Stanway of Millicent and Miss Rosa Dawson, third daughter of Mr William Dawson of Dingley Dell, Robe, were joined in the bonds of matrimony. The officiating clergyman was the Reverend R. Kenny, MA, incumbent of St Peter's.'

After their marriage, Alf's father, also called Alfred, came east to the Wimmera, and his brother went further east to Paynesville, as a pioneer there. This was over one hundred years ago. A story is

1

told of Alf's parents setting off on their honeymoon in a horse-drawn buggy. So starry-eyed were they and so oblivious of everything but themselves, that the horse was left to his own devices and eventually led them back home!

They were very different in temperament. Alfred was phlegmatic, calm, sensible and business-like. He was tall, six foot three in height, while Rosa just reached five foot. She was outgoing, emotional, musical and very fond of poetry. Alf often said of himself that he could feel the Dawson and Stanway strains fighting within him. He was easily moved, often to tears, but then the Stanway strain would take over and restore his calm! Their first home was at Salisbury near Nhill, where Alf's father managed the Kiata Hotel.

Five children were born of this marriage — Grace, May and Jean, then Alf and Gordon. Their father insisted that each child be given only one name and it must be short. It was a very happy home balanced by the good-natured common sense of the father and the care and devotion of the mother. Grace, the eldest, was like her father — tall, strong, disciplined and business-like, but also very musical. In later life, she and her Scottish husband John Balderston set up business, first in Millicent and then in Mount Gambier.

When Alf came along he was in a great hurry to get into the world. True to his nature he didn't give his mother time to get to hospital in Nhill — he was born in Salisbury on 9th September 1908. Fortunately his mother's sister Ida, a trained nurse, was staying with them at the time and she ushered Alf into life with a prayer. Thereafter she prayed for him until she died. In a letter written to him following his appointment to Central Tanganyika she said:

> My heart is still more than full of the little boy whom I helped into the world in the little house in the lane — a place so full of happy memories and oh, how proud Rosa was of her little son! Do you know you gave us all a shock by arriving there and then instead of a week later in a private hospital in Nhill. Your father galloped home and just wouldn't believe he had a little son!

Alf was called 'baby' by all the family until Gordon's birth eighteen months later. Then he graduated to 'Boy' and Gordon became 'baby'. Even when Gordon was called 'Gordon', the family and Grace in particular continued to call Alf 'Boy', even to the end of her life.

There was no local Anglican Church, so the Stanways worshipped at the Methodist Church. The children all attended the one-teacher rural school at Kiata. Alf started school in January 1914 at the age of 5 years and 5 months. It was a two-teacher school at the time: there was a kindergarten teacher as well as the principal teacher. Also in those days there were no motor cars, radios, aeroplanes or electricity. Alf remembers the coming of each of these things as modern marvels. Often, his father would carry him in his arms to see the great Adelaide express train go thundering through the night, not too far away.

Alf's memories of those days were of great teams of horses five or six abreast, mighty Clydesdales harvesting the huge wheatfields of the Wimmera. He and Gordon ran barefoot in the country and one of their tasks was to bring home the cows in the evening for milking. Each boy had his own large bowl of milk which stood at the side of the stove waiting for the cream to rise. This was lifted off for their porridge in the morning and the milk was theirs to drink whenever they felt thirsty.

Alf and Gordon had a special language of their own which no-one else understood. Whereas Grace, May and Jean were musical, Alf and Gordon were tone deaf. Both had speech difficulties. Gordon mixed up *r*'s and *l*'s and Alf stuttered badly: his thoughts came far too quickly for his speech. His father was however very patient and almost completely cured him of the problem. Throughout his life he found the letter *s* hard to sound and an *s* followed by a *p* was particularly difficult. In music he could recognise a beat, but had no tune recognition and if the national anthem was played, Alf would quickly guess it to be 'Yankee Doodle'! He often recognised hymns by the beat and concentrated on the words in hymns; his favourites were chosen for their **thought** content.

Years later in Africa, he spent his first Christmas at Kahuhia in Kikuyu country. He was with the Bewes' family who were all gifted musically. Alf shared in the singing of Christmas carols. Peter, Richard and Elizabeth Bewes were singing melodiously and little Michael was sitting on Alf's lap. At the conclusion Michael called out — 'Mummy, why doesn't this kind uncle sing in tune like everyone else?'. Alf was very chagrined to think that such a tiny child had tune recognition while he did not. Grace had tried to teach him to play the piano. His mathematical mind grasped the theory of the scales and enabled him to play a few simple pieces. One day he overheard Grace tell his mother that Alf's playing was like someone tapping a typewriter. It mystified him that Grace would call out from another room and tell him he had made a mistake — how could she possibly know without looking at his hands? Sometimes he would touch a black note out of place to find out whether or not Grace would notice. Of course she always did. He did not pursue trying to master the piano.

Grace helped in disciplining the boys. If they did not put away their toys when asked, they were confiscated. Alf and Gordon soon got the message. Later I discovered that Grace followed the maxim, 'a place for everything and everything in its place'.

Tree climbing was a favourite pastime for the boys and this brought great anxiety to their mother. On one occasion while they were climbing a tree near the house, their mother spotted them and appealed to their father to tell them not to climb trees. Pointing to the tree in question he wisely said, 'Boys, don't let me see you climbing **that** tree'. The boys perceived their father's meaning.

The boys very much wanted a bicycle and were told to save up their pocket money. Their father would put in as much as they did, and when they had enough, the bicycle would be bought.

Both boys calculated carefully and saved. On the great day when they had the full sum they called on Dad to buy a bicycle for them. To their utter joy he went to an inner room and brought out the bicycle and laid down the rules — no squabbling about turns or it would be impounded, and no squeakiness. Alf remembered how highly they regarded their father for having the bicycle ahead of time.

Alf remembered with less joy about being asked one day to bring in some kindling wood. He was sitting by the fire reading and pretended not to hear. When his father asked him why he did not answer his mother, Alf's reply was that he did not hear. Very sternly he was told, 'Son, don't say you didn't hear, say you didn't **heed!**'. He never forgot that lesson either.

Both boys were taught chess by their father, who played them without a queen until they began to beat him and the queen was restored. Alf and Gordon both became very good chess players. As an adult, Gordon frequently played blindfolded or over the telephone, remembering moves from the previous day or week.

As the Stanway children grew older, the family moved to Horsham and Alf's father managed the Horsham Hotel. It was here that Alf was prepared for baptism and confirmation at the age of twelve, in the church of St John's, Horsham. He was baptised on 21st April 1921 and confirmed by the Bishop of Ballarat on 30th October 1921.

When the girls had completed school in Horsham the family moved to Melbourne. Grace attended the Conservatorium, May and Jean began nursing training, and Alf and Gordon attended the Melbourne High School.

Alf's parents, 1900.

Earliest portrait of Alf, 1910.   *The schoolboy at Horsham.*

CHAPTER 2

MELBOURNE

When the Stanway family moved from Horsham to Melbourne in the early 1920s, they bought a home in Alphington and Alf's father opened a newsagency in Fairfield. They worshipped at St Paul's, Fairfield where the Reverend Arthur Mace was the Vicar. Melbourne High School, which Alf and Gordon attended, was at that time at the top of Spring Street, where the Royal College of Surgeons now stands. It was co-educational. Both boys joined the St Paul's Scout troop, where their Scout Leader was the Reverend Joseph Booth, later to become Archbishop of Melbourne.

When Alf completed his intermediate certificate examination he left school, being keen to make his career in the business world. His best subjects at school were the various branches of mathematics. He was a 'whiz' at mental arithmetic and usually scored full marks in Maths. He was aggrieved if marks were deducted for untidiness!

He began as an office boy with the Gas Company and then moved to the law firm of Hedderwick, Fookes and Alston as a junior clerk. He was very happy there and became a committed Christian during that period of his life. He started to study accountancy at night school.

One of Alf's daily tasks was to confirm that the outgoing mail contained the requisite legal documents, before closing the envelopes. Some aspects of legal decisions, especially regarding property and wills, remained in his memory and were to be very valuable to him in his later career.

He joined in the regular pleasures and entertainments of the youth of the day. He was fond of dancing. When I asked how he managed to dance with his tone deafness, he told me he could follow a beat. His worldly ambition at that time was to be successful in business or politics. He had a high regard for the Reverend Arthur Mace and he and Gordon were fairly regular in attendance at church and scouting activities. After a while, Alf became very dissatisfied with his lifestyle and felt something was missing but couldn't discover what it was.

On the night of 29th July 1928, he was sitting in church when a visiting preacher was announced. It was the Reverend C.H. Nash, who preached on the text from Luke 12:4-5:

> I tell you my friends, do not fear those who kill the body, and after that have no more they can do. But I will warn you whom to fear; fear Him who, after He has killed, has power to cast into hell, yes, I tell you, fear Him.

As Mr Nash preached, Alf followed his argument closely and decided to commit his life to God. At the conclusion of his address, Mr Nash asked those who were Christians to bow their heads and pray for those who were not. Alf told me that he knew instantly that he was now in the former group and so was able to pray for others. He was just a few months short of twenty years of age.

Shortly afterwards, he had a great desire to experience how he could live the Christian life more fully. He was reaching out for a deeper Christian experience, convinced that there was something more meaningful and of the fulness of God's Spirit than what he already knew. So deeply was he concerned, that he was moved to spend a night on his knees praying that God would reveal to him the secret of a truly victorious life. He opened his New Testament and these words seemed to leap at him from the page: 'One is your Master, even Christ' (Matt. 23:10). Here was the answer for which he had asked: the Lordship of Christ. He invited Christ to be his Lord and Master and he arose from his knees with great joy and peace flooding his heart. He was to become an enthusiastic evangelist, keen to introduce others to his Lord.

Just nine months after Alf committed his life to God, there occurred the most momentous experience of his life to this time. The Church Missionary Society produced an advertisement as shown.

Alf went to this meeting. It was a small gathering, but as Mr Long developed his illustrated talk, God was talking to Alf in such a manner that he couldn't keep still. He got up and walked about for a while to try and contain his emotions and response to the message. Finally he sat down next to a sympathetic person and burst out with: 'God is calling me to Africa!'. This printed advertisement for the talk he preserved for 60 years, and it is before me as I write.

From that time on, he became very involved in youth groups in Fairfield, and more and more active in the League of Youth of the Church Missionary Society. At Fairfield there was a combined Fellowship of Presbyterian and Anglican young people, and a tide of revival of spiritual power and enthusiasm seemed to arise among

CHURCH MISSIONARY SOCIETY.

ST. PAUL'S PARISH HALL, FAIRFIELD

IN DARKEST AFRICA
THE CHALLENGE OF TANGANYIKA

Moving Picture and Lantern Talk

by

Rev. R. C. M. LONG, B.A., Th.L.,

Home Sec., C.M.S.

Slides mostly from the camera of the Bishop of Central Tanganyika, the new Australian Diocese in Africa.

WEDNESDAY, 22nd MAY, 8 p.m.

TELL OTHERS ———————————— ALL WELCOME

COLLECTION FOR C.M.S.

them. Evangelistic campaigns were organised and open air meetings in the City, as were large rallies aimed at winning people to Christ, and back-up prayer meetings. God enabled Alf to lead many young people to the Saviour.

When he had qualified in accountancy he joined the Lawrence Publishing Company as its accountant. He acquired a great deal of knowledge about publishing and was introduced to the pitfalls in that field. He had a flair for figures and could add up columns of these quickly and accurately. Later, during his missionary career, as he checked mission accounts, he had a gift for spotting just where an error lay and was able to trace it and produce a correct balance. Sometimes he even solved problems by algebra, which always mystified me!

By now it was the early 1930s. The world-wide economic depression was at its peak. There were many unemployed people in Melbourne and those with jobs were anxious to keep them. At just such a time, Alf offered to CMS and was advised to undertake a theological course at Ridley College with ordination in view, as preparation for a missionary career.

In his own words, Alf has reduced this to writing:

The time came to leave the world of business and enter Ridley Theological College. At that time the great depression, which affected

Australia so severely, was at its height and unemployment was the highest ever known.

I had enough money for a year. The duration of the course was three years. I determined before God, having been encouraged by reading the lives of Hudson Taylor and George Mueller, that I would not tell anyone of my needs and trust God for all I required. Even so, stipendiary lay work which would help a little was hard to obtain. I ran out of money after one and a third years and sought the Lord in a manner that was intensified by need. After three days I was told of a post in Gisborne where they needed a lay reader. Would I like it? Would I need it? It meant £1 a week which was a princely sum in those days.

I told no-one of my need, not even those who were closest to me.

As far as I recall, only one person gave me something more than once, and the amounts were small. I walked to save fares and went without what I did not need, and found that all my essential needs were met. College fees had to be paid in full at least at the end of each term. I could always do this.

Then came the last day of the last term and I still owed £5. I waited for the mail, just a forlorn hope, but there was nothing. Perplexed, I went to see the Principal. He greeted me and told me he had good news. I had won a cash prize, the Gair prize for Comparative Religion. It was £3 for first prize. He said, 'Let me read you Dr Law's letter!'. It stated that all the other candidates were bunched together and none therefore was to receive the second prize among these fellows. So I was to receive the second prize as well, the further £2. 'Where shall I send it?' the Principal asked. 'To the Bursar, please', I replied and went down the stairs three at a time.

Such experiences as this strengthened Alf's faith and trust in God, so that in all his later missionary life he had great confidence that God would supply all the needs of the work in answer to believing prayer. Regarding answered prayer he quoted Archbishop William Temple who said, 'I have noticed that when I pray, coincidences begin to happen'. Every time a real need was met in this way Alf called it not just the fulfilling of a need but 'an experience of God'.

Alf enjoyed his three years at Ridley. He disciplined himself to regular study and kept regular quiet times, rising early in the morning to meet with God. He began to condense spiritual principles with easily remembered aphorisms which he constantly applied to himself and to others. One such was, 'No bible, no breakfast', and 'Pray last and get nowhere fast'. He was often asked to wake up other students who wanted to rise early. He kept this early prayer time all his life, even during the long years of illness. He was a 'morning' person, always at his brightest and best first thing in the morning. Conversely, because of his enormous output of energy, he needed a good long rest at night. He did not make long prayers at the end of a day. He could close his eyes at any time and anywhere for ten minutes or so of refreshing sleep.

He made it a practice never to take his burdens to bed with him. He committed these to the Lord and was usually asleep as soon as his head touched the pillow.

During the years after his conversion and for the remainder of his time in Melbourne, Alf was fully involved in all the activities of the Church Missionary Society League of Youth, whose watchword was: 'Whatsoever He saith unto you, do it' (John 2:5). He was Chairman of the Council for years and greatly influenced them into habits of prayerfulness, especially in decision making, and strove for unanimity in their decisions. He chose the right people for the right tasks. Great numbers of League of Youth members in those and subsequent years went to the mission field, mostly with CMS. One went to China with the CIM (China Inland Mission). Some of them have retired only recently. Even more members went into full-time service in Australia. I hesitate to name them lest I leave out someone.

As well as this, Alf was one of the founders of the Inter-School Christian Fellowship. This was a movement to introduce a voluntary Christian witness in the government schools following the methods used by the Crusader Union in the Private Schools. As Alf had a gift for devolving responsibilities, I found the Minute Secretaryship of this movement (ISCF) my task for a while.

Another of Alf's great interests was the Upwey Convention, affiliated with the English Keswick Movement and held in a large auditorium at Upwey in the Dandenong Hills. (In later years (1950) it was transferred to Belgrave Heights, where it remains to this day.) In December 1934, Alf was invited, along with Charles Sandland, to join its Council. To have such young men on the Council was quite an innovation for those times.

Alf was ordained deacon on St Thomas the Apostle's Day, 21st December 1934. He, with the other ordinands, had gone into retreat at Bishopscourt, and it was Archbishop Frederick Head who ordained him. He received a New Testament with the inscription:

'Be thou faithful'

'God is faithful'.

He went from his ordination to the Convention at Upwey. By this time, the League of Youth had bought a block of land, and a large marquee was erected on it as a dining area. This was the year (1934) when the famous Bible Scholar, Dr Graham Scroggie was leading the Bible Studies and the gifted evangelist, W.P. Nicholson was taking the evangelistic meetings. It was my first experience of a League of Youth camp, and of this wonderful fellowship of young people. I had been converted on 4th June 1934 and I was inspired by the teaching at the Convention meetings.

Alf was offered several curacies, some in Sydney and others in Melbourne. Archbishop Head advised him to take the toughest challenge, that of St Alban's in the suburb of St Albans, and St John's, Deer Park, assuring him that it would be good missionary training.

For some time, Alf had had a friendship with Ruth Crawford. She was a fine Christian employed in secretarial work. Her parents lived in Traralgon in Gippsland but she worked and boarded in Richmond and taught Sunday School where I did at St Stephen's, Richmond. Alf was later to become engaged to Ruth.

On commencing work in St Albans, Alf began to get the small congregation to come to church on time by starting the service five minutes earlier every week, until they were more prompt. The McKechnie family, regular attenders, declared they left home five minutes earlier every Sunday but even so always entered church to: 'Dearly beloved brethren . . .'. However, Margaret McKechnie — later to become Alf's secretary in Africa — was already there, as she taught in the Sunday School!

Alf found accommodation in the Hale household, where he was joined by John Alder, who had been converted under his ministry. Before Alf's coming to the parish there was combined Presbyterian-Anglican fellowship, a Christian Endeavour Society which met weekly in alternate churches. The Church funds were low and members of the Vestry wanted to hold a dance in the hall to raise money. Alf was against this form of fund-raising. Mr McKechnie said to the other Vestry members, 'If the Lord doesn't want us to do it, then don't hold the dance. You'll remember Jack Nash didn't like us holding dances to get church funds.' Alf was grateful for this encouragement and support. He did not therefore have to go public over a contentious issue such as this for church funds.

In the year 1934, Alf was in Sydney, and he met Marcus Loane for the first time in the grounds of the Gladesville Rectory. Neither was to know that this was to be the beginning of a deepening friendship of 55 years' duration. Although their careers were fixed in different continents, they maintained a regular correspondence and met whenever opportunity afforded.

When Alf had been at St Albans for a few months. he had a very searching experience. He sometimes quoted this incident when he gave convention addresses. I first heard it at Durban in 1941. He told of how he had to husband his resources when he first started to receive a salary. He needed an overcoat and had prayed about it but God seemed to be saying 'not yet'. One day he set out to attend the City Men's Bible Class. Mr Nash taught there once a week, always using topical illustrations and often with prophetic insights.

On this day, on his way to the class, Alf walked up Elizabeth

Street and passed by a men's outfitters called Fred Hesse. This shop specialized in sales and quick returns. Across the window was a sign which said, 'OVERCOAT SALE — NOTHING OVER 30 BOB'. Alf's attention was caught. He really needed that overcoat. But he had prayed about it and knew God was saying 'not yet'. He turned to walk on but a salesman at the door said, 'Coat, sir?'. 'No, sir', said Alf. 'Why not?' said the man. Alf replied, 'You don't have the kind I want'. 'Come in and look', said the man. Alf was tempted, walked in, saw just the kind he wanted and bought it. He put it on and went to the class. He sat down and bowed his head to pray but the words would not come. He tried to analyze the reason and all he could come up with was 'the coat'. He felt rather petulant thinking 'Why shouldn't I have an overcoat?'. However he told God, 'If it is the overcoat breaking my communion with you, please give me a sign and I'll own up'. Peace came, he prayed and the class commenced. During the study Mr Nash said these words, 'I would rather go without a topcoat than deny my Lord. Judas sold his Lord for a thirty bob bargain'.

You can imagine how Alf felt: very small indeed and very repentant, but this proved a valuable lesson to him. He never forgot it and in buying material things, he waited on God to get the timing right.

In 1936, Alf invited Marcus Loane to come to St Albans and conduct a mission for him. It was held from 2nd-9th February 1936. This was a very blessed time, with conversions taking place, and the friendship between Marcus and Alf deepened.

Alf told me about one of the happenings connected with St John's, Deer Park. It was his custom when he took an evening service there, to have a meal with the Ross family. Mrs Ross was a regular attender but Andy, her husband, made it quite clear that he was a non-attender and had no intention of becoming one. Alf replied that he would not put any pressure on him but that on the day he asked Andy to go he would do so. That day came some months later. After the meal Alf said, 'Come on Andy, get your hat, you are coming to church tonight'. Andy protested but Alf said, 'We have all these young folk coming down from Melbourne, you must make them feel welcome'. Andy took his hat, went to church and thereafter went every Sunday!

Alf once told me that if God had not called him to Africa, nothing would have attracted him away from parish ministry. He really enjoyed it and found it very fulfilling, perhaps the most fulfilling of a clergyman's life.

Early in 1936, Alf was advised to take a Primary Teacher's course at the Teacher's College. This was to make it possible for him to work on the mission field, where teaching grants were given by the government in East Africa. He was priested early in 1936, entered the Teacher's College in March and in May left St Albans to go to a curacy at St John's, Latrobe Street, assisting Mr Nash. This church was joined to St James under the Mission of St James and St John. Alf was delighted to be working with the beloved 'Chief' as Mr Nash was fondly called. Since his conversion under Mr Nash, he had had many opportunities to absorb his teaching and spiritual wisdom, and to wonder at the depth of his prophetic ministry. So those few months with him in 1936 were very valuable.

I was able to lend Alf some of my college notebooks, as I had graduated from the Teacher's College in 1935. I gather they dismayed him. At one stage he suggested to me that I should offer for work in Africa, where teachers were needed. I laughed and told him it would be about the last place I would go! My father had been working with the British Government on the projected Cape to Cairo Railway after the Boer War ended, and his stories of Africa were very off-putting. In fact, I was busy reading everything I could about China, all the Hudson Taylor books and everything that alluded to China in any way.

As it seemed unlikely that the Australian CMS would be able to support a missionary in the immediate future, Alf asked for his papers to be sent to CMS' parent society in London. He and Ruth Crawford announced their engagement in September. Their papers had gone to London and been accepted, and they were located to the coast of Kenya, where Alf would work in a Diocesan Boys' Primary Boarding School.

At the end of October, Ruth became seriously ill, was rushed to Epworth Hospital for immediate surgery on a Saturday, but died the following Wednesday. On the Sunday, Alf appeared at the door of St Stephen's Church Hall in Richmond where I was teaching Sunday School. Thinking that he was looking for Ruth, I said she hadn't come, but I didn't know why. He told me she was in Epworth Hospital and gravely ill following the operation. He asked how to get to the hospital and I said I would take him there. On the way he said he had been in church praying, and had read Psalm 37 and had meditated on the words, 'Delight thyself in the Lord and He will give thee the desires of thy heart'. He had tried to analyse his desire. Was it that Ruth should be healed completely or that she should see the Lord? He was trusting God's love to do what was right for her.

Her death was a deep sorrow for her family and Alf. Her friends in the League of Youth were shocked — we were not used to young people dying. Alf was given much comfort and support in the following weeks, as he completed his studies at the Teachers'

College and made his preparation for departure to Africa on Australia Day, 1937.

He had been appointed a member of the Upwey Convention Council in December 1934 with other young men, an unusual move on the Council's part, and he was invited to give one of the morning addresses on Boxing Day 1936. Since Ruth's death, Alf had been very concerned about a bachelor existence. He knew he could not cope at all with domestic things. He was in a dilemma. The time was still close to Ruth's death but he felt God was leading him to consider a possible partner for his future, so he began to pray and ask God for positive guidance. If his thinking was wrong, he prayed that God would reveal this, but if right he asked that he would be shown without doubt whom he should consider. As he prayed, his thinking was directed to Marjory Harrison. On the morning of the day he was to speak at the Convention, he was given a small Christmas gift with a distinctive card, about 3″ by 3″ printed with the words:

The Lord shall Guide thee continually.

Isaiah 58, 11

Was God telling him his thinking was right? If so, he prayed that his convention message would be blessed and God would confirm it, with signs following. He preached at the Convention on the text from 1 Samuel 15:22, 'To obey is better than sacrifice and to hearken than the fat of rams'. The address was very moving and as

he came away he was given another small gift enclosed in a card
exactly identical to the first one — 'The Lord shall guide thee
continually'. Isaiah 58:11.

Alf was always one to go straight to his goal, so he decided to
speak to me regarding the possibility of our marrying at some
future date. I remember he did a lot of talking. I asked myself why
it was that God was guiding Alf so clearly, while I was completely in
the dark? Eventually we came to an understanding to be unofficially
engaged, until such time as a marriage could be considered.

As I write today, those two identical cards are with me. To Alf
they were proof of God's clear guidance and the seal on our coming
marriage. Alf cherished those cards and that is why I have them
today.

CHAPTER 3

KALOLENI EAST AFRICA — FEBRUARY 1937–AUGUST 1944

Before Alf left Melbourne for Africa, he paid a visit to my father, who told him, among other things, that Africa was no place for a white woman! My father also told me: 'That young man fills the house'.

Alf sailed from Melbourne on Australia Day 1937, on board the P&O liner *Mongolia* bound for Bombay. A great crowd gathered at Port Melbourne to assure him of their prayers and to see him off. On board, he had good fellowship with other missionaries going to India. He spent several days in Bombay before setting out for Kenya. He was appalled by the poverty he saw on all sides in Bombay, and the sight of so many homeless people sleeping on the streets at night. He rebuked himself sternly: 'Stanway, you are a hypocrite! You are thanking God that he didn't call you to India!'.

About ten days later, Mombasa hove into view. It is a coral island surrounded by coral reefs, so the ships have to go into port on a high tide. Late February, when they arrived, is the hottest time of the year but, regardless of this, Alf dressed in a suit and wore a clerical collar. He was met by Kenneth Stovold, the Headmaster of Kaloleni School. Soon he regretted his formal attire and wished he had donned an open-necked shirt and shorts! The thirty mile journey to Kaloleni, travelling in a west by north direction, is over dirt roads, through bush country and past huge coconut palms, doum palms and fairly thick vegetation. *Kaloleni* is in the language of the local Giriama people; it means 'go and look'. On arrival at the station, Alf was made very welcome by the other missionaries.

Kaloleni is on slightly higher ground than the surrounding countryside. Formerly a look-out post, it had been built in case marauding Maasai should make an attack. Alf was pleasantly surprised at the well laid out grounds of the mission station. There was an attractive hospital building and nearby dispensary, both roofed with Bangalore tiles; neat school buildings and dormitories; a football (soccer) field and staff houses, in a setting of green lawns, croton bushes and flamboyant and mango trees.

A neat rondavel hut with a thatched roof was prepared for Alf, but he ate with the Stovold family whose home was adjacent to his hut. At night, the living quarters were sprayed to kill off mosquitoes which flocked in at dusk, and the lamps were trimmed. These were kerosene pressure lamps for the living-dining area and hurricane lamps for the sleeping quarters. The missionaries slept under mosquito nets which enclosed their beds like a small room.

The Kaloleni School selected boys from the small bush schools throughout the Giriama country. These schools were established by the Anglican Church, and served as places of worship on Sundays as well as schools on weekdays. The buildings were a simple mud and wattle type, but open and airy.

The classes consisted of standards 1 and 2, but there were three stages in standard 1, so that children from primitive backgrounds could be eased slowly from stage to stage. At first they were taught in their vernacular language, but by standard 2 they were being taught in the *lingua franca* — Swahili.

After standard 2 was completed, the next step was Kaloleni School, which taught from standards 3-6. This completed primary education. Many of the students were quite 'old'. Few knew the dates of their birth and most started to 'read' when the opportunity opened up in their districts. Only the very best students could go on with further education, as there were very few secondary schools in Kenya in those days.

Alf was involved in the church and school life of Kaloleni itself and in the whole of Giriama country stretching right up to the Sabaki River.

The routine of the day at Kaloleni commenced at 5.30 a.m., when the boys in the school drum and fife band marched vigorously around the football field, playing either 'Colonel Bogey' or 'Sussex by the Sea' — their repertoire was meagre! After that they drilled before the sun became too hot. Sometimes Alf had to be present at these sessions. School assembly followed after breakfast at 8 a.m. and then classes began. Alf taught mathematics primarily, but was involved in many other aspects of a schoolmaster's life. Instruction was chiefly in Swahili. English was taught as a second language.

Lunch was at 12 noon. When possible, the expatriate staff had a brief siesta after lunch and this became a 'must' for Alf. He could sleep for ten minutes and awake refreshed. More classes followed from 2 p.m. to 4 p.m., and in the cooler hours afterwards, football and sports were played. After the boys ate their evening meal, they had preparation work in the school library and then bed. Alf enjoyed getting to know the dormitory boys, and often had good opportunities for spiritual counselling at that time.

At dusk, the missionaries met together at Dr Allen's house. They sat on his verandah steps and had prayer together, arising out of the joys or problems of that day. The CMS Secretary, who lived in Nairobi, wrote to Alf and instructed him to learn the Swahili language and not the local Giriama. All the men and boys spoke Swahili fluently, since it was the major language of the Coast. The women heard it but would not speak it, because women of ill-repute were usually of the Swahili race, a mixture of Bantu and Arabic origin, and were Muslim. The Giriama were primal or animistic people, of pure Bantu origin. The church services at Kaloleni followed the Giriama Prayer Book, but the sermon was usually preached in Swahili.

In the church, there was a wheezy old pedal organ and a huge drum. As the organ played, the drum was beaten to keep the time. There was a hard-packed earthen floor and forms for seating. The men and boys sat on the left-hand side of the church and the women and girls on the right.

Alf was soon able to hear quite a lot of Giriama, though he could not speak more than a few words in it. As well as English missionaries Kenneth and Hilda Stovold and their children, there was Sister Amy Sparrow at the hospital, and Elinor Bodger in women's pastoral work, both from England. Dr Kenneth Allen was a Canadian and his wife, Ruth, American.

After some months, Alf learned that the nickname given to him by the boys was *Kitendawili*, which means 'riddle'. Why? Perhaps they could not make him out? He assisted Dr Allen with hospital accounts, no mean task, because the doctor often only wrote 'blue soap' on the cheque butts, with no amount shown and Alf had to go searching for the correct figures. Some years later he was called *Bwana Daftari* (Mr Accounts), so his fame must have spread in that direction.

On the following Australia Day (1938), our engagement was announced. It took a little while for my confirmation of this to reach Kenya, but when it did on 14th February, St Valentine's Day, Elinor Bodger, or 'Bodge' as she was affectionately called, sent him this little verse in mixed English and Swahili. A copy was also sent to me.

St Valentine's *siku* (day) was *karibu kwisha* (nearly over)
and the *mwezi* (moon) was shining *sana* (brightly)
when the *posta* (postman) his precious *mzigo* (load) did *fisha* (deliver)
nyumbani (at the house) *kwa* (of) the lovesick *bwana* (master).
Oh mail, *umeleta habari gani* (what news have you brought)?
upesi (quickly) the tidings scan.

Is the fairest maiden in Melbourne's *pwani* (coast)
Betrothed to the Reverend Stan?
Furaha kuu (great joy) on our Alfred's *uso* (face),
He *cheka(s)* (laughs) with bashful glee
His Marjory is starting to *pata* (get) her trousseau
tayari kuvuka (ready to cross) the sea.
So, *fanya haraka* (make haste) and *taja* (name) the date.
We *piga makofi* (clap hands) with thanks
That Marjory soon will be pulling her weight in
the 'm' *wadogo* (little) ranks.

So now we come to the place where I must explain what a 'little m'
is, as used in the sub-title of this book.

In those days of over fifty years ago, the formal lists of missionary personnel were based on 'who' the actual missionary was. If a
male missionary was married, his name appeared on the list as the
Rev. Alfred Stanway (m). That 'm' represented me! It meant he
was married and this was my only official identity. Many years later
it improved considerably. It graduated to the Rev. Alfred Stanway
(Marjory). But, in the meantime, missionary wives liked to refer to
themselves as the 'little m's'.[1]

Alf's Bishop in Kenya was R.S. Heywood, who was soon to
retire. Many years later, he was one of the presenting bishops, on
the day of Alf's consecration. He was succeeded as the new Bishop
of Mombasa by Bishop Reginald Crabbe, whose Diocese covered
the whole of Kenya.

At the end of Alf's first year, he had passed his first Swahili
examination and had to start studying for the second. This entailed
a tremendous amount of set work study: all of the New Testament,
two books of the Old Testament and several sections of the Swahili
Prayer Book. Missionaries were expected to pass the second
examination before marriage, so the goal of marriage gave him
great incentive to study. Unfortunately for Alf, Ken Stovold
became very ill, and he and his family returned to England. This
meant that Alf had to take on Ken's duties as well as his own. He
was assisted by some very fine African teachers, but with his
duties in the church and district, he was soon very busy indeed. He
grew very fond of the carpentry teacher, John Wilson Samuel,
known to all as Fundi John, a very talented craftsman.

---

[1] Extract from the Church Missionary Society (London) Diary for 1940:

Kenya Personnel

....

....

The Rev. Alfred Stanway (m).

At the end of the school year, Alf was preparing to travel up-country to speak at a 'Keswick' convention. He was in great need of a tailor for the new school year as the current one was soon to leave. The 'freshers' were taught to make their own white shirts and khaki shorts — the school uniform. They were barefooted. Although Alf advertised widely, no Christian tailors applied and he did not wish to employ a Muslim. He had to leave Kaloleni without this need being met and he was afraid that the burden of it would cloud his convention message preparation. He asked God to lift this burden from is mind. So completely did God answer this prayer that Alf forgot the matter completely until his return. He went to the office and saw his clerk, Joseph Hanjari and the anxiety flooded back. Alf said, 'Oh! Joseph, the tailor!' 'Yes sir,' said Joseph. 'He has arrived sir, and is in the tailor shop.' Not only was he an answer to prayer, but when Alf asked him his name he said, 'Hudson Taylor, sir'. He was a wonderful provision from God, a fine man with a fine wife. Alf praised the Lord for this further experience of God in his life.

During one school vacation, Alf made a special safari up north beyond the Tana River, with Canon and Mrs Butcher of Mombasa and the Reverend Wilson Kajoro, a fine Giriama clergyman. They went to make contact with a nomadic tribe of elephant hunters called the *Sanya*. Wilson had found an evangelist who could speak the Sanya language and took him along as well. They had a large white sheet to stretch between two trees as a screen and a 'magic' lantern worked by carbide. They planned to show gospel pictures while Wilson spoke to the Sanya in Giriama, and the evangelist translated into Sanya. Wilson was keen to play on the Sanya curiosity. They rarely saw white people and avoided those men sent by the Government to collect taxes. Wilson told them that these white men were very clever, they could make fire come out of water (using carbide) and could take out their teeth and put them back in again. Alf was not party to Wilson's suggestion but, as he told me afterwards, 'for the sake of the Gospel I took out my teeth (he had a top set of dentures) and they all ran away!' However, they soon came back and begged him to do it again. Then they challenged him to eat a roasted corn cob. This incident secured their co-operation and they gathered round to see the pictures and to hear the Gospel.

During these days at Kaloleni, Alf was beginning to feel 'under the weather'. He was constantly tired, and could not get 'on top' physically. One day he felt so unwell that he wondered whether he would be able to continue to work in Africa. He decided to read that evening's *Daily Light* portion, and on turning to it he read: 'Is it well with thee?'. The reading goes on to encourage believers when they are tempted to faint, and ends with the words, 'Beloved, I wish above all things that thou mayest prosper and be in health, even as thy soul prospereth' (3 John 2). The day in *Daily Light* was 12th November, and Alf took it as comfort from God. Although as it turned out he was a day out on dates, it was the right message for him! Also, the daily dose of quinine he took had been insufficient to suppress completely the sub-tertian malaria in his system. This was discovered and he was treated and sent away to the Taita Hills to stay with Peter and Elizabeth Bostock to convalesce. He never forgot this passage and marked it in his *Daily Light*. Every year as we read it, he was reminded of God's promise of health.

The Giriama people of the coast still live in their traditional lifestyle. They worshipped their ancestors. Whenever an animal was killed for food the blood was collected and poured on the graves of their forebears, as were food and beer offerings. Hyenas and ants usually managed to clean this up. Ebony sticks were erected on the graves, with cloth tied to them to indicate a man's loin cloth or a woman's *rinda*. They feared Satan and his power and placated him with prayer and offerings of food and drink. Charms were worn on various parts of their bodies to ward off evil spirits, and fetishes guarded their cultivated plots and houses. God was regarded as good but remote. Witchdoctors were in abundance and they preyed on people's fears and beliefs. It was a difficult area to win for Christ.

The very change of atmosphere of removing boys from this environment and placing them under Christian influence brought many to real belief in Christ. Alf made a habit of visiting the dormitories as the boys prepared for bed and found good opportunities to counsel them and witness to them for Christ. One boy, for example, told him that his father had carved out a great image and erected it in his hut. He spoke to it every day and offered it food, and prayed to it. The boy knew he would have to go home to the challenge of this situation and was very apprehensive and in need of the good counsel that Alf could give.

When Alf heard that I was about to leave Melbourne at the beginning of May 1939, he prepared to sit for his second Swahili written and oral exams. He had not been able to cover all the set books, but satisfied the examiners. They had regard to his lack of time for study and agreed that our marriage could go forward; so a date was fixed for the wedding at Kaloleni on Tuesday, 6th June. Some months prior to this, Alf had written to the CMS Bookshop in Nairobi and asked them to send me a Swahili Grammar book. Then he wrote to tell me that the book would be coming and suggested I study it as well as I could as it was the recommended book to be used in learning the language.

In due course the book arrived and I opened it eagerly only to find, with dismay, that it was wholly written in Swahili, no English at all! Later I realised that the Bookshop people had taken Alf literally. What he had in mind was *Swahili Exercises* by Steere, but understandably they took him literally. In later days, I advised Africans to try and understand what Alf was thinking about and then they would understand what he was saying. I learned to apply this principle almost daily to myself!! There was a happy ending to the story of the book I was sent. I never used it but kept it clean and nice and when we left Africa thirty-two years later what had cost four shillings (4/-) fetched 150/-! By that time the University was keen to buy it as it was out of print.

The time came for me to leave Melbourne and I travelled with three others destined for East Africa. Callon Wilkinson was returning for a second tour in Uganda; Grace Camm was to teach at the Butere Girls' School in Western Kenya and Madge Dunsford was to help with educational work in Uganda and to be married to the Reverend Kenneth Prentice the following year. It was the beginning of May 1939 and we left on the *Narkunda* with a great group of friends to see us off.

Marjory leaves Melbourne for East Africa, 2.5.39. (Photograph: Moviegraph Co., Melbourne)

When we reached Bombay, I received Alf's letter saying that the wedding date was 6th June at Kaloleni, and that he had ordered the invitations from Harrod's in London, to come by airmail. We trans-shipped in Bombay to the *Takliwa* and a little over a week later, were approaching Africa. On 1st June — Thursday — I received a radiogram in the evening to say 'Wedding Saturday Mombasa'. This caused quite a flurry since there was no reason given.

Next day we came into Mombasa very early at dawn, on a high tide and berthed at Kilindini. There was Alf waiting on the dock-side. He had told me he would be wearing a blue shirt; in fact he was wearing a white one! Later, when I asked him about this, he said the blue one was in the wash. My private reaction was, 'Aren't some men funny?'.

Alf came aboard and had breakfast with my travelling compan-ions. He explained that the rains had been very much heavier than anticipated and the earth roads were badly rutted. It wa. unwise for ordinary cars to travel on them and guests coming out to Kaloleni could be bogged down. It was thought wiser to have our wedding in Mombasa: Saturday the 3rd was the more convenient time for all concerned.

Our party of four stayed in the quiet but pleasant Palm Court Hotel near the Cathedral. That Friday afternoon, we went to Canon Butcher's residence in the Close for a prayer meeting with all the missionary staff. Alf spoke at this but I cannot recall now what the message was. Afterwards I chose the hymns for the wedding ceremony with Canon Butcher. The choice was restricted to those hymns available both in English and Swahili, since Alf's senior school-boys were to come in by lorry for the service. I chose 'O perfect love, all human thought transcending' and 'How sweet the name of Jesus sounds'. That night Grace and I went to dinner with Alf at Desmond Givan's home. He was to be best man, and was a CMS missionary clergyman engaged in school work in Mombasa.

Next day there were minor troubles such as having to press a lace frock with a monstrous charcoal iron (Callon did this), and having to find decorations for the cake I had brought out from home. Everything went fairly smoothly except that there was a mix-up about my getting to the Cathedral on time, so I was late and Alf, to quieten his over-active mind, read through all the collects in the prayer book! Canon Butcher preached to us from John 2:5, 'Whatsoever He saith unto you, do it'. He did not know that to four of us standing before him, that this was the text which had shaped our lives in the League of Youth in Melbourne. Later he told us he had been awake the previous night and had asked God for a message and this was given to him. Next day was Pentecost

Sunday and Peter Bostock preached in Swahili in the Cathedral. I could understand nothing, but one could sense God's presence with us.

Peter and Elizabeth Bostock furnished a cottage for us in the Taita Hills and there we spent our honeymoon. The next phase in life for me was settling into a Stanway lifestyle. The day started at 5.30 a.m., aroused by the school band. A servant then came and lit the big old black Dover wood ('one fire') stove in the outside kitchen (kitchens were outside because of the heat) and soon brought us a tray of tea. Alf departed to a small outside room for his quiet time. Breakfast was early. Quinine tablets kept company with the salt and pepper and as we had to take a tablet each morning to suppress malaria, by 10 a.m. our ears were buzzing with the after-effects! After breakfast, Alf read the *Daily Light* portion and we used our prayer diaries. Later we introduced *Broken Bread*, which I read. This is a brief commentary on the theme verse of the *Daily Light* reading. We have kept up this practice for 50 years and now I carry it on.

We then left for school assembly. This was a great help as it was conducted in Swahili and it was vital that I should hear the language as often as possible. After that I usually took Swahili prayers with our domestic staff. All this Swahili was overwhelming but it was essential for me to learn the basics as quickly as possible. I had a

Mombasa Cathedral where Alfred and Marjory were married, 3.6.39.

little desk in the sitting room and Alf insisted that I keep available on the top of it, my Swahili Old and New Testaments (these were in two different dialects), my Prayer Book, *Swahili Exercises* by Steere, and the English-Swahili and Swahili-English dictionaries; all of this was meant to catch my eye and entice me to study at every available minute!

Whenever I accompanied Alf to visit outstations, while he was driving he put me through my paces with the noun class concords and their agreements with adjectives, relative pronouns, etc. It was quite good fun and a great help to memory. I was surprised how quickly one could hear what was being said although it took very much longer to master the speech forms. This latter ignorance, however, saved me from cultural mistakes. By the time I knew *how* to say things I also knew *what* to avoid saying. Alf was excellent in grasping the meaning and even the inner meaning of what Africans were saying. He was fluent, but his accent was not good and he was prone to concordal errors, out of his haste to converse.

One day in the early hours of the morning, we were awakened by 'Spridge' (Alf's name for Miss Sparrow). Dr Allen was not well, and a patient had been brought to hospital with a strangulated hernia and she wanted us to drive him into the Mombasa hospital. Alf had a third share in an old A-Model Ford (called 'Dorcas, the kangaroo' — it was full of good works but a trifle jumpy). A stretcher was put between the flaps at the side of the back seat and we drove in the dark to Mombasa. The patient was moaning a lot of the time, but we delivered him to hospital and drove home. He made a good recovery. He was from the Pokomo country north of Giriama and some years later he walked out to Kaloleni to thank us for our help.

Alf decided to teach me to drive after we had been enabled by CMS to get a reasonable car — a Ford V8 — for our work. We went to the football field. Alf pointed out the mvuli trees (African mahogany) to me and said to avoid those but the pawpaw trees would present no threat! He evidently intended to teach me everything in one lesson — he said that was how he had learned. He explained the gears etc. and what to do and said how important it was to learn to stop. Then as I slowly started to steer the car around the ground he said, 'I am going to ask you to stop suddenly'. He did and I did. I took my hands and feet off everything and rolled slowly into an mvuli tree. It took me thirteen years to recover from that lesson. Even then I meekly submitted to letting him teach me once more — though we took several lessons to get over it.

When war broke out in September of that year, cars were going into Mombasa and not coming back. We had no radio and it was some days before we knew that there was a war on. The Government decided to give a radio to our mission station. It was the big, old-fashioned valve set worked from a battery. We put it on a table on the verandah, and when the news session came on in Swahili the announcer said, *'Jambo, watu wote'* (hello everybody) and to our delight the Africans who were gathered around solemnly said *'Jambo'* back to the box.

By the close of 1939, Alf was due for home leave. Three years in the coast climate was considered a long enough tour. However, because of the war, travel was inadvisable just then, so CMS decided that we should have a change up-country for three months in a better climate. We spent a month with friends on a coffee farm near Kapsabet in the far north-west of Kenya. This time was enjoyable and the climate bracing, and both of us spent hours in language study.

After that we spent two months in Nairobi, where Alf helped the Reverend Rowland Pittway, a Welshman, with African services at Pumwani and in the big church of St Stephen's, on the Station Road Mission Compound. This included a Lenten Mission. During this time we also made contact with several people in the Revival Fellowship Movement. In those days it was associated with the local Oxford Group movement, but they separated soon after, as the Revivalists felt that the Group did not put enough emphasis on the Cross. Up to this time the Revival had made little headway at the Coast but then neither had any other group.

Christianity and Islam alike met with apathetic responses, perhaps due to the health problems of the Giriama. Most of them had several illnesses all at once: malaria, bilharzia, worms, yaws and other maladies. While we were away from Kaloleni, Alf was relieved by David Symonds, an English educationalist who was a bachelor. When our three months break was up, we rejoined David at Kaloleni and we all shared the one house.

David and Alf were keen to keep informed about the war news so we listened to the 9 p.m. BBC news each night. David and Alf were very different in background and temperament, but each respected the other. In April 1940, David's fiancee, Eula Carr came out from England, flying to Uganda and then travelling to the coast by train. Very early one morning, David met her at our nearest railway station, Mariakani, and she stayed with Miss Bodger, a single lady missionary, until the school term finished. After this, they were due to go to Nairobi for their wedding. We four, and Miss Bodger, with a teacher, Japhet Mumba, set off by car for Mombasa. The road was wet and muddy and rivers flowed over the drifts; we could not get through until the waters subsided so we all spent many hours on the road that day.

After their wedding and honeymoon, Eula and David returned to share our house for a few months more. As David and Alf worked together in the school, they began a lasting friendship and we kept in touch with them over the years right up to the present. Later that year they were posted up-country and we were alone again until our home leave.

We left Kaloleni in January 1941, and after an exceptionally interesting voyage in the *Mauretania* between Colombo and Melbourne, we arrived home. My mother's greeting was followed by, 'that's the same old coat you went away in!' Indeed it was, since it was never cold enough for me to wear it on the Kenya coast. We had a great welcome home and it was wonderful to meet up with family and friends again. We were also able to be guests of Marcus and Patricia Loane in their home at Gladesville, and Alf and Marcus resumed their friendship and enjoyed long walks together. During this wartime period, our Melbourne CMS Secretary, the Reverend Lawrence Nash, had left to serve as a Naval Chaplain and Alf was asked to help out in the CMS Branch. The following is a quote from a CMS General Committee minute:

> During their first furlough in 1941 Alfred was of great assistance to the Victorian Branch. In May he was appointed organiser of a Temple Day the Branch planned at St Paul's Cathedral. On the 7th July he was appointed Acting General Secretary and this continued until 7th September. (The General Secretary at this time, the Reverend L.L. Nash was serving in the Navy.) He did a considerable amount of work re-organising the Branch finances during that period, and the Committee passed a special resolution of thanks on 1st September.

Our return to Kenya after this leave was a lengthy trip. We left mid-November and travelled to Newcastle by train. Everything was hush-hush in wartime and we did not know the next step until we were told to go aboard the *Themistocles*, an old World War One ship. Once aboard she turned south, then through the Bass Strait and on to Albany where she loaded frozen meat for England.

There were many young RAAF airmen on board en route to England. While in Fremantle, we heard that the *Sydney* had been sunk and a little later — when we were at sea — we heard that the *Prince of Wales* and the *Repulse* had gone down in the Indian Ocean. We had to carry our life jackets with us everywhere we went. Miss Marjorie Moulton, Dr Wellesley Hannah's fiancee, was travelling with us, going out to marry him. He was then at the Mvumi Hospital in Tanganyika.

We sailed into Durban harbour on Christmas Eve and disembarked there. Early in the New Year, Alf went north by flying boat as he had to be back for the new school year. Marjorie Moulton was able to get a passage, but I had a seven-week wait. Eventually I sailed in a little Chinese cargo ship which was carrying arms and ammunition to Burma. The month was February. It was extremely hot travelling up the coast and at night we were blacked out, so it was a great relief when Mombasa was reached. I could not get any transport to Kaloleni on arrival, but I sent a note by the *Daily Mail* lorry to say I was in Mombasa. I understand Alf was chairing a Teachers' Meeting when he opened my note. He said, jumping up, 'My wife's in Mombasa, the meeting's over!', and he and Ken Stovold came to Mombasa and took me back at once to Kaloleni.

There was a new young English surgeon, William Kirkaldy-Willis at the hospital with his Canadian wife, Peggy. Ruth Rampley and 'Spridge' were the nurses and 'Bodge' was still there doing pastoral work. She had lived on that mission station longer than any of us, and was very attached to her very old mud-brick thatched house. It was unsafe and riddled with white ants, but she loved it. Alf had been supervising the building of a new house for her, but as she saw it going up in concrete blocks, she disapproved strongly. It would be hot, etc., etc.

Alf wanted to get her out of the old house and into the new without straining relationships, so when it was ready he went to her and said, 'Bodge, what kind of offer did you make to CMS?'. 'What do you mean?' she said. 'Well, was it an open offer?' 'Of course! Anywhere in the world for Christ.' 'Good', said Alf, 'In that case you won't mind moving from your old house into the new one, will you?'. She agreed with a little reluctance.

About this time there came to the school two lads who were later to become famous. One was Ronald Ngala, who was to become a member of Parliament and a Minister in the post-Independence Government of 1963. The other was Thomas Kalume. He came from the Dakacha area in the very north of Giriama. When he was born his mother called him 'Kalume', which means 'little man'. His home was in a traditional tribal situation, in a beehive-shaped hut among uneducated people. He did well in the bush school, won entry into Kaloleni and applied for the baptism class. On interviewing him, Alf asked if he were a Christian believer and if so, how did that happen.

Kalume said that one day he was walking along a road when he came to a man who was seated on the ground reading from a gospel. Kalume politely stopped and greeted the man then said, 'What are you doing?' 'I am reading', said the man. 'What is "reading"?' asked Kalume, since he had never seen a book in his life. The man held up the book and said, 'This is a book, it is talking to me.' 'Is it?' asked Kalume. 'I can't hear it. Make it talk to me!' The man explained that was impossible. 'For the book to speak to you, you must go to the place where the book is' (i.e. school = *chuoni*). He explained to the boy that there was a little bush school nearby, but he would need his father's permission to attend. Kalume was very excited and his father agreed that he could go and stay at night with an uncle whose hut was near the school.

'So', Kalume told Alf, 'I went to school and I found the book was talking to me; then I discovered it was not the book talking to me, but God talking to me'.

In due course, Kalume was baptised 'Thomas'. He was a brilliant student. Alf taught him mathematics at which he excelled, and in his senior year I taught him English. He passed out with many credits, went up-country to secondary school, and then on to teacher training. Later he returned to Kaloleni as the School's Principal. He was highly regarded and was elected to Parliament as the Coast representative, even winning the Muslim vote. He was given a scholarship to America.

Kalume trained for ordination, was priested and also worked for the Bible Society, putting the Gospels into basic Swahili. We saw him only once again, when he visited us in Dodoma in 1961 and we reminisced about the old days. He told me he had used my grammar notes when he took on teaching English. Soon after this, he died quite young from a heart attack. He was a burning and shining light in Giriama.

Another boy whose life touched Alf's was Mashaka Birya. Mashaka means 'troubles' and he hated his name. He had a cast in one eye and maybe the name resulted from that. He decided to read for baptism and chose as his new name 'William Walter Wilberforce', thenceforth to be called Walter. In his senior year, he became very ill with empyema and of course there were no antibiotic drugs in those days. Alf visited him regularly in hospital. Dr Allen said he would have to have an operation to drain all the pus from his lungs if he were to live. He refused the operation. Alf tried to induce him to agree by telling him that he had a 'King's disease'. 'What, King Georgie?' Walter asked. 'Yes', said Alf. 'Did he get better?' 'Yes', said Alf. So Walter had the operation and slowly recovered and Alf prayed with him daily. More than thirty years later, Dr David Milton-Thompson, who was then the doctor at Kaloleni hospital, wrote and told us about an old man who was gloriously converted by Revival teaching. His name was Walter and he said that his teacher, Stanway, used to pray often for him when he was ill in hospital. We praised God for this late fruiting.

Alf used some unique forms of punishment in his school. Once when almost the whole school was found guilty of a punishable offence, Alf was having some building work done and needed large stones for the foundation work. So the boys were told to go and fetch three large stones each. They were to place them in individual groups where he would inspect them. If they were not large enough they would have to bring two more. The results were highly satisfactory and the offence was never again repeated.

All through our second tour I had been studying for my second language exam, working at night by the light of the pressure lamp when Alf was asleep. The two Old Testament books, Deuteronomy and Isaiah, set for the exam, were packed with new and unusual vocabulary but I should have done more work on the New Testament. However, I managed to pass in time to be told that we were to move to Maseno, in the far west and on the equator. Then, it was stated, we were to study the Luo language! This was the language of the Nilotic people in the Kavirondo area around Lake Victoria Nyanza.

The coastal people who were engaged in educational work, implored Bishop Crabbe to leave Alf for a few more years. He was getting the educational system working so well in Giriama country that they did not want to lose him. Bishop Crabbe told them politely that he was merely moving him from one part of the same field to another.

During our time of service at Kaloleni, Alf recorded two instances of God meeting a need we had which no others knew about.

During the war it became more and more difficult to obtain imported goods, e.g. motor-car tyres and inner tubes. The Kenya Government rationed what was available and car owners were sent permits for two each of tyres and tubes. The cost of these was 300 shillings (/-) and if the offer was not taken up by a stated date, the permit was cancelled. We needed these items but did not have the money so we philosophically accepted the fact that we would lose the permit.

About this time, our doctor was on holiday and Dr Norman Green came down from Maseno to relieve him. He knew nothing of our need. When the time came for him to return home, he asked Alf if he would cash a cheque for him for 60/-. Alf agreed and went to the office to collect the money. When he returned, Dr Green handed Alf a cheque for 360/-. Alf said, 'I thought you asked me for 60/- only?' Dr Green replied, 'Last time I was in England, a friend gave me a large sum of money. He stated which proportion I was to keep myself and what I was to give away. I have given away all but 300/-. I have asked God many times what I should give this to, without any guidance, but since I have been here God has been saying to me, "Give it to Alf Stanway, he needs it!" I cannot see any lack in your home but if I know the voice of God he is certainly telling me to give it to you. Do you need 300/-?' Alf then told him about the tyres and the tubes — another clear experience of God at work in our lives.

The other instance happened close to the end of our time at Kaloleni. Because of the heat and perspiration and continual laundering, clothes wore out very quickly and Alf had almost exhausted his own supply and there was no opportunity to replenish them. About this time an old Melbourne friend, the Reverend Reg Gray came to visit us. He had gone to live in England some years past and had joined the British Navy as a Chaplain. The Navy Headquarters were in Mombasa at the time and Reg asked Alf if he knew a reputable tailor to outfit him for the tropics, as he had only clothing for cooler climates. Alf took him to a tailor he knew in Mombasa who did superior work and Reg ordered several outfits, safari jackets and shorts to match in white and khaki drill. They were beautifully made and Reg was delighted, but almost at once he was ordered back home and had no need for them. So he parcelled them up and sent them out to Alf who recorded:

They were right for size, better quality than I could afford and a greater quantity than I had ever known.

Thank you, our loving Father, for the remembrance of this wonderful and timely gift. Each time we think of it we know you have broken into our lives.

We loved the Coast and the people, but the prospect of a better climate cheered me up and Alf always liked a fresh challenge. So, in August 1944, we travelled up country by car, spending a few days in Nairobi en route before going on to the West. Farewell happy days at Kaloleni, our first home together.

CHAPTER 4

MASENO
AUGUST 1944–MARCH 1947

The journey by car to our second Mission Station took us from the extreme east of Kenya to the extreme west, from the Indian Ocean to the great Lake Victoria Nyanza, a distance of approximately 700 miles. We traversed the coastal plain of the Nyika bush country, then began to rise to increasing altitudes the further inland we travelled. Up on the great interior plateau we reached an altitude between 5000-6000 feet at Nairobi. There we broke our journey and Alf conferred with the Bishop and the CMS Secretary, Mr F.C. Smith. On the next section of our journey we mounted even higher, coasting along the embankment of the Great Rift Valley, seeing the crimson of myriads of flamingos below on Lake Elementaita. The railway climbs even higher at this point to 9000 ft then slowly descends to Lake Victoria, a fresh water lake which lies in a great basin at an elevation of just over 3000 ft. Finally we reached Kisumu, then the Provincial Headquarters of Nyanza Province and an important port on the Lake (previously called Port Florence). A regular steamer travelled around the Lake once weekly, from Entebbe in Uganda to Bukoba and Mwanza in Tanganyika, then to Kisumu and back to Entebbe. The Lake is said to be the size of Ireland and it takes half an hour to fly over it in a modern jet plane. The Ripon Falls, tumbling out of the Lake in Uganda, are the source of the River Nile.

From Kisumu, the terminus of the railway, a small branch line runs out to Butere. The distance from the Coast to Kisumu is greater than the usual time zone of 500 miles, but the same time was kept throughout Kenya. When the sun rose at Mombasa, it was still very dark at Kisumu, and this was to affect us as I shall explain later.

Some eighteen miles from Kisumu, Maseno because of its altitude and despite the fact that it lies astride the equator, has cool nights but warm days, and we needed more blankets than we used at the Coast. For a great part of the year there were very heavy thunderstorms, usually around four o'clock in the afternoon, and we rarely needed to water our garden except in January, during the driest season. After the Coast we found this climate delightful.

We had been instructed to leave off taking prophylactic quinine because there was thought to be a connection between irregular doses of quinine and blackwater fever, and there was a history of this disease in Nyanza and Uganda. So we abandoned quinine until we left Maseno. If malaria occurred, we were to take large doses of it by injection.

The Mission Station at Maseno consisted of three sections. Furthest to the west was the hospital with its staff houses, etc., and contiguous to it was the prestigious secondary boys' school, second only in its academic record to the premier secondary school — the Alliance High School — in Kikuyu country. Our school consisted of a chapel, school buildings and dormitories, staff houses and a football field. A boundary separated the Mission from Government Offices, a Government Hospital, a Veterinary Centre and staff houses. Then there was a stretch of open country, and our house called *Sunrise* further east, a good mile from the hospital. Here the pastoral missionaries lived and it was set close to African villages.

The house was set in large grounds and was built to what was called the 'Uganda Plan'. This consisted of a very large and wide entrance hall off which opened five large rooms. The kitchen was a separate building outside, with the standard Dover stove fed by wood. We understand that when the house was first built it was intended for a girls' school. Africans in those days saw no need to educate daughters, and by the time they did, it was decided to build two girls' schools elsewhere, one in Luo country at Ng'iya and the other in Luyia country at Butere. So the house was occupied by a succession of pastoral missionaries, but had been empty for some time when we arrived. There was very little furniture of any kind and because of war-time restrictions, it was difficult to buy any, or even to buy curtain material. I remember cutting up two folk-weave bedspreads to make curtains for our bedroom. I also made other improvisations.

Our CMS Secretary on a subsequent visit authorized us to purchase four single bedsteads, two for us and two for guests, so little by little we made it a home. The central room off the hall became Alf's office, so he now worked from home, although he was so often away on safari that it did not have a maximum use.

Something which intrigued us on our arrival was the question of time. We were asked, 'What time will you keep?'. At the Coast, we were used to keeping Standard Time, and decided to follow that as all Government Departments and the Railway and the whole township of Kisumu did so. The hospital, however, kept to 'sun-time', i.e. sunrise became 6 a.m. This suited Africans. They kept suntime (without watches or clocks) and it was they who were to be considered when they came as patients — although even on the equator there was a maximum difference in sunrise of 53 minutes in the year. The School kept a steady half-hour behind Standard Time, whilst out at Ng'iya Station, Archdeacon Walter Owen, the most senior of the Nyanza missionaries, calculated meridian time at noon from the sun with the use of a sextant! This time factor had to be reckoned with. When people asked us out to meals we would say, 'Seven p.m. Your time or our time?'

To make the time issue a little more confusing, time in East Africa is calculated in the various languages as beginning at sunrise. So 7 a.m. in our time is 1 a.m. in theirs, twelve noon for us is 6 o'clock for them. This means their twenty-four hours ends just before sunrise, which affects the date of the day. What we call last night, they call 'the night of today'. We always kept our clocks at European time, but Africans could look at a clock saying 4 p.m. and call it ten o'clock, and we did the same if we spoke in their language. So what was 6 a.m. in Mombasa and daylight, was thick darkness with us!

Alf was immensely interested in large scale planning, and he began to study the distances between various outposts of the work, the boundaries of parishes and so on. A parish was the sphere of a pastor's work and could contain up to ten churches. Lay readers and evangelists conducted services and the pastor itinerated to celebrate communion. These parishes were established among the two large tribes in the Nyanza area, the Bantu speaking Luyia and the Nilotic Luo people. There were an estimated three quarters of a million Luo people in Nyanza, the second largest tribe in Kenya, and at that time the Luyia were thought to number around 700,000 people. There were many tea estates in that country, and there was a need for Chaplaincy work among the expatriate workers on these estates. There was no resident chaplain. Alf himself took services for them when he visited the estates, usually in a club house, and other clergy who were able to visit also held services.

The Luo work extended far south to the Tanganyika border, and some of the Luo Christians, who had no real knowledge of geographical boundaries, crossed over and established a church at Kowak in Tanganyika. They appealed to Alf for shepherding, but Alf had to explain to them that it was another country. So he wrote to Bishop Wynn-Jones, then the Bishop of Central Tanganyika, to inform him of this little church at Kowak and asked if they could be pastored from his Diocese. When Alf went down to Central

Tanganyika, he found his letter waiting in the (too hard!) basket, to be answered when possible.

The Luyia people had penetrated the Nyanza many years before the Luo. They were conservative agricultural people, and occupied the most fertile areas. Much later, the Luo came down from the Nile region. They were pastoralists but also engaged in fishing in the Lake. They were progressive and aggressive and of a sturdy build. They found it difficult to speak either the Bantu language or Swahili, and their grammar related better to English than to Bantu languages. Their words were short and disjunctive like English; their noun plurals were at the ends of the word, whereas the Bantu was agglutinative and the noun plurals stood at the beginning of the word. While the Bantu people coped easily with Swahili or Luo, the Luo people were not good at Luyia or Swahili.

This needed thoughtful consideration. Archdeacon Owen, the senior and leading pastoral worker spoke Luo and most of the council meetings for the Archdeaconry were in Luo, since the Bantu Luyia could cope with it. Alf thought it would be wiser to have these meetings in Swahili, as all the clergy did their ordination courses in Swahili and Alf himself could cope with it. So after Archdeacon Owen was no longer there, this occurred. Alf did not think it would be wise for him to spend a lot of time in learning Luo as he could read any prayers he needed to take in Luo, and preach in Swahili, which could then be translated by an interpreter.

I, on the other hand, settled down to learn Luo. Shadrack Malo, a teacher at the Secondary School, came regularly to teach me. He had spent a few years at the Coast and was fluent in English and Swahili. He would teach me by sometimes using an English or a Swahili equivalent for the Luo. The New Testament was available in the language and the Prayer Book, but no dictionaries at that time were comparable to what was available in Swahili. I felt that it was important for me to get a little Luo, as I would be going to women's meetings and they would be unlikely to speak Swahili.

There were three diocesan Mission Stations in the Province — Maseno, which was on the boundary of Luo-Luyia countries, Ng'iya in Luo country and Butere in Luyia country. Miss Pethybridge from Victoria had worked as a nursing sister at Butere for many years but suffered badly from asthma in that country and had been transferred to Nairobi, where she lived in an African location and did pastoral work among the women. When we were at Maseno, Grace Camm was the headmistress of the Butere Girls' Boarding School and Lee Appleby, also from Melbourne, who had lived at Butere for many years and was involved in school work, was now doing full-time translation work in the Luyia language. There was also a Teacher Training Institution at Butere staffed by English CMS missionaries.

A strange custom originated from Butere. When Alf began celebrating marriages, he found that people always asked to be married on Monday. This intrigued him and he made enquiries as to why they wanted that particular day. It turned out to have originated with a pioneer English missionary, Canon Leech, who lived at Butere. He was doing translation work and was constantly being interrupted to conduct weddings, so he made the rule that weddings shall take place on a Monday. He also made himself a room up a tree, where he could not be interrupted when working on translation.

At Ng'iya, Archdeacon Walter and Mrs Olive Owen lived. They had started their missionary career in Uganda. It behoved Alf to meet his senior pastoral worker Archdeacon Owen as soon as possible after our arrival. A date was fixed and we were invited to lunch. However, when we arrived I was directed to go and have lunch with Lottie Extance, a single lady missionary. I felt like a schoolgirl and not a wife, while Alf was 'grilled' successively by Walter and Olive. They were both exceedingly strong characters and were nearing retirement. Walter Owen was almost a King in this country. He came from Wales, was a gifted linguist and a scientist, and very interested in digging up fossil remains, but on the other hand he was a very liberal theologian. Olive was the daughter of a well-known authoress, Mrs O. F. Walton, who wrote *Jessica's First Prayer* and *A Peep Behind the Scenes*, a book I remember weeping over in my teens. It was Mrs Owen who ordered Grace Camm to let down all her (Grace's) hemlines , when she arrived as a new missionary at Butere in 1939! Grace did not even like sewing.

Archdeacon Owen allowed Alf some latitude to try out his views, especially regarding finance. When Alf tried to convince the clergy that there was a more effective method of raising Central Church Funds, Walter decided to 'give the young man a chance' to prove it. By the use of carefully accounted receipts, the scheme worked well and Alf was to apply it thenceforth. When the Archdeacon completed a large translation work in Luo that he had been engaged on for some time, he said to Alf, 'Stanway, it's finished', with great joy, like someone who had reached a long set final goal. He and Olive then set out for a holiday at Limuru. He took his manuscript and put it safely in the hands of the publishers, and on reaching Limuru suddenly died.

He was not replaced and as Lottie Extance was alone on the Station, Alf was asked to be responsible for her and the school from

Maseno. The diocesan powers-that-be, authorised him to take over the Archdeacon's files, which Alf of course, carefully read. He had done the same with the files that his predecessors left at Maseno. Whilst reading them, Alf noted that many of them came from the African Education Board in Nairobi and were minutes of its decisions. He thus retained in his memory information that was to have a startling result when he was in Nairobi some years later, as Secretary of the African Education Board. Alf had a fairly retentive memory for details, although he wasn't one to work at details himself; he liked the broad sweep better.

As well as the many Diocesan schools in Nyanza, Alf was in charge of some 320 churches. While Miss Moller, the headmistress of Ng'iya was still on leave, Grace Camm was due for leave, and as a berth aboard a ship to Australia just post-war was impossible, she was requested to take a short leave in South Africa. This left Alf with the responsibility of the running of the two girls' boarding schools — each about twenty-five miles from Maseno. A little later, the teacher training institute at Butere was added to the list. When Miss Moller returned from leave he quickly off-loaded the accounts, etc. on to her and she remarked, 'Do you need to let out the clutch so quickly?'. She was a fine Headmistress and a fine missionary.

Sometimes, I was included in gatherings of the clergy of the area, and when Alf wished to make a careful definitive statement which was important, he would say it in English and then ask me to translate it into Swahili, so that a correct minute was recorded. One of the senior clergy, Canon Yeremia Awori, often stood up to speak. He was very tall, well over six feet, and invariably, he would start to speak by saying, '*kwa ufupi*' (in short) and then continue at great length. His nickname was thus '*Kwa Ufupi*'. Another clergy-man, Nathan Sila Awor, spoke eight languages, and was a great asset in work in townships where many tribes mingle.

Alf helped to train Festo Olang', a Luyia who was a deacon. Festo had been in charge of educational work at Butere, and was an exceptionally fine man. Alf was able to procure a British Council scholarship for him, and he went to England for study under the terms of the scholarship. In 1955, he was consecrated Bishop in Kampala by Dr Fisher, the Archbishop of Canterbury. He was to become the first African Archbishop of Kenya in 1970.

The Revival Movement had penetrated to a small extent through Nyanza at this time. It became clear that the people affected by it accepted Christ in their hearts, rather than as a verbal acceptance. It led to a new morality, better living and in most cases a life-long commitment to Christ. Its members regularly met together for prayer, confession and hymn singing.

I remember an African who came to see Alf very early one morning. I had to tell him that Alf was not at home and was not expected until late afternoon. He said he would wait, so he sat down under a shady tree for some hours until Alf came home. He said that some years earlier he had been a patient in the hospital at Maseno and on discharge he had gone off with a hospital blanket. Since he had committed his life to Christ, he had no peace about this; his theft came between him and his Lord. But he had a problem, the blanket was worn out. So he produced ten shillings to pay for a replacement, then went off with peace, having made restitution.

As well as his wide range of responsibilities, Alf was always able to relax. He was fond of counselling others, 'Do not organise your life on the basis of extreme busyness. You must keep margins, even if these sometimes have to be used'. He was in his office by 8 a.m. in the morning, but by 4 p.m. he was ready to go up from *Sunrise* to visit colleagues at the hospital or school. We often dropped in on Cicely and Bertram Bowers. Bertram was on the school staff. They had four lovely children and Cicely and I shared common interests.

Sometimes Alf would play billiards with other members of the school staff — Lawrence Mayor, the Principal, Fred Ainsworth and Bill Lewis. On our way back to *Sunrise*, we often called on Peter and Madeline Akehurst. Peter was a Government Agricultural Officer and a keen Christian, and Madeline had worked as a travelling Secretary for the Inter-Varsity Fellowship. We usually drank coffee with them and Alf introduced them to 'Vitamin L' which he maintained was very important and only found in chocolate! From the Akehursts, we went home to dinner and an early night. Later Peter went home to England and studied for Orders and served in a church near Capetown for a few years.

During this time at Maseno, Alf contracted shingles in the nerve circuit surrounding his left eye, and up into the scalp, which was very painful. In those early days, there was an African doctor at our hospital and he was unsure about the diagnosis. He tried Alf with antibiotics, but they did no good. Finally Alf's eye swelled up, the lids were puffy and covered with blisters and he felt wretched. So he was driven one Sunday afternoon into the Kisumu Hospital. It was a one-doctor hospital, and as it was the doctor's day off, he did not see Alf until the evening. The doctor took one look at him and declared him to be a classic case of shingles. He brought a textbook showing a patient whose eye condition matched Alf's. The caption underneath read, 'patients complain bitterly'. At Kisumu he received good treatment and recovered slowly.

Five months after we left Kaloleni, I ran a daily temperature of

100°F but we could not pinpoint the cause of the trouble. Nothing showed up in blood slides, as long-term doses of quinine prevent the malarial organisms from appearing on a slide. We left for a holiday in Limuru and at the high altitude of 7000 ft with very cold nights, this brought out a crashing attack of malaria. Since I had long ceased to take suppressive quinine, the disease was now emerging. I was treated with a drug discovered in the early war years called Mepacrine, which sent my skin a bright yellow colour. On returning to Maseno, I had two more such attacks. The onset was marked by very cold fingers, toes and nose, and shivering. Blankets were piled on. Then came raging high temperatures and heavy sweats which left me feeling like a damp wrung-out cloth; but the fever left me completely and I never again had a bad attack.

Another time, Alf and I travelled to Kisumu from Nairobi. We had an evening meal at a *dak* bungalow at the Lumbwa Station. I sensed that the environment wasn't very clean. A day or two later I went down with a heavy attack of amoebic dysentery, confirmed by our hospital. So Alf drove me into hospital in Kisumu, by which time he had also contracted it. But the prompt treatment we received prevented it from becoming a chronic disease, or from spreading to other parts of the body (it could also invade the liver and cause amoebic hepatitis). Apart from these illnesses we kept very well.

We had a Hudson Terraplane car which served us very well, but it was rather skittish in mud, and there was plenty of that about with so many heavy thunderstorms occurring which affected the red earth roads. One day Alf left home early in the morning to open a new church in Luo country. They were to give him lunch afterwards and he expected to return before dark. He returned on schedule but that was a miracle where we again experienced God's intervention in a tight corner. He arrived at the church, but as he had never visited it before and as he knew he would be there for several hours, he looked around for a shady spot in which to park the car. He saw a good place where there was a thick grass cover, but as he parked the car, a concealed stone punctured the petrol tank. An inspection revealed that petrol was seeping out continuously, so he borrowed a basin and put it under the leak, knowing that he had now a major problem. He decided to put it out of his mind until the service was over.

While he was robing, two Africans came to see him in the vestry. They told him that his tank was leaking badly. 'I know', said Alf. 'We can mend it Bwana', they said. 'What?', said Alf, who knew the problems of welding a petrol container. 'Do you know how to mend a tank like this?' 'Yes, Bwana', they said. 'We are apprentices from the Railway Workshops in Nairobi, and we are home on leave and thought we would come to the service today. We can't mend it here, but if you permit us to take it home to our village where we have our tools, we can mend it all right. It may not be perfect, but you will be able to get home, and then next time you go to the garage in Kisumu ask them to inspect it for you.'

With a deep feeling of relief and thanksgiving, Alf entrusted the car to them and went to a very blessed service and a splendid lunch, after which the two men came back with the tank well mended, put it back on and poured back the petrol collected in the basin. With beaming faces, they saw Alf start the car and move off as though nothing had happened. On meditating on this incident, we saw how God had ready two black angels, with the requisite knowledge in the very spot where they were needed at the crucial time. We could not think what the alternative might have been. It was a long way from home and a long way from a garage. Alf would have had a long walk home and the car would have been stranded for weeks. It was a mighty blessing to us and a great encouragement. 'Before they call I will hear' (Isaiah 65:24).

During the blessing arising from the Revival Movement, converted Africans were concerned to regularise their marriages. The Luo people in particular were very polygamous, but their language had a special name for a first wife. As they were cattle keepers, it was a real temptation to them to invest the increase of their cattle in a dowry for another wife. Many were convicted and wanted to start life again with a Christian lifestyle and only one wife. Their problem could be dealt with by the Bishop only, but usually they were able to arrange other suitable marriages for their extra wives.

During our time in Nyanza, we had fellowship with Christian missionaries of other denominations in that area. There were some delightful American Quaker missionaries at Kaimosi to the North. Their African people were of the Luyia Bantu group. There were other missions, the Assemblies of God and the Church of God. We had an Inter-Mission Conference annually, when we met together on one or other of the Mission Stations for Bible messages, prayer and fellowship.

I remember going with Alf to the Quaker Mission at Kaimosi for one such conference. The Hoyt and Ford families became well known to us. Mr Ford once told me, 'Mrs Stanway, generally speaking your husband is generally speaking'. This was said with due appreciation of Alf, but it was an apt remark. Mr Hoyt told us of an incident which showed his humour. An African whose home was at Kaimosi, went a long distance away for work for a time. While there, he attended a Baptist Church whose missionary wrote to Mr

Hoyt saying, 'We discovered that so-and-so has not been baptised, so we have baptised him'. Mr Hoyt said, 'That's all right. We'll dry-clean him when he comes back'. I had not previously known that the Quakers do not practise baptism.

Around our home, we had a vast area of lawn. The house had two verandahs with a galvanised iron roof and tanks to catch the water when it rained. As there was a very large expanse of roof, and much intermittent rain, we were never short of a good supply of beautiful rain water. At the edge of each lawn was a wide herbaceous border, and the perimeter of the plot was planted with a large cypress hedge which needed constant clipping. Because of all this bountiful garden, made before we moved there, we needed to keep two gardeners. The toll on lawnmowers, the old-fashioned push type, was very heavy. Also the gardeners were constantly taking the mowers to pieces and filing the blades. They were not the best of mechanics, nor were we!

The garden gave us great pleasure, and Alf began to preach aloud his sermons to the flowers and birds. He used to walk up and down, with his faithful dog, Cobber, walking behind him. Eventually the dog would realise this had no future and gave up before Alf did!

One day, Alf went into Kisumu with a long shopping list of the groceries I needed. As we were eighteen miles from Kisumu, it was advisable to stock up on household requirements whenever a visit was made there. On his return home, he had bought two new lawn mowers and we inspected them with pleasure. When I asked about the groceries, he said he was so taken up with the mowers that he had forgotten to return to pick them up! We managed somehow or other.

By the time we were well settled in, Alf acquired a Luo clerk called Ayuo. He married soon after and some time later, he burst in on us to tell us excitedly that he had a little son, and to ask me for a loaf of bread. He wanted this as a gift for his wife. In those days bread to an African was like a delicious cake to us. However, we had run out of bread that morning, so my cook had made a fresh loaf and we were looking forward to having it with an omelette for our evening meal. I never gave away anything with more reluctance but Alf was not concerned — as long as I could rustle up something to eat he was happy.

Dr Bullen, an English doctor at the Government hospital at Maseno, frequently came with his wife to the English service in the School Chapel. As a rule Alf took these services. In our last year there, Mrs Bullen developed cancer and after an operation had to go to South Africa for radiotherapy, as at that time none was available in Kenya. This meant she was away for three months. Dr

Bullen was very concerned for his eighteen month old daughter, Gillian. She had a good *ayah* (children's nurse or nanny) but as the doctor had to be at work every day until 4 p.m., he did not like to leave her without some European supervision. He asked me to help them out. Gillian was brought to *Sunrise* each morning with the ayah, but was extremely unhappy in the unfamiliar surroundings and without her mother. So I agreed to take whatever work I was engaged in to the doctor's house, where I could be on hand to supervise. This proved satisfactory, but I was happy when her mother came back well and could take over.

Although our time in Maseno was only two and a half years, it seemed so much longer, as so much was crammed into the time. I sat for my first Luo exam and succeeded in passing. And, as happened when I finished my second Swahili exam, we were moved again! So it was off with the Luo and on with the Swahili once more.

We left in March 1947 for our second home leave. Alf went ahead to Nairobi to confer with Archdeacon Cecil Bewes, from whom he was to take over. Cecil was leaving the Colony for good, as his four children were ready for higher education in England. It wasn't an easy decision for him and his wife to make. They loved Africa, the work they were doing, and the people too.

We had an eventful trip home. After I had packed up everything and seen Desmond Givan settled into our house, I followed Alf to Nairobi. In Mombasa, we met up with Dr and Mrs Hannah and their son Lister who were to travel with us, and Winnie Preston and Faith Ward, nursing sisters from Tanganyika.

On reaching Colombo we found in this post-war year of 1947 that it was extremely difficult to obtain berths on any ship. The ships were not yet running to a schedule, so Alf and I decided to fly to Singapore to catch a ship which might have sailed already! We travelled on an Air Force York plane, not furnished for passengers. When we arrived in Singapore we heard that the ship, the *Marella*, was in port and due to sail for Australia the next day. British prestige was very low in Singapore in 1947, and we found it difficult to find accommodation for the night. Eventually, Alf managed to get into Raffles Hotel, by sharing a rather run-down room with three other men, and I found a room in the YWCA.

Next day, we boarded the *Marella* for home, and we arrived without further incident. So our Maseno chapter closed as we were expected to live and work in Nairobi on our return. On reviewing the Maseno experience, we found once again that the loving kindness of God had met us at every turn of the road, and that we had had many opportunities to serve Him and witness to His grace.

Alf had come to know his Bishop, Reginald Crabbe, much better as they journeyed together on many confirmation safaris. The uprooting was not as painful as was our leaving Kaloleni. Our time had been much shorter and in our living conditions at *Sunrise*, we had been more isolated from close companionship.

CHAPTER 5

NAIROBI FEBRUARY 1948– DECEMBER 1950

Our leave in Australia was drawing to a close. Alf had gone to the Upwey Convention in the Dandenongs just prior to Christmas. I had developed tonsillitis and followed later, when we both attended the CMS Summer School. After these events, Alf began to seek a passage back to Africa, but shipping was still unscheduled. The route via Colombo or Bombay was affected by the many British expatriates seeking shipping back to Europe following the Independence and Partition of India. Ships going via South Africa were few and far between.

I urged Alf to go ahead alone, as I was not well enough at the time to accompany him. Day by day he enquired at travel agencies about a ship. He was needed back in Kenya, as Archdeacon Cecil Bewes was soon to leave Nairobi, and it was advisable for them to have meetings together about the work Cecil was to hand over to Alf.

For several days, every Christian address Alf heard was about the ocean or ships! He attended a CMS meeting where the Reverend C.W.T. Rogers spoke on 'Toiling in Rowing', based on Matt. 14:24-25 — '... but the boat was now in the midst of the sea, distressed by the waves; for the wind was contrary ... and in the fourth watch of the night He came unto them'. Mr Rogers said several times, 'Don't worry about your ship. God knows all about your ship'. Strangely enough he said 'ship' not 'boat'.

Alf felt comforted by this message, and within a few days he secured a passage for one on board the *Misr*, an Egyptian ship which was going back to Egypt via Durban, then up the coast to Mombasa to pick up refugee Poles who wished to return to Europe. It was not a very comfortable ship, but Alf willingly took a passage on it and was farewelled at the Victoria Docks by family and friends.

On arrival at Mombasa, he journeyed by train to Nairobi and

went to the CMS Guest House until his own housing was settled. He was able to meet with Bishop Crabbe and discuss matters of importance, and as the Bewes' house was next door to the Guest House, he and Cecil had a very good opportunity to arrange a smooth take over.

Here I would like to say a little about Bishop Crabbe. He and Mrs Crabbe came to Kenya when the Bishop was over 50 years of age. The Archbishop of Canterbury had specially required him to work on a constitution for the Diocese of Mombasa. Since 1844, the gospel had been preached, converts won and churches established throughout the land, but as yet there was no officially approved constitution for the Church.

All missionary dioceses are extra-provincial, and are attached to the See of Canterbury. Archbishop Geoffrey Fisher wanted constitutions brought into being for these and nearby dioceses to prepare them to become provinces of the Anglican Communion. During Alf's tour of duty in Nairobi, he became involved with Bishop Crabbe and others in the preparation of the constitution. At each step of its development, it was returned to Archbishop Fisher for consent or alteration. Finally, the draft constitution was approved to the extent that Archbishop Fisher used it as a model for future constitutions. Later, when Alf went down to Central Tanganyika, he was also to work on a constitution for that Diocese, and for a model he chose that of Mombasa and was able to get the constitution into a form which was approved quickly because of the experience he gained with Bishop Crabbe.

Bishop Chambers of Central Tanganyika had joined with Bishop Crabbe and other East African Bishops in regular conferences. When Alf had been working in Kenya for some years, Bishop Chambers had thoughts of asking him to go down to Dodoma in Tanganyika to work but Bishop Crabbe had asked him to promise not to offer Alf work down there. Bishop Chambers kept this promise reluctantly. After he retired in 1947, Bishop Wynn Jones became the new Central Tanganyika Diocesan.

In early 1948, Bishop Crabbe asked Alf if he and I would occupy Bishopsbourne while he went home on leave. His daughter, Betty, was a statistician with the Government and wished to stay in the house. So Alf agreed and as I was not yet back, Miss Dorothy Bowlby, an elderly English lady agreed to be chaperon until my return.

When I was ready to return to East Africa, it was still difficult to get a passage. The number of British people leaving India had increased and there was a long waiting list of passengers for East Africa. There were several other CMS missionaries likewise waiting — Dr and Mrs Hannah and two children, also Lee Appleby and

Mary Newell. We were advised to send all our heavy luggage aboard the *Pemba*, a cargo ship. Eventually passages were secured on the *Moreton Bay* to Colombo, and from there we would have to seek onward passages ourselves. On the departure date in March we were all on board, ready to sail in a few hours, when our Victorian CMS Secretary came on board and suggested we disembark and wait for a more favourable ship about to arrive the following week. We all refused to budge. We had said goodbye to family and friends and the new suggestion was unthinkable.

So, without any further incident we left Melbourne and reached Colombo safely. As the Immigration Officer stamped my passport he said, 'Oh! I see you are going to Kenya. There is a ship leaving for Mombasa next Wednesday'. I laughed and said, 'I haven't a chance to be on her'. When we arrived at the Colombo Guest House in which we were booked to stay, we found the Pearson and Bakewell families there, on their way home to Australia. On the Monday, George Pearson volunteered to go to the office of the British India Line and register my name for a passage. He was told there were no berths available.

Then occurred what to me was the strongest example of the gift of faith that I have ever experienced. Without any evidence that it could be so I just **knew** that I would be sailing on that ship. It was an extraordinary feeling of a quiet confidence in God working out the implications. George went again the next day to the shipping office and was told there were still no spare berths. I set about doing my laundry and re-packing for Africa. The ship was due to sail at 5 p.m. the next day, so on the morning of the day the ship was to sail, I went to the office of the Shipping Line myself.

The officer who saw me said he had a berth, but it was near the engine and he was unsure whether to offer it to me or to an elderly lady. I told him to offer it to her, but he vacillated. Finally he said, 'You must get a clearance from the food control'. As he said that I knew he would give me a ticket. I secured the clearance, then went to the Bank and changed travellers cheques into local currency to pay for the ticket. I also went to the Post Office and sent a cable to Alf announcing the date of my arrival in Mombasa. Finally, I received the ticket and returned to a late lunch and announced I was leaving that evening. Everyone was astonished.

The end of the story is extraordinary too. Alf had taken over from Cecil Bewes as Secretary of the African Education Board and of the African Council (the executive body on the African side of Synod). In connection with his educational responsibilities, he had arranged meetings of local boards in Nyanza, Kikuyu and at the Coast. The meeting at the Coast was the day before my arrival, and he was to proceed from there to Kisumu the next day. This was perfect. He was able to meet me, take me up to Bishops-bourne and then rejoin the train for Kisumu.

Bishopsbourne was situated in the Kilimani (= on the hill) area of Nairobi, and from nearby, one could look down and see All Saints' Cathedral and other buildings below. In that area on Bishop's Road was the CMS Secretary's house, then Mr Willoughby Carey. It was near here that the new CMS Guest House would be built in the future, which is now known as the CPK (Church of the Province of Kenya) Guest House.

For some time, the diocesan authorities had been working on having all land titles for schools and churches in the name of the Diocese, instead of CMS. CMS was a foreign society. No African was eligible to belong to it, and in view of the increasing political awareness of the time, it was advisable to make the changes quickly. A political party called the KAU (Kenya Africa Union) with its forceful leader Jomo Kenyatta, who had studied in England and Russia, was getting a lot of press attention. The political stirrings were strongest among the Kikuyu, the most populous tribe in Kenya, but there were movements in Luo country as well. The Kikuyu people were pressing ahead to establish independent schools in their country — independent of Government and volun-tary agencies alike. So Alf was involved in title changes, and found his meagre knowledge of legal procedure from his days in a lawyer's office of great help.

Alf also had to give much time and attention to the Diocesan educational work, with its interaction with Government ministers and Mission Boards. He had good relationships with Government English personnel, often yarning about cricket, especially during the Test Match seasons.

Alf's office was on the CMS property, or compound, in Station Road. Mr Carey also had an office there with an office 'boy' (rather elderly!) called Melchizedek. Alf had a Kikuyu clerk called Par-menas. (I remember him mixing up his r's and l's as many Africans do. Once Alf sent him to me for a copy of the 'Rambeth Lipoti'. After a moment's reflection I asked, 'Lambeth Report?'. 'Yes', he said, not conscious that he had said otherwise.)

One day, an African from Kikuyu Country came to collect his Provident Fund money. His signature tallied with that lodged in the office. Alf checked the total owing to him and was about the write the cheque, but found himself unable to do so. He had what the Quakers call a 'stop', so he went to an inner room to pray and ask God 'why' he was unable to write the cheque. Then the light dawned. He remembered that when he was at Maseno reading up the past minutes of the African Education Board Meeting, the name of a man in Kikuyu country who had embezzled money from the church was recorded there. Their local board had ruled in these circumstances that he was not to claim any Provident Fund money. So Alf taxed the man with this fact and he admitted to it and left the office. He must have waited until Cecil Bewes had gone to try out his luck on the 'new chum', but this didn't work because God was in the circumstances.

While we lived in Nairobi, a new form of theft became fashionable. It was called 'pole fishing'. Most houses had expanded metal across the windows, but if the windows were open, a pole with a hook on the end could be inserted through spaces in the metal, and any garment lying around pulled through. Often at night when people were asleep their clothing was stolen. Men's trousers were particularly fancied as the pockets often contained money. One night Bishop Crabbe woke up to see his trousers apparently floating through the air, and thought at first he was dreaming, but the next second he sprang out of bed and retrieved the trousers just in time. What the thief did not know was that the Bishop had been an Olympic athlete in his youth and was still very spry. Thieves also sometimes entered houses in daylight and stole men's clothing from bedroom wardrobes. Again, trousers were the most fancied article.

One Monday morning, I was about to go shopping and decided to lock the bedroom door. I had not confided in the servants as to where the key was. During this time, Alf was approached to take the funeral of an Englishman. Bodies could not be left for long and funerals were often hastily arranged. As it was a Monday, the other Nairobi clergy were taking their weekly 'day-off' and could not be contacted, but Alf was in his office and agreed to help. He came home to get his robes, but they were in a case under the window in the locked bedroom. So he had to resort to 'pole fishing'. He found a box to stand on, and with the aid of a walking stick inserted through the fanlight above, he was able to hook up the suitcase and pull it through the fanlight window. I was very unpopular for a day or two but I reflected I may also have saved his trousers for him.

During our occupation of Bishopsbourne, Alf was too far from his office to go back at night, so we three ladies (Dorothy, Betty and I) coaxed him to read to us as we knitted or sewed. He usually chose a humorous book. I remember one such he read was Grossmith's *Diary of a Nobody*. Alf being a morning person was rarely able to sit up late. One night we all rose to go to bed, Alf leading the way. Betty and I were dealing with teeth cleaning, etc., but when I reached the bedroom Alf was already sound asleep with his head and shoulders on the pillow but his legs had not made it — they were still outside the mosquito net. I called Betty to see this, lest I be told the next day that it was a tall story. We pushed his legs in, and tucked him in, all without his knowledge. This gift he had of easy relaxation, made it impossible for him ever to seem to be under stress. It was a real gift from God.

During 1948 and 1949, the number of committees Alf was on amounted to over sixty, and he often had to travel long distances to sit on area committees. When Bishop and Mrs Crabbe returned from leave, Alf and I moved into the house vacated by the Bewes. We were able to employ an excellent servant through the Labour Exchange. He was a Luo called Ony'ango who was quiet, efficient and respectful.

The CMS compound was in a strategic position in Station Road, set around the huge bluestone church of St Stephen which could hold one thousand people comfortably. Next to the church on one side was our house and next to that the Guest House. In the centre of the plot were the offices and the bookshop, also single ladies' quarters, and at right angles to us were staff houses, where the Beechers and Pittways lived. There was also a Bookshop Manager and a few other staff members' houses. Alf saw to the administration of the Bookshop, in which he was vitally interested. In a letter to a friend dated 15th October 1950, Alf wrote, 'I re-organised the Bookshop and as a result made £5000 last year. The Publishing Department, my baby, made £1000 on its own. The turnover was 370,000/- and this year it will be higher'.

All through his ministry, he tried to 'get it over' to missionaries that they should always travel with Christian books in their cars. Later, after we left Nairobi, a huge new office block and bookshop was built. This was made possible as the Independent Government of Kenya wanted the land where we lived for Government Headquarters. With the compensation money, the Diocese put up a multi-storied building in the business area of Nairobi city for our work. It is now owned by the Anglican Province of Kenya and called Church House.

A regular weekly prayer meeting was held for all the CMS staff. Miss Pethybridge, who lived among the Africans in the Pumwani location, used also to come across and meet with us. Later in 1948, Bishop Crabbe appointed Leonard Beecher and Alf as his archdeacons. Leonard's citation was worded 'primarily but not exclusively' for the European work and Alf's was 'primarily but not exclusively' to work among Africans. They were also appointed Canons of both All Saints' Cathedral and the Mombasa Memorial Cathedral at the same time. They were instituted into these offices in All Saints' Cathedral and were allotted stalls there side by side.

The reason in those days for distinguishing between European and African work was a matter of language. The majority of Europeans could not understand standardised Swahili. Many spoke

All Saints' Cathedral, Nairobi where Alfred Stanway was installed Archdeacon of Kenya and Canon of the Cathedral, 1948. (Photograph: Pegas Studios, Nairobi)

Synod of Diocese of Mombasa, Nairobi, 1948: the two Archdeacons, Alfred Stanway (L.) & Leonard Beecher (R.), flank Bishop Reginald Crabbe. (Photograph: Kenya Information Service)

what we called Ki-settler, using the infinitive of the verb for all verb usage. Also, most Africans could not understand English, and they preferred to worship in a language they understood. Gradually over time, a few Africans began to attend the English services in the Cathedral and most missionaries attended the Swahili services.

When we moved to Station Road, Alf's office was only a few yards from the house and he was frequently tempted to go across there for a couple of hours after dinner if we had no guests or if he had had many interruptions during the day. If it grew late, I would lift up the phone to call him and remind him to come home. As it was lifted he would hear the click before the phone rang, and usually closed the call immediately and came home.

Alf acquired a splendid English lady secretary, Susan Ward. She was bright, cheery, outgoing and efficient, and was to prove not only a great asset but a valued friend, right up to the present time. He could trust her and rely on her absolutely and she soon knew how best to handle government officials. She was a happy presence in the office and used regularly to retrieve Alf's hat from the various places he had visited and generally tie up 'the ends'. After we left Nairobi she married Dr Hugh Sansom, a meteorologist with the Kenya Government and we frequently stayed with them on future trips to Nairobi.

The Government Education authorities asked Alf to find for them a qualified teacher, proficient in Swahili, to correct the vast number of Swahili history papers written by candidates for the KAPC (Kenya African Primary Certificate) examination. On the candidates' total performance lay the possibility of selection for the few coveted vacancies in secondary schools. Alf was anxious to help the Government, but he didn't look too far away — he looked at me! (I have mentioned previously that he was good at devolving responsibility!)

I quailed at the thought of marking at least 1000 history papers in Swahili! They offered 75 cents for each paper but this was no inducement (75 cents represented the old 9 pence — ¾ of a shilling. The currency is shillings and cents — 100 cents = 1 shilling.). CMS missionaries were not allowed to own land in the country where they worked and their wives were not allowed to earn extra to their husband's salaries. So with a great deal of reluctance, I started on this marathon task, which by dint of perseverance was finally accomplished. When the task was done, I was very relieved but delighted to be told that CMS had relaxed the rule about wives' earnings, owing to the stringency of living in expensive city conditions, so I was allowed to keep a portion of the grant.

We discussed how best to use this unexpected windfall and

decided that Alf should have a new suit. I had recently had a small legacy and was set up for clothes, but Alf had to wear a suit daily, as was the custom for people in business in Nairobi. He was gradually wearing out his second-best suit and had kept the best one for church services. We found a good tailor who made a suit to fit him and we were both delighted with it. Alf put it on and paraded before our neighbours. We were reduced to laughter when Dorothy Pittway called out to her husband, 'Rowland, do come and see Alf, all wrapped up in his wife's history papers!'. Nairobi was the first place in which we had electricity in our home so we were able to have a small refrigerator, quite a luxury then.

Alf was often free to take chaplaincy services on Sundays in centres such as Limuru, Karen, Kabete, Machakos, and Nakuru. From his early days in the ministry, he made it a habit to be in church and usually robed, twenty minutes before the start of the service. You can imagine how I was organised to be ready too! I remember going with him to spend a weekend at Machakos, where he preached from Matthew 4:4, 'Man shall not live by bread alone, but by every word that proceedeth out of the mouth of God'. He stressed **every**, we are not free to discriminate which Scriptures we shall choose. We cannot accept our Lord's teaching on marriage and not his teaching on money, or his teaching on money and not on marriage. We must accept **every** word.

On another occasion we stayed with the Percival family. He had been a noted 'White Hunter', and on entering their dining room, dozens of heads of different animals mounted on plaques looked down on us. It was an eerie feeling eating in their presence.

Bill Kirkaldy-Willis and Dr Allen, both of whom worked with us at Kaloleni, were now in Nairobi and it was good to renew our friendship with them. Alf also came to know Carey Francis very well. He was an outstanding teacher and a bachelor. Alf admired him very much for his Christian qualities. He was a Cambridge Wrangler and a great disciplinarian. He was Principal of the premier secondary school in Kenya, the Alliance High School. He was honoured and respected by the boys whom he taught, and they never forgot him when they grew up. Sometimes Alf would go out to Kikuyu to preach in the School Chapel which he always enjoyed and we usually had lunch with Carey afterwards. He and Alf enjoyed their conversation and sometimes I felt as though I could tiptoe out and not be missed!

We entertained many visitors when we lived in Station Road. Among those who came were Canon Max and Mary Warren, General Secretary of CMS England; Bishop Stephen Neill and the Reverend Clive Kerle, then General Secretary of the NSW Branch of CMS. In September 1950, Marcus Loane came also.

Alf and I used to relax by taking a quick trip out to Embakasi, a few miles out of Nairobi, to the Game Park. This was a natural park where most of the African animals — except elephants — were to be seen. Alf came to know all the routes and paths in the park and we came to know all the habits of the various prides of lions which hunted there. One lion was universally known as 'Spiv' but Alf had names for the others too. I can remember one whom he called 'Old George'.

One day we took Bishop Stephen Neill to the Park. Alf kept up a running commentary on the animals and pointed out the lions by name. Bishop Neill later wrote in a church newspaper that the Archdeacon 'knew his lions'. It was a wonderful relaxation and we came to understand how the lions stalk and hunt their prey. Contrary to popular belief, they do not roar when they are hungry and hunting, as that would frighten away their prey. When they roar it is to establish their territorial rights; it is as if to say 'I have arrived'.

Once Max Wiggins, with whom we were to work in Dodoma, heard lions roaring not far away. He asked the African pastor who lived nearby if he were not afraid? 'Oh, no' said the pastor, 'don't worry when he roars, but when he grunts "ugh, ugh, ugh", then you must watch out'.

We would see a male lion make a diversion by allowing himself to be seen by a group of animals. As he was running, his flanks were heaving and caused the 'ugh, ugh' as the air was expelled from his lungs. The game would all look at the lion to see where he would move next. In the meantime the lioness was crawling on her belly downwind from the game. When she was within reach of a short run, she would spring up and with incredible speed hurl herself on the back of the quarry, already marked out, then swing around to the jugular vein and make the kill. Once the prey was killed the male lion moved in and ate first, followed by the lioness and the cubs. After that, the waiting circle of hyenas and jackals would follow with the vultures, and last of all the ants, so that nothing was left but a heap of bones.

During the time of political unrest in the surrounding Kikuyu country, the Revival Movement was holding huge conventions in various centres around Nairobi. Thousands would gather out in the open, seated on the grass, and the preaching would begin. Sometimes there would be translation into two or three languages, with the people of each language group seated near its translator, while minor language groups would have 'whisperers' translating for them. It all seemed highly organised, and yet there was no evidence of the kind of careful planning that Europeans seem to need to get results. Sometimes in the background there would be huge clay pots on 3-stone fires, and enough food would be cooked to feed the multitude afterwards. Many Africans came to new life in Christ through Conventions like this, and were to hazard their all in the Mau Mau rebellion.

Alf and I had three experiences of looking after missionaries' children. Peter and Elizabeth Bostock paid a brief visit to England and left their twin daughters with us. They — Joy and Jane — were also our godchildren. Alf delivered little sermonettes to them at bedtime and heard their prayers. They used to watch me preparing food and said, 'Our mother doesn't do it like that!' Apparently, when they went home they said it in reverse, 'Auntie Marj doesn't do it like that!'

Another time, the boarding section of the European school was closed. Lessons were available for day children, so David Bowers from Maseno and Arthur Langford-Smith, came to stay with us. Arthur was obliged to write home, but there was little in his letter except 'I like it here, the breakfasts are good, the lunches are good, the dinners are good'. That about filled the page but it taught me how important little boys' stomachs are.

The next child to stay with us was Tony Bowers, David's brother, who had contracted typhoid fever on a half-term holiday. He had recovered but was producing positive tests, and was not allowed to travel home with his parents when they went on leave. When his tests were negative, I took him up to Naivasha and put him on the flying boat for England. He arrived safely, carrying the largest pineapple I could find in the Nairobi market.

When Clive Kerle had visited Tanganyika in the early months of 1950, he came up to us afterwards with the news that Bishop Wynn Jones was seriously ill in Dar-es-Salaam hospital. He died there in May, and it was a heavy blow for the Diocese of Central Tanganyika, a great loss to all who knew him. In mid-September, Sue Ward came bustling into Alf's office with the news that there were two airletters for him from the Archbishop of Canterbury. Alf took them and came over to our house to read them. They were dated 11th September 1950.

Among other things the Archbishop said:

> Lambeth Palace SE1
>
> . . . I am going to invite you to allow me to appoint you Bishop and in so doing I am going to make a condition.
>
> I am entirely satisfied that it is right to call you to this office. You will command the confidence of the missionaries and natives in Central Tanganyika; you will command the confidence of Australia; you have had valuable experience; you have a good knowledge of Swahili; great gifts as an evangelist; first rate powers as an administrator, the zeal and love and wisdom to make you a Father in God . . .

the call comes to you now and I do not hesitate to put it.

Now for the condition. It is that before you take up your office you should spend three months in this country . . . it is important that you should have first-hand knowledge of the people who shape policy whether in things civil or ecclesiastical in this country. It is important that you should get to know the Church of England and some of its leading persons so that you can understand the various facets of our Church life and of its relations to the Anglican Church in East Africa and indeed in West Africa as well . . . for these purposes and more I think that you and your wife should come to England. The experience I believe would be an immense help to both of you and also of immense help to us in every way . . . I have already arranged a consecration of Bishops on February 2nd . . . this is the first occasion on which I could consecrate you and it would be a very suitable one . . . so my dear Archdeacon, I commend this whole matter to your attention and you to the guidance of the Holy Spirit that you may perceive and know His will and have grace and strength to follow it.

> Yours sincerely
> (signed)   Geoffrey Cantaur

This letter was a tremendous shock to us both. Alf could not share the news with local friends until his letter of acceptance was received and the appointment made public. But, just at that time Marcus Loane had come to stay with us, so Alf had a trusted confidant and friend with whom he could pray and share. As so often happens when God is leading one into fresh ventures for Him, He brings comfort and help just when needed.

There arose now in Nairobi waves of political unrest. I usually attended the Sunday morning services in St Stephen's Church next to our house unless I was accompanying Alf to a service in the district. In the evening we usually went to Evensong in the Cathedral. During the morning services I began to notice that the singing was better. The church was still packed but it became clear that most of the Kikuyu people were staying away. They used a five note scale in their tribal singing and, unless taught as children, could not adapt to our scales and this was obvious in their singing.

One morning a group of Kikuyu Church Elders from Kabete, about ten miles away came to see Alf. They asked if they could see him in private, so he brought them across to our house where they began to tell him about the Mau Mau movement. They were all very keen converted Christians, and were greatly agitated as they had been rounded up by Mau Mau oath administrators, who tried to force them to take the oath. If they did not, they were threatened with death. The oath was disgusting — a filthy thing to be drunk and so totally repulsive to Christians that they utterly refused to do it and were viciously beaten. Alf asked them what was their response to this beating and they said, 'We rejoiced that we were allowed to suffer for Christ's sake as He suffered for us'.

Once a person was oathed, he was forced to obey the Mau Mau leader who could order him to kill someone or perform some other vicious act. The movement aimed to convert the whole of the Kikuyu tribe to its aims which were, 'Out with the European and back to the tribal religion'. Alf had a session with the Police to report what the Elders had told him, but by this time special intelligence was bringing news of similar happenings all over Kikuyu country. The keen Christians stood out against it, even to death for many. We were just seeing the beginning of it in 1950 and it was to continue for a few years yet and more openly.

September 23rd was the date chosen by the Archbishop of Canterbury for the announcement of Alf's appointment as the 3rd Bishop of Central Tanganyika. It was to be announced simultaneously in the English papers, *The Times* and *The Daily Telegraph*, and in the East African and Australian papers. Owing to the time difference between England and Australia, it appeared first in the Melbourne evening paper, *The Herald*, in which many of Alf's friends saw it.

On the day itself the CMS Secretary notified Alf's missionary colleagues as follows:

> CMS Box 360, Nairobi
> 22nd September 1950
>
> Today the Archbishop of Canterbury announced the appointment of Archdeacon A. Stanway as Bishop designate in Central Tanganyika and on behalf of you all I assured Alf of our delight in the honour which has come to him and of our thankfulness to God that Tanganyika is to have so able and so good a man for Bishop. Our delight is mingled with a sense of dismay at the thought of the great gap Alf and Marjory will leave. But the work is the Lord's, and the calling is the Lord's, and where His will and purpose are honoured He will surely provide men and women of His choosing, and enable them for every part and detail of His service.
>
> The consecration is provisionally arranged for February 2nd 1951 in Westminster Abbey . . .
>
> Willoughby Carey

Mr Carey also wrote to me the following:

> 22nd September 1950
>
> Dear Mrs Stanway
> On behalf of all the CMS missionaries in Kenya I would like to say how delighted we all are in the appointment of Alf as Bishop in Central Tanganyika.
>
> We are thankful also that Tanganyika is to have such an excellent missionary as Bishop, and one who has by his service, ability and gifts proved himself so well fitted for such a responsible and demanding office.
>
> Alf has won the trust and love of us all and the confidence and

affection of Africans throughout Kenya and he is known and loved in Tanganyika. His contribution to the building up of the African Church in Kenya is quite outstanding and his experience and knowledge will be of great service to the African Church in Tanganyika.

It has been a joy to work with him here, and his drive, ability and energy in all things, and especially in the re-organisation of the Bookshop, have been most valuable to the whole missionary cause in the Church of Christ here.

How we are to fill his place I don't know; and, but for the knowledge that God does and will provide in the sending of men and women of His own choosing, we should feel something akin to dismay.

Nevertheless our great loss will be Tanganyika's great gain. For all that you and Alf have been enabled to do during these past thirteen years, for the love and fellowship you have both given so freely, and for the gift of your friendship, we shall always be grateful to God and to you both. You are and will be very much in the thoughts and prayers of all your friends now and in the great days to come.

> Yours sincerely
> Willoughby Carey
> Secretary

Alf's reply to Mr Carey's letter was dated 23rd September 1950, in which he said:

Dear Willoughby

Many thanks for your gracious letter about the appointment to Tanganyika. I do appreciate all that you have said and the promise of your prayers and those of my friends in Kenya.

I have always appreciated the liberty that you have so fully given me to try and work out in my own way the solution to the many problems that face us.

My roots go deep in Kenya soil and, were it not for the assurance of His call it would be a sore day for me leaving the work here. Even so, I feel a great wrench which is softened to some extent by the knowledge that in a modern world we are really still neighbours.

I am conscious of lacking many of the gifts and grace needed for my new task — all I can do now is to bring to Him what I have and trust Him to equip me for the task.

> With many thanks,
> Yours in Him,
> Alfred Stanway

Congratulatory telegrams poured in from England, Australia and East Africa and many letters. I would like to quote from what came from some East African friends and colleagues. One of the most senior of retired missionaries living in Kenya was Mrs Sybella Burns, Archdeacon Burns' widow who lived in Limuru and with whom we had enjoyed many happy hours, who wrote:

Limuru

I must confess to something of a shock when I saw Alf's photo and the announcement of his appointment to the Bishopric of Tanganyika and my first thought was, 'How will they get on without him in Nairobi?', but I have been praying that God would show the man of His choice to fill the need of Tanganyika, so I put my first thought to one side — we may make mistakes but our father never does — so surely He has chosen you for this new work . . .

> With loving joy and sympathy,
> from your friend,
> S. Burns

P.S. I am afraid I shall never be able to call you 'Bishop Stanway'. I am afraid I shan't get beyond 'Alf' with you! Forgive me?

Lawrence Mayor, the Principal of Maseno School wrote on 24.9.1950:

> Maseno

Dear Alf,
Congratulations, but you won't want them, I know. It's our prayers you'll be asking for.

If the Bishop one worked under were the chief factor influencing one's choice of mission, I'd ask for a transfer to Central Tanganyika . . .

All the very best, and thank you now, in case I get no other chance, for all your help and friendship to me and to the school.

> Yours, Lawrence.

Come and see us all when you can.

Alf's best man, Desmond Givan wrote this:

> Mombasa
> 22.9.50

Dear Alf,
So the great news is out and you've managed to keep mighty quiet about it. The Mombasa Times this morning, so David tells me, says that you are to be Alfred Tanganyika, and a more worthy appointment could not be.

I am ever so glad to hear the news both for your and Tanganyika's sake, though what the Bishop here and the Diocese as a whole will do without you is hard to think.

Everyone here who has heard the news agrees that this time, at any rate, there has been no misguidance. I hope you won't go too soon but I suppose that your Diocese will not be left empty for long and you must have a bit of leave first.

Well, all the very best to you and may you live many years 'in the land the Lord thy God giveth thee', (unless you come back when R.P.C. retires, which would fulfil the conditions I hope).

See you next week at D.C. (Diocesan Council).

> Yours ever,
> Desmond.

Eula and David Symonds, our colleagues with whom we shared our home and work in Kaloleni, wrote immediately too.

PO Box 72
Mombasa
September 23rd

Dear Alf and Marj,

I must confess my first reaction to reading your news in the Mombasa Times was one of sorrow. A selfish reaction perhaps, but there are few, if any people out here with whom we feel so 'one' as with you, and the roots of those good old days at Kaloleni went down deep.

Though I am not very keen on bishops as you know, or rather their paraphernalia, but perhaps you will realise my whole attitude to the subject . . .

Well Alf and Marj., tho' we may not see so much of you in days to come, we will try to be to you the kind of friends that you will need, supporting you by prayer, and sympathising with you in the 'loneliness of high places' which you may feel at times.

God bless you and use you abundantly.

With our love, as ever,
Yours, Eula.

David added a letter in which, among other things, he said:

I would not be human if I did not point out that this is a fulfilment of my prophecy put in writing to Willoughby Carey on 6th June last . . .

Maude Pethybridge, the women's pastoral worker at Pumwani, a fellow Australian CMS missionary had this to say:

Miss you! The whole church in Kenya will, and I will ever so much. Are you not from my own home town? Are you not 'my ain folk' more than others? Blessings on you. May the Father love others more and more through you. May the Saviour save you more and more and use you. May the Holy Spirit give you life in abundance . . .

With much love,
from Pethy.

There was a very touching and lovely letter from the Reverend Canon Samuel Kuri, a very old saintly retired clergyman, born to freed slaves last century. I translate what he said:

Rabai
16.10.50

Sir, my child and friend,

Perhaps you have not known what I have written above, for I have not written from time to time, or at all since (your) leaving the coast.

First, I thank God that I met you at Limuru on that last Sunday before returning to Rabai after our refresher course. I do not know that I shall hear you preach again as on the Sunday evening at Limuru. Many people came and spoke to us and each had his message.

What was granted to you to expound was received by the older people and the few young ones who were there, especially those of the S. Mission **reference unclear MS** and us also. I praise God for the news I received about you of how you are called to the greater work of the episcopate and to serve Africa even more for our country of Tanganyika. I say 'thank you' to God and I considered it no wonder in my heart. So, 'He who began a good work in you will perfect it even to the day of Jesus Christ'.

I rejoiced when we met Mrs Stanway at the opening of our new school, the Isaac Nyondo Secondary School, she also rejoiced with us.

We are praying for both of you that God will continue to bless you there in Tanganyika as he did when you were with us. Please greet Mrs Stanway for me.

I beg you to let me know the day of your Consecration that I may share in Spirit with you on the day.

> Greetings for now.
> I am your friend.
> S.B. Kuri

Canon Samuel Kuri, son of freed slaves. Priest-in-charge at Rabai. (Photograph: Kenya Information Office)

Members of the Friends Mission at Kaimosi, with whom Alf had a happy relationship and for whom he had done some auditing, wrote to him through their Superintendent who once, instead of calling Alf Archdeacon, addressed him as Archbishop!

> Kaimosi
> 20 October 1950
>
> Dear Bro. Stanway
> Through neglect I have not written as I intended to congratulate you on your appointment as Bishop. I felt the choice was a wise one and that God will use you in a larger way in the days to come to His glory.
>
> I recall very clearly how you once stated that when you became Archbishop I would be the President of the United States. It appears you are making more headway toward your goal than I am toward mine.
>
> All from the Mission here are wishing you God-speed and blessing in all your undertakings for Him. We hope you will feel free and find opportunity to visit us here frequently, but as your duties will take you farther the opportunity will probably be more remote.
>
> With every best wish and a prayer,
> Leonard and Edith Wines.

Our dear friend, Bodge, from Kaloleni wrote:

> ... Yes, we saw the news of the appointment of the Bishop of Central Tanganyika in Friday's Mombasa Times — but I might tell you that I was in Mombasa when the news came of the death of Wynn Jones, and the comment of someone was, 'I guess they'll be wanting our Alf as his successor'.
>
> So the definite news in the paper was in the nature of confirmation of supposition.
>
> Well, God's biddings are enablings, so all Power to you both for the big task. I am glad about the well-deserved honour, but we shall miss you *Sana* (very much).
>
> Much love from Bodge.

Others from East Africa who wrote included the recently consecrated Bishop Leonard Beecher, Alf's co-Archdeacon, Ronald Ngala, one of Alf's old pupils, at this time headmaster of the Mbale Secondary School in the Taita Hills; also the Reverend Obadiah Kariuki, a keen Kikuyu, later to be consecrated as an assistant bishop in Kenya. Ruth Wynn Jones wrote from Dodoma, very happy at Alf's appointment, saying that Bill, had he recovered, was intending to invite Alf down to help him. Chris and Lionel Bakewell wrote from Western Tanganyika, also Jean Meyer and George Pearson. Hugh Evan Hopkins, Provost of All Saints' Nairobi, and Max Wiggins, Provost of the Cathedral of the Holy Spirit in Dodoma, all sent their congratulations. Welles Hannah in writing said:

If I were in the privileged position of giving a newly consecrated bishop advice, I'd say, 'For the love of Mike, forget you're a bishop!' But, for you I'd say, 'Don't forget you're a bishop!'.

Many letters came from Australia, from relatives and friends. His former vicar, the Reverend Arthur Mace, Alf's vicar at Fairfield long ago, and at this time Vicar of St John's, Toorak, wrote on 24th September saying:

I wanted to be amongst the first to congratulate you . . . our long and particular association together gives me the privilege of saying how much you have my prayers and good wishes in your new appointment . . . I am sure you will fill the office with humility and dependence on God, and that capacity for hard work which you have already exhibited. I am sure your many friends of Fairfield days, including the Archbishop will be proud that you have come to this office . . .

Arthur R. Mace

Margaret McKechnie from the St Albans days and later to become Alf's personal secretary and our long-time friend and helper wrote:

It was grand to hear about the new BISHOP OF TANGANYIKA. Of course a few of us really wished we had been members of the Nominating Committee as we had the same idea . . .

Archbishop Booth of Melbourne wrote with his congratulations, also Bishop Donald Baker, then Principal of Ridley College.

From England, Bishop Heywood who was to be one of the presenting Bishops at the Consecration, sent his best wishes. Mrs Head, the widow of Archbishop Head who ordained Alf, wrote inviting us to visit her, saying she hoped to be at the Consecration. The last letter that I shall note came from Norman Larby, the Officer in charge of African education with the Colonial Government in Nairobi. He wrote that he was pleased at the preferment but would be very sorry to see Alf go.

Bishop and Mrs Crabbe arranged a farewell party for us at Bishopsbourne and all the local missionaries came to it. Alf was presented with a handsome briefcase and I with a pigskin writing wallet, and there was a beautiful carved camphor wood chest of Chinese origin as well. We were scheduled to fly out of Nairobi on Monday 1st December 1950.

On the Sunday evening, Alf had been asked to preach his farewell sermon at the evening service in Nairobi Cathedral. On the way to the service he discovered that he had forgotten his sermon notes. Gordon Mayo, the priest-in-charge of the service was very agitated and offered to go back for them, but Alf said he was not to worry, they were only a few lines on the back of an envelope. Alf was reputed to be able to think on his feet and did not rely too much on notes. Gordon Mayo maintained afterwards that Alf had preached from his travel itinerary!

We had enjoyed our time in Nairobi very much. We met many interesting people and made many friends, and were never bored. Among those we valued highly was Dr John Winteler, a consultant physician who had spent some time in Tanganyika. He was a fine Christian of ecumenical outlook, and his friendship with Alf and me was to continue and grow over the years. Healthwise, we also kept well; Alf worked hard but relaxed easily. We never really said goodbye to Nairobi, for we were to go there frequently in the years to come, and it always seemed like going home, as long as we had friends still living there.

CHAPTER 6

INTERLUDE IN ENGLAND

We left Nairobi for London on a Hermes plane on 1st December 1950. Our route was via Kampala in Uganda, and then we followed the Nile from its outlet on Lake Victoria at the Ripon Falls to Juba in the Sudan and through the desert, looking from far above like a silver snake edged with green. We saw the Blue Nile from Ethiopia join the White Nile and then we came down in Khartoum to refuel. It was extremely hot and we were wearing warm outfits for England and so we were glad to embark again for the next stage. Unfortunately, engine trouble developed and we had to return to Khartoum to spend a further uncomfortable twenty-four hours. However, we were taken to Omdurman to the Mahdi's tomb and to see other relics of General Gordon's day, and were accommodated in a vast hotel of Victorian splendour.

Next day we left for Egypt, following the widening Nile and crossing its huge delta after leaving Cairo. With the morning light we were crossing the Mediterranean and saw the northern lands as clearly as though looking at an atlas. The whole of Italy and Sicily stood out, and Greece and its islands. I wondered at the skill of the early cartographers who portrayed it all as accurately as we were seeing it now.

It was still early morning when we landed in Rome and we decided to see some of its splendours. As we had no Italian, we hired a taxi and said, 'Thomas Cook?', which proved effective and we were able to join a tour of the Borghese Gallery and St Peter's Basilica that morning. In the afternoon, we did another tour of the Catacombs of Callixtus and the Church of St Paul's Without The Walls. We passed the splendours of the Colosseum, the Forum and other notable places.

Before dinner, we set out to buy warm gloves. We had hoped to do a little more sightseeing but our bodies were exhausted, so we had an early night, feeling very happy to have had the privilege of seeing historic Rome. Way back in the early thirties, I remember our Latin teacher saying, 'Girls, now when you go to Rome ...'. I certainly didn't believe her then, but how right she was!

Next day we set off for London, flying over France and feeling sad at the sight of the huge bomb craters so clearly visible below; it brought the past war closer to us.

We reached London in the afternoon, and as we travelled out to Streatham where we were to stay, we had the joy of recognizing the Houses of Parliament, Westminster Abbey, Trafalgar Square and other famous landmarks as we passed. The CMS Wigram House was well heated and we felt welcome. On our first Sunday, we travelled by bus to St Peter's Vere Street, and heard John Stott preach. This was the first of many meetings we were to have with him over the years.

Alf became involved in the many appointments arranged by Canon Max Warren. These lasted until the week before Christmas. Interviews were arranged with Church and Government authorities, with Lord Reith of the BBC, the Colonial Office, and the Colonial and Continental Church Society (later to be the Commonwealth and Continental Church Society). Then he met with Miss Dennant, the secretary of the Central Tanganyika Diocesan Association (CTDA). She operated from a house owned by the diocese in the King's Road, Windsor, in which she also lived. The CTDA had been set up by Bishop Chambers to inform its members about Central Tanganyika and to manage its financial affairs in England. Miss Dennant was handling all the ticket arrangements for Alf's consecration in the Abbey and the luncheon to follow in the Mary Sumner House in Westminster.

Alf also went to Wippell's, the tailors and robemakers in Westminster, to be measured and later fitted for his episcopal robes and suit with gaiters. The cost of these clothes was covered by gifts from many friends. Carey Francis asked to be allowed to give Alf his cassock, and Mrs Givan, the Irish mother of his best man, and a member of the Brethren Assemblies, took great pleasure in giving him his gaiters! Alf always referred to them as his 'givans', to her great delight.

The week before Christmas, we travelled to Paris by air. It was glorious to get above the clouds and see the sun again! We were met by Bishop Chambers. He was at this time the Chaplain at the British Embassy Church, a Colonial and Continental church appointment, and he and Mrs Chambers welcomed us warmly to their apartment. The two men had much to discuss and Bishop Chambers was to come for Alf's consecration and to be one of his presenting bishops, together with Bishop Heywood.

There was a thick blanket of crisp snow lying over Paris while we were there. We travelled on the Met., walked down the Champs

Elysees and Alf spent any spare moments he had in the Louvre. Bishop Chambers had a French curate who took me on a funicular up to Montmartre and also to see Napoleon's tomb, the Eiffel Tower and the Place de la Concorde.

On Christmas Day, we were up early for a coffee and rolls breakfast and then driven first to Maison Lafitte and later to Versailles. Alf celebrated Holy Communion for expatriate English people in both places while Bishop Chambers took the Communion service in the Embassy Church. Then we met up at the International Club in Paris for a traditional Christmas dinner. Alf, resplendent in gaiters — which he said kept him beautifully warm — went across to Ireland. He enjoyed his visit — there was no food rationing there as in England. He said the atmosphere of the Church of Ireland in those days reminded him of Trollope's novels. On his return we travelled by train to Devon, to Lee Abbey, an Anglican Community where Alf went into retreat with reading and prayer in preparation for his consecration. I enjoyed the Devon countryside and the warmth of the Community.

On returning to London, we heard that Archbishop and Mrs Fisher would soon be returning from Australia and New Zealand. When CMS authorities heard that they would be visiting Australia, they enquired of the Archbishop whether it would be possible to consecrate Alf at home. However this was not possible, as there were legal requirements connected with the Archbishop's role as Metropolitan of the missionary dioceses, and these could only be met in England.

Alf received the following letter as the day of the consecration drew near:

Lambeth Palace SE1
25th January 1951

Dear Archdeacon

The Archbishop and Mrs Fisher are looking forward to welcoming you and Mrs Stanway here next Thursday night, February 1st. You may like to know that Evensong is in the Chapel at 7.15 p.m. and dinner is at 7.30 p.m.

Yours sincerely,
(signed)   J.S. Long
Chaplain

This was followed the next day by a letter from the Archbishop:

Lambeth Palace SE1
26th January 1951

My dear Archdeacon,

One of the things I had hoped to do as soon as I got home was to see you well in advance of the Consecration, but I do not see how it can be arranged. You may be otherwise occupied and between now and next Thursday evening I have no spare moments. I think, therefore, we must wait until you come on the Thursday evening to stay here, but I should like to send you this note just to tell you that I am looking forward to meeting you and that you are in my prayers.

Yours sincerely,
(signed)   Geoffrey Cantaur

LAMBETH AND THE SERVICE OF CONSECRATION

We arrived at Lambeth Palace with the other Bishops Designate and their wives and were shown to our rooms which were in the hostel accommodation. Since the end of the war a section of the Palace had been set aside as hostel accommodation for visiting dignitaries of the church.

We attended Evensong in the chapel and then we all had dinner with Archbishop and Mrs Fisher. After coffee, and a short time of conversation together, the Bishops Designate, Sherard Falkner Allison, Principal of Ridley Hall, Cambridge (to be Bishop of Chelmsford) and Percy James Brazier (to be Assistant Bishop of Uganda) and Alfred, withdrew for interviews with His Grace, while the ladies talked together. Our menfolk were provided with notes on their procedures in the Abbey for the following day and we all retired to our rooms. It seemed as though we were right under Big Ben, as it boomed out the hours during the night.

Next morning the hostel guests had breakfast together and prepared for the service. It was a cold, wintry day with wet snow lying in untrodden places. We were driven to the Abbey by a Lambeth chauffeur. Alf and the other Bishops Designate were received by the Dean of Westminster in the Jerusalem Chamber. Robed in cassocks and geneva gowns, they awaited the arrival of His Grace the Lord Primate of all England, and the Presenting Bishops, and in their presence they took the oath of allegiance to the King's Majesty, tendered to them by the Registrar of the Province of Canterbury. They were then conducted to the Jerusalem Chamber, where the clergy of the Collegiate Church and the Bishops Assistant were robed and assembled. They were marshalled in order and prayer was offered before they were taken by the vergers of the Abbey to the western alley of the Great Cloister.

I had been taken to my seat, which was the first in the North Lantern, and on my right sat Mrs Head, the widow of Archbishop Head, late of Melbourne, and there were seven other personal friends including the Akehursts. Other friends present included the Reverend Eric Constable of Melbourne and Dr Norman Powys of Mvumi, Tanganyika, some of the Trustees of the CTDA and Canon Cecil Bewes.

The two processions, that of the Church of Westminster and that of the Archbishop of Canterbury, moved to the West Cloister door and up the central aisle of the Nave to the choir, while Psalms 121 and 122 were sung in the ancient plain chant. The Archbishop proceeded to the Holy Table and commenced the service of Holy Communion. After the collects followed a reading from Acts 20:17, the Gospel for the day and then the Creed.

Canon Max Warren preached from the Epistle to the Galatians 6:14, 'God forbid that I should glory, save in the cross of our Lord Jesus Christ, by whom the world is crucified unto me, and I unto the world'. Among other things that Canon Warren said was, 'The man of God is not to glory in pomp and circumstance though he may have to endure them, he is not to glory in authority though he will have to exercise it, he is not to glory when all men speak good of him, nor, as is perhaps more likely, when they speak ill of him, is he to glory in being misunderstood . . . God forbid that I should glory save in the cross of our Lord Jesus Christ . . . the apostle is being intensely personal here . . . it is not the cross which he carries for Christ of which he is thinking, but the Cross Christ carried for him. His only glory is that he is a sinner saved by grace . . . '.

After the sermon the Bishops Designate were conducted to the Chapel of the Holy Name to put on their rochets. The Archbishop being seated, the Presenting Bishops took their places and received the Bishops Designate and presented them to the Archbishop to be consecrated.

The Principal Registrar of the Province of Canterbury then read the King's Mandates for the consecration of the three Bishops Designate and the oath of due obedience was ministered. The litany was chanted and Questions of Examination then put by the Archbishop to those about to be consecrated. They were then taken to don the remainder of their episcopal robes.

The Bishops Assistant formed a semi-circle around the Archbishop. The Bishops Designate knelt as the 'Veni Creator Spiritus' was sung and then the consecration in the appointed form took place; then the Archbishop proceeded with the Communion Service.

The communion was administered first to the newly consecrated Bishops and their families, then to the other Bishops and close friends. The procession reformed and the newly consecrated Bishops walked with the Archbishop as hymns were sung. As they reached the front of the Abbey the bells rang out a wonderful peal.

The consecration was a truly inspiring and moving service, never to be forgotten by Alf or me. We then joined with many friends in a luncheon party given by the CTDA in Mary Sumner House. After

With Archbishop of Canterbury, Geoffrey Fisher, after Alfred's Consecration as Bishop of Central Tanganyika, Westminster Abbey, 2.2.51. (Photograph: Universal Pictorial Press, London)

this we returned to Streatham and during the following days, Alf fulfilled other appointments.

The Archbishop of Canterbury had arranged for Alf to go and see him at Lambeth on 21st February which would be the last opportunity for discussion. Alf received this letter:

Lambeth Palace SE1
8th February, 1951

My dear Bishop

Thank you very much for your letter. The service in the Abbey was most moving and its memories will ever remain with you.

Thank you also for letting me know of the matters you would like to discuss with me when you come to see me on February 21st.

There is another matter. I noticed that at your consecration you were not described as a Master of Arts. It would give me much pleasure to confer on you a Lambeth MA which carries with it the Hood of an Oxford MA. There are fees to be met but I have already made enquiries and friends of yours are ready to find the fees. If you are ready to accept I can confer the degree upon you at 12 o'clock on the day upon which you come.

Yours sincerely,
(signed)   Geoffrey Cantaur

This gracious move of the Archbishop came as a great surprise and gave Alf much pleasure. We learned with interest that an Archbishop of Canterbury by his office is a University, and can confer degrees in different faculties if he wishes.

There is one other interesting matter connected with the Consecration. Subsequently the names of Sherard Allison, James Brazier and Alfred Stanway were inscribed in the Abbey. They are to be seen on the inner wall of the archway — under the organ screen, leading from the nave to the chancel. On a later visit to England we went to see them.

One of the churches in which Alf preached before returning to East Africa was St John's, Harrow which had supported our Diocese for a number of years. Alf flew back alone to Dodoma in Tanganyika at the end of the month, thus completing the three months in England stipulated by the Archbishop as his condition in September 1950.

Mr Dashwood, the Registrar of the Province of Canterbury, sent to me the grant of the Lambeth Degree of Master of Arts, after it had been registered in the Crown Office. There was also the legal document called the Notarial Act, confirming the consecration, to take with me as well.

I left London in the first week of March aboard the *Durban Castle* and sailed for Dar-es-Salaam.

CHAPTER 7

TANGANYIKA 1951 AND 1952

Alf returned to Nairobi on 2nd March. He was driven the 440 miles south to Dodoma in Tanganyika by Russell Girling, a New Zealand CMS missionary in the Diocesan Office there. They broke their journey at Arusha to meet diocesan personnel and the next day they arrived in Dodoma. Ony'ango, our Luo servant, accompanied them and Dodoma seemed the end of the world to him.

Tanganyika had been a German Colony from 1885 to the end of the First World War. It was then mandated to Great Britain by the League of Nations, later to become the United Nations. The three East African countries were the Protectorate of Uganda, Kenya Colony and Tanganyika Territory. The Diocese of Central Tanganyika covered about three-fifths of Tanganyika.

The Kenya border in the north was one of the boundaries of the diocese. In the west it was Lake Tanganyika, with the Belgian Congo on its further shore and to the north-west it bordered on Ruanda-Urundi, former German colonies now mandated to Belgium. The eastern boundary was contiguous with the Diocese of Tanga and Dar-es-Salaam, and the southern boundary with the Diocese of South-West Tanganyika. These other dioceses were formed by work pioneered by the Universities' Mission to Central Africa.

Throughout Alf's new diocese other missions and churches were working e.g. Roman Catholics, Lutherans, Moravians and other smaller voluntary agencies. They all worked in defined areas and as a rule did not overlap each other's work. Alf was due for home leave in August so he had just five months in which to visit each Mission Station or centre and to conduct a backlog of confirmations. He realised that he needed a quick overview of the extent of the work before going on leave.

His enthronement as Bishop took place in the Cathedral of the Holy Spirit in Dodoma on the morning of 11th March. This was to be an ideal opportunity to meet the diocesan clergy, all of whom

Alfred Stanway requesting entry into Cathedral of the Holy Spirit, Dodoma for his Enthronement Ceremony.

were able to attend together with all the missionaries who were able to travel to the ceremony. The Provost, the Very Reverend Maxwell L. Wiggins, and the Archdeacon, the Venerable Oliver Cordell (who had been the Vicar-General during the interim period without a bishop) conducted the service and the African Archdeacon of Ukaguru led the sentences of obedience and loyalty. I was still travelling by sea at this time and was disappointed that I could not be present, but there is a record of Alf's sermon for the occasion, and in view of the developments which were to take place I think it is important to record it here.

First he looked back to those who had laboured there before him. He recalled the start of the work at Mpwapwa in 1876 and its

The Rev. Charles Maling (L.) and the Ven. Archdeacon Oliver Cordell, install Alfred as Bishop of Central Tanganyika, 11.3.51.

association with Uganda, its incorporation into the Diocese of Eastern Equatorial Africa, its being then cut off to belong to the Diocese of Mombasa, until in 1927 it became the Diocese of Central Tanganyika. Alf went on to say that there was a present link with the past in that Bishop Chambers had presented him at his consecration and Alf spoke of his great vision of courage in the early days. Alf referred to Bishop Wynn Jones as an apostle of friendship with a true pastoral heart and he paid tribute to a great body of clergy, lay men and women who had worked for the Lord — some of them for 40 years — in the days past. He then stated that we cannot look back only.

The Church must have a message relevant to the contemporary situation in which we live. We believe our Church has a message for these days. We claim to be an Apostolic church and though many in our Church rest their claim for this upon the succession of bishops down from apostolic times, I always feel we are on more secure ground when we claim to be apostolic because we possess the teaching of the apostles, and when we are certain that the same Holy Spirit that led them is our guide, and when our preaching, like theirs, is to set forth Christ and Him crucified, as the only hope for a sinful world.

We are also Catholic; part of the great universal church of Jesus Christ which knows no ecclesiastical boundaries, but is made up of all those who are really Christ's. Because of this it has been, and I hope will be, an increasing mark of this Diocese that we stretch forth the right hand of Christian fellowship to fellow Christians of other denominations.

We are also a Reformed Church. The Reformation set forth again in clear unmistakable terms the doctrine of Justification by Faith, and stressed the need for individual personal experience of Christ. A man may dwell in a nominally Christian land, he may be born into a Christian family, he may by baptism be admitted into the privileged position of one of the family of the Church, he may by confirmation be admitted to partake of the emblems of Christ's death and passion; but these things alone, though they are all helps and though they may bring him into covenant fellowship with God, are insufficient of themselves to save him from his sins. We need to come one-by-one to the Cross of Christ, for Christ died for our sins, the just for the unjust to bring us to God, if we would know the cleansing and healing power of Divine forgiveness and enjoy the richness of the peace of God which passes knowledge.

The stress on individual conversion is a mark of all true churches, and our Anglican Church goes further and stresses not only the need for individual conversion but teaches that the only proof of such conversion is a life manifestly showing forth the fruits of the indwelling Spirit of God. Conduct and character spring from individual experience. If such spiritual experience is true it will bring forth life that commends the Gospel of Christ.

We are also in a church of today. We live in an age when not only Dictators, as individuals, but where even States themselves interfere from time to time with religious freedom and personal liberty. The trend of our time is for the outside world to ask the Church to conform to the world's standards; whether they be of conduct, of home life or of nationalistic aims. We must, however, be ready to reply in the words of Paul to the Romans. I quote from J.B. Phillips' translation:

> Do not let the world squeeze you into its mould, but let God remould your minds from within, so that you may prove in practice that the Plan of God for you is good, meets all his demands and moves towards the goal of maturity.

One of the great problems of East Africa is the racial question. We of the Church must oppose all divisions which are merely based on prejudice or colour or race. There are great problems to which we do not yet know the answer but we are certain of this, that no answer that is not based on justice and righteousness can hope to survive. The Church of Jesus Christ recognises no such unjust barriers which men in their folly seek to raise.

Naturally I should like to see great strides made in the church life of this Diocese where we dwell in a developing country, and today in this very personal service between the Bishop and some of his flock, I ask your prayers. Some of you, I know, have formed regular habits of personal prayer. I know you will remember me. Some of you are more spasmodic in your prayers, but do seek to remember me and the work. Some of you gave up praying long ago, except perhaps for odd occasions, but now in later life the prayers of children are obviously not the prayers you could pray. You need to start again to talk to God in your own everyday language, for He knows, He loves and He cares. Perhaps you do not know how to pray for yourselves? You might begin afresh by praying for me and for all the ministers of the Gospel of Christ in this territory, that they might be true shepherds of the flock of Christ.

I want to set out just the main line along which I would like to see the Church develop. We need to aim at increasing self-support in both the African and European work. Here the African congregations are ahead of the Europeans in providing for those ministering to them, but there is need for increase on every front.

We have no right to seek to build a church which will be ever dependent upon the resources of the home countries, but must aim to build up our own support as rapidly as possible. It is perfectly natural to expect support from home while we are young and developing but this cannot be a permanent arrangement.

I would like to see work among the Indian community developing.

We need to raise the standard of entrance for the ministry, and to pay more attention to the training of the clergy.

Along with this there is need for longer and more efficient training of African evangelists.

We need to make greater use of the laity in every branch of the Church's work.

I would like to see the production and distribution of Christian literature to all races increased.

I come to you and to this great task just as an ordinary man who twenty odd years ago found life and peace at the foot of the Cross of Christ our Saviour and who soon after was called to be a minister of the Gospel of Christ in Africa.

I have only a few of the very many gifts required for this office, and I could not have come to you at the Archbishop's call were it not for two great facts: first, the consciousness that it was the God who called me long ago who was calling me afresh and bidding me come; and secondly, He was promising me, 'Have not I commanded you, be strong and of good courage. Be not afraid, neither be thou dismayed for the Lord thy God is with thee withersoever thou goest'. Joshua 1:9. Go in this thy might. 'Surely I will be with thee'. Exodus 3:12.

The presence of Christ our Master is the most enabling force in the whole world, for all power in heaven and on earth is given unto Him. Where He is, there is pardon, and where there is pardon there is peace, the peace of God that passes all understanding, and where that peace is, there is the power to do the will of God. As I seek to give myself afresh to Christ for this great task, I trust that you too will see that He has His rightful place in your life.

After his enthronement, Alf carefully reviewed the Diocesan properties at Kikuyu and in the town of Dodoma. Kikuyu as used in this instance has no connection with the use of Kikuyu in Kenya. *Mkuyu* is a fig tree and *kikuyu*, a little fig tree, but this *ki* particle can also refer to some outstanding feature. In this case it was an enormous fig tree standing alone which must have been very, very old. It gave great shade and was a local landmark.

There were at Kikuyu the Alliance Secondary School buildings, dormitories, assembly hall and staff houses. There was also the

Alf outside the Chapter House of the Cathedral, Dodoma.

house in which both Bishop Chambers and Bishop Wynn Jones had lived.

Alf also inspected the Diocese's town properties, some of which were built of the local grey granite. These were adjacent to the Diocesan Offices which were constructed of the same material. On the opposite side of the road were two semi-detached houses built in pise-de-terre with granite lower courses, and it was in one of these that Alf decided we should live. He wanted to be in touch with the everyday commercial life of the town and to be near his office, rather than commuting back and forth to Kikuyu which was beyond the town boundary.

I arrived in Dar-es-Salaam at the end of March and Alf came to meet me by train. We travelled up together, arriving in the middle of the night at Dodoma station, where the Dodoma carriage was shunted into a siding. In the early morning we were met and taken to our temporary quarters with missionary workers in the town.

Meanwhile in Kenya, the Mau Mau rebellion had become open warfare, with many deaths and injuries inflicted, especially on Africans who refused to be oathed — though a few Europeans were killed also. Alf received a death threat in a letter, which he took to the Police. He was given an African *askari* (soldier or policeman) who was to follow him everywhere he went. The poor man found it well nigh impossible to keep up with Alf! I remember that Alf went to rest at Kongwa one day and the askari took his position outside the door of our room. By the time Alf was ready to go back to work the askari was sound asleep, so Alf carefully stepped over his body and took off. The services of the askari were later dispensed with and no new threats came.

On his visit to the various mission stations in the Diocese, Alf took stock of all the properties, noticing things which needed to be upgraded. He determined to supply where necessary, new beds and mattresses. The missionaries usually provided the Bishop with the best bed they possessed and often that was very poor. Also, he determined as soon as it could be achieved, to install water-borne sanitation on all the mission stations. He was very moved by the condition of the Mvumi hospital buildings, wondering where and how he could look to finance such a large project. The Leprosy Settlement at Makutupora also needed upgrading. So much of the planning that he now did was to be on a wide scale and could not quickly be brought to fruition but it occupied the forefront of his thinking from now on.

From his experience in Kenya Alf realised the need for Africanisation on all fronts in the Diocese. Political movements in Uganda and Kenya were stirring up national pride and it was inevitable that this would soon follow in Tanganyika. There was tribal rivalry in

Kenya between the dominant Luo and Kikuyu people, which exacerbated political activity, but fortunately there was no such conflict among the Tanganyika people.

A Conference was planned for East African Bishops in the Upper Nile, and Alf decided we would attend it and then go south-west from Kampala, following Lake Victoria to where our Diocese met the Ugandan border at Kagera. A visit to Katoke, Rubungo and Bukoba was planned and Charles Maling drove up in the Bishop's car — a rather unreliable old Ford V8 — to meet us at Bukoba.

By that time the car needed a new main spring, so while Alf took services, Charles rooted around among car parts at the local garage and found what he needed. This was adjusted and we set off for the far north-west, crossing the Malagarasi River on a primitive ferry and arriving at the mission station at Murgwanza, in Bugufi country. We reflected on the fact that Bishop Chambers, and soon after Lionel Bakewell, had **walked** there! There was a commanding view from the high ridge on the station from which one could see the great sight of the seven volcanoes in the Congo beyond Ruanda. The Wahangaza people of Bugufi were closely related to the Ruandans and their languages were very similar. The hospital at Murgwanza was started originally as a clinic by a Church Army nurse and is quite a big hospital today. After fellowship with the missionaries and Africans, Alf took confirmation services and next day we headed south-west for Kibondo in Uha country. The car performed badly. There seemed to be something wrong in the petrol system but neither Alf nor Charles could fix it. 'You pray, I'll drive', said Charles, as we made poor progress. As we drew near the Kibondo mission station, we had a very steep hill to conquer and wondered whether or not we would make it. From up on the hill the Kibondo people watched our poor progress, but eventually the car succeeded, only to stop dead at the very top.

Next morning Captain John Spencer of the Church Army, with Alf and Charles, took the petrol pump apart and found that the trouble was a broken diaphragm. So, there we were, about 70 miles from the nearest garage — and it was unlikely that even there we could procure the particular spare part to fit this model of car. When they went to see the District Commissioner whose child Alf was to baptise the next day, they discovered that he had suffered a similar mishap with his car and had vowed that he would never be without that particular spare part again. When examined, it proved to be the exact part that our car needed. This was a further case of 'Before ye call I will answer', and God meeting our need in a tight corner.

From Kibondo we went south to Kasulu to the next mission centre, where the Reverend Erisafati Matovu and his wife Edita lived and worked. Pastor Matovu had built up a work for God among the Waha people, and there was evidence of spiritual fruit and blessing from his labours.

Our last stage by car was to Kigoma on the eastern shore of Lake Tanganyika. This lake is about 500 miles long and more than a mile deep, and is said to be a rift in the earth's surface. The great railway, built by the Germans and only completed as the First World War broke out, terminated here at Kigoma, and this town saw the last episcopal act of Bishop Chambers in Tanganyika. He dedicated St Michael's church and then he and Mrs Chambers said goodbye to his diocese and crossed the lake by steamer to Albertville in the Belgian Congo, and from there went to South Africa and on to Paris.[1] We decided to visit Ujiji just close by. It was an Arab township and was the site of the famous meeting between H.M. Stanley and Dr Livingstone in 1871. It was a moving experience to look at the memorial built on that spot — a map of Africa with the Cross overlying it. A section of the original mango tree (under which Livingstone used to sit when this was his base) is mounted on a plaque in the Dodoma Cathedral. Alf earnestly desired to start work in Ujiji and prayed very much for a plot of land there, but this was never granted while it was still in his Diocese. The Muslim influence was very strong.

We put the car on the train at Kigoma and travelled back with it to Dodoma. Alf had now seen all our mission centres: the centre, the west and the north and he had realised how strategic it was to develop the perimeters of the Diocese.

At this point I want to say something about the Revival Fellowship Movement and its influence upon the life of the church in Central Tanganyika. This was undoubtedly a great movement of the Holy Spirit, breaking out first in the Church of Uganda in the 1930s and spreading from there in all directions. It reached Tanganyika by spreading south to Ruanda and Urundi and south again to Bugufi and Uha. The Revivalists based their specific teaching on the passage in 1 John 1:5-9 which teaches openness of life, walking in the Light, fellowship with each other, the cleansing blood of Christ as the antidote for sin, also open confession of sin in public with forgiveness, restitution and blessing. To illustrate how important this teaching was to become, I will refer to three outstanding leaders of Revival Teaching in the Diocese.

In the East — the first by birth was Yohana Majani Omari
In the West — Erisafati Matovu
In the Centre — Festo Kivengere

[1]See *Dare to Look Up: A Memoir of Bishop George Alexander Chambers*, by Nancy de S.P. Sibtain. Angus and Robertson, Sydney 1968, page 87.

Majani Omari was born at Songe in Unguu country, beyond our mission station at Berega. His people were Muslims. He wanted very much to go to school but there were no Muslim schools out in the bush. The nearest school was ours at Berega and we were Christians! Eventually his father allowed him to become a boarder at the Berega School but with strict rules attached; he must on no account stay and listen to Christian teaching of any kind, nor was he to read the New Testament. If he disobeyed he would be disowned.

Omari made good progress in all the rudiments of primary education. Being told not to read the New Testament made him very curious. 'Why not?', he thought. He secretly stole a New Testament and took it away to read it by stages. He had managed to read all through Matthew, Mark and Luke and was working through John when he was stopped by verse 6 in Chapter 14, which says, 'I am the way, the truth and the life; no one comes to the Father but by me'. Many years later he told Alf and me, 'That text, that very text, pushed me out of Islam into the light of Christ'. He decided to disobey his father and to become a Christian, so he took instruction in the class for baptism and was duly baptised *Yohana* (John) after the gospel which changed his life. His father did disown him, but the teacher at Berega took him in and cared for him. In later life there was reconciliation with his father and brothers, though they all remained Muslims.

When Yohana completed his schooling he trained as a dresser (a male nurse) at Berega Hospital and afterwards was entrusted to dispense simple medicines in rural dispensaries. During this career he did voluntary Christian work at Berega, teaching adults to read and assisting with baptismal and confirmation instruction. He showed gifts as an evangelist and so Bishop Chambers met him and challenged him to go up to Uha and win the primitive people there for Christ. Yohana refused even to consider this. He had only recently married and Ana was expecting her first child. Bishop Chambers then said, 'Well, pray about it!' 'No', said Yohana, 'I will not'. 'Then I shall', said the Bishop. A few days later Yohana had a dream in which someone stood near him and told him to read Ezekiel, Chapter 2 and verses 7 and 8. He awoke and remembered the dream and felt it had something to do with the Uha challenge, and tried to put it out of his mind. About a fortnight later he had the identical dream again. This time he told Ana about it, and she suggested they open the Bible and read it. This is what he read:

You shall speak my words to them, whether they hear or refuse to hear; for they are a rebellious house.
But you, son of man, hear what I say to you; be not rebellious like that rebellious house; open your mouth and eat what I give you.

Yohana knew this to be his call to go as an evangelist to Uha, leaving Ana behind. He set out with a few possessions and a bicycle and boarded the train at Morogoro bound for Kigoma, thus going from the extreme east of the diocese to its extreme west. Ana joined him before long. He learned the Giha language, and setting out on his bicycle he organised groups of people under trees all up and down the country. He started teaching them the gospel and so lit a fire in those parts that never died down. Bishop Chambers took him from there and sent him to Kongwa for theological training and in due course he was ordained.

When we arrived in Dodoma Yohana was serving in the Cathedral Parish so we saw a great deal of him and Ana. He spoke beautiful Swahili. (The nearer people live to the Coast the better Swahili they speak.) Later he was a much sought after speaker at Revival Fellowship Conventions.

In the west, located at Kasulu lived Erisafati Matovu and Edita his wife. They had no children. He was an intelligent Ugandan but had not gone very far educationally. He was a successful businessman with a small *duka* (shop) in which he sold the basic requirements of the local people, sugar, salt, matches, kerosene, maize meal, beans and such like. He prospered but was often dishonest and sometimes defrauded people. The Revival movement caught up with him and he was gloriously saved, made restitution where he could and decided to set out with Edita — also a committed Christian — to evangelise people. Edita had been born in a very polygamous household, her father having had many wives. She and her husband found their way to Tanganyika where he began to witness for Christ. He likewise was 'found' by Bishop Chambers and sent to Kongwa College for theological training and was ordained to return to minister in the West, Kasulu being his main base.

He had a long ministry there and was full of sanctified common sense, a wise and much trusted counsellor of people. Unfortunately we did not see as much of him as Alf would have liked because he lived so far from us. However, whenever there were clergy refresher courses, usually held in those days in Kongwa, we were happy to renew fellowship with him. Alf was very drawn to him. I remember on one such course that Alf had told the gathered clergy not to ask permission to be absent from the course as it would not be given. During that time, Yohana Omari was expected back from overseas and Alf invited Matovu (he was a great friend of Yohana) to go into Dodoma with him to meet Yohana. As they drove along Alf said, 'You did not expect to be meeting Yohana today, did you?'. 'Yes and no', said Matovu. 'What do you mean?', said Alf. 'Well, you told us not to ask you for leave, so I didn't, but I took it to a Higher Court'.

Once the Western part of the Diocese was divided we did not see Matovu again, but he was a great warrior for Christ and will be long remembered. He retired back to Uganda.

From the West the Revival came down to the centre with the visit of a team of four Africans and one missionary. They spoke in schools in Dodoma and Mvumi and many people gave their lives to Christ. Old grievances and resentments were confessed and healed. The work at the centre was strengthened by the arrival of Festo Kivengere. Some little time ago Alf was asked to write about Festo by his biographer. At that time Alf was not physically able to write very much but this is what he said:

When I left Kenya to be Bishop of Central Tanganyika, Festo was employed as a Secondary School teacher at the Alliance Secondary School, our Diocesan Boys' School in Dodoma. He was already accepted as the local leader of the Revival Movement. His linguistic gifts marked him out. He was a gifted speaker and this was enriched by what God was doing through the Revival Movement.

In those days missionaries, pastors and local evangelists were regarded as the vanguard of the Church. Many of the revivalists had difficulties with church teachers, pastors and evangelists whom they suspected, and often rightly so, of opposing the gospel. Festo, while being keen on the Revival message, was able to bring better relationships between the two groups.

As Bishop, I maintained that we look on the Revival Movement as one of, but not the sole, method of evangelism in the Diocese. They ran their meetings on the basis that the revivalists should have complete charge, and this outlook often brought about difficulties when persons chosen by committees were replaced by others more open to the Revival Movement.

It was true that a great work was going on. The best of the clergy responded to the Movement and conversions were many and encouraging.

On recognising Festo's potential, I offered to ordain him, but his friends in the Movement gave other advice. I was able to obtain a British Council Scholarship for him that I considered would widen his experience. When Billy Graham visited Tanganyika, Festo was asked to be an interpreter for him. His talent was not lost on the evangelist and this prepared the way for a Billy Graham Foundation Scholarship for him to study theology at the Presbyterian Seminary at Pittsburgh, USA.

Prior to this I was able to arrange for him to accompany Bishop Yohana Omari to Australia. Yohana's English was weak so Festo's help was invaluable. This introduced Festo to the Australian scene.

Later Festo was asked to take a posting as a Supervisory Education Officer in his home Diocese, and from that posting he was chosen to be Bishop of his own native area. This led to his acceptance of an increasing responsibility in his career. Bishop Omari was a great friend and a true companion in the gospel. Festo's love of the Word of God and his exposition of it kept these two in touch even though their lives kept them in different countries.

On one occasion Festo and I discussed the idea of him being a freelance evangelist. I said that three options were open to him. The first way was to be a Church employee and paid by them, secondly, if that would be too restrictive, to organise a group of friends together and let them be responsible for his travel and livelihood. The third option was to run his own show and raise the necessary finance. I deplored this last method. Billy Graham gave up the method of accepting love offerings. Festo recognised that the third method was unsatisfactory.

Festo aimed high in his role of evangelist. His preaching was scriptural and anyone listening to him was able to recognise that he was a careful student of the Word. It was obvious that his was an outstanding personality marked out for great things for God and time has proved this to be so. It was a privilege to have known him.

The Revival Movement developed a pattern of convention meetings where crowds gathered together for three or four days of intensive preaching. This followed a chosen theme, for example a typical theme would be 'Jesus satisfies'. Several speakers would take different teaching sessions but they would all point to the chosen topic. The Revival chorus 'Glory, glory Alleluia' was sung continuously, usually (especially in the west) with Luganda words, but also in Swahili as 'Utukufu Aleluia'. The whole pattern of the singing, enthusiasm and feeling of brotherhood was typically African. It was joyous, cheerful and emotional. They did not tire of endless repetition, long addresses and continuous singing and there was a strong bond of community among them. Public confession of sin was common and restitution usually followed. Excesses happened from time to time and Alf decided to notify the clergy that in public meetings, if sin was confessed openly there must be no details given, no naming of other people, no dates or times of the offence and 'no picture to be painted in words which could defile the mind of another'. As the movement spread, and with time became widely accepted, it moderated and good people emerged to be splendid and continuing Christians. There was no schism in the church.

Now to revert to Alf's quick overview of the Diocese. He still had not visited Kaguru country in the East where the Reverend George Pearson had large numbers of candidates for confirmation, because there had been a long period without a Bishop. The only way Alf could fit in a visit to the east was on his way to Dar-es-Salaam where we were booked to sail home via Bombay on 10th August. It was decided that he would go down by train from Dodoma to Morogoro where George would meet him and take him on a tour of several days to all the confirmation centres. They were to conclude with a service in Morogoro after which they would leave for Dar-es-Salaam where they expected to arrive on the evening of the 9th ready for us to sail at 9 a.m. the next morning.

Meanwhile I was packing our possessions for storage and our suitcases for the journey. I then took the train to Dar-es-Salaam, collected our steamer ticket and travellers' cheques and was all ready for Alf to arrive that night. But alas! He didn't come and next morning there was no sign of him or George. I was in a dilemma! What should I do? Go aboard without him or miss the ship and see what happened? I thought it best to go ahead as planned. When I boarded the ship and tendered the ticket to the Purser he said, 'Where is your husband?' Feeling rather foolish I had to say, 'I don't know'.

We sailed from Dar-es-Salaam at 9 a.m. and made Zanzibar Island four hours later. We berthed out to sea and I decided to wait until 4 p.m. to go ashore when it would be less hot. But before that time came, Alf burst in jauntily. Apparently, his brief case containing his passport had been put away safely in his room at Berega and on packing up he omitted to collect it. George Pearson made the 70 mile journey to Morogoro, conducted the service and as they were preparing to leave for Dar-es-Salaam, Alf realised the brief case was still at Berega. George nobly did the double journey of 140 miles there and back and they travelled all through the night, reaching Dar-es-Salaam as the ship was well out to sea, though still visible.

There certainly was recourse to prayer now, so they went to the Airways depot to enquire whether there was a flight to Zanzibar that day. On being told there was but it was fully booked, they asked if Alf could have the seat should there be a cancellation. There was a cancellation and Alf was in Zanzibar twenty minutes later. However, first he and George had a few hours to fill in, so never daunted, Alf went to the Education Department, where they had profitable discussion with Government officials which proved most helpful to the Diocese. It seemed to me that even Alf's mistakes turned out well!

We continued to Bombay where we were to trans-ship, but there Alf had word from his brother that their father was not well. He wanted Alf to fly from Perth and he would pay for the ticket. So now I could see that I would be chief custodian of the baggage at the end of the voyage as I had at the beginning! So I penned this little verse which originally had stick figure illustrations:

This is how he missed the ship
which waited not to right his slip
but hasted off upon its trip.

This is now he took a plane
The hasting ship he overcame
by stepping off Unguja's main.

This is how he spent each day
in restful pursuits, sleep and play
until at last he reached Bombay.

There it was he found a letter
saying, it obviously was better
to fly alone to Melbourne city
leaving his spouse, it seemed a pity,
to carry on alone!

So when he reached the Golden West
he took a plane, the very best,
and soon stepped off in Melbourne town
looking fit, and well and brown.

But, what about the little 'm'?
Well, she's the maiden all forlorn
who counts the baggage night and morn
and copes with sundry manly duties
which need performing.

But, what she really wants to know is,
does she always have to do it??

I handed this to him on a scrap of paper next morning and his reply
to my question was, 'Yes, of course!'.

We were reunited again in Melbourne and Alf soon began a
heavy programme of meetings, deputations and lectures in Victoria
and interstate. He conferred with the Federal Council of CMS,
renewed ties with friends, especially Marcus Loane, and tried out
some of his ideas and thoughts for the extension and consolidation
of the work in Central Tanganyika. It was a valuable time for
strengthening the ties between the Home Base and Mission Field.
During this time he interviewed Kevin Engel, with a view to his
serving in Tanganyika after finishing his priest's year in Sydney.

We returned to the Diocese by the end of June 1952. Alf was
convinced that it was not good to have such long leaves in
Australia, and in future he was to cut down lengthy times away
from the Diocese. Three weeks after our arrival, Alf celebrated the
marriage of Mary Baker, the daughter of Bishop Donald Baker, a
Principal of Ridley College, Melbourne and a Sister Tutor at Mvumi
Hospital, to the Reverend Edmund (Ted) Arblaster, one of his
chaplains. The reception was held afterwards in the grounds of our
house.

The following months were very busy with Diocesan affairs and
safaris. We began to look forward to some of the long safaris we
had to take, especially those going north, first to Arusha where

there was a large Diocesan boarding school — in those days for our European children — then on to Moshi for chaplaincy (i.e. English language) services and so on to Nairobi. These journeys proved very relaxing opportunities for uninterrupted conversation which was not easily achieved at home.

The biggest event ahead was the Silver Jubilee of the Diocese on 1st November 1952, so Alf began to plan for it. He established regular prayer meetings for the missionary staff (later English-speaking Africans were to join in) each Wednesday evening. Some-times these were held in our home, and if Alf was away, at the Provost's home at Kikuyu. In later years they were regularly held in the Bishopsbourne Chapel on the first Wednesday night of each month and the meeting was followed by supper. During these sessions Alf formed the habit of stating the present needs of the work and recording what was prayed for. Then over a few weeks a review would be held and we would praise God for the answers he had granted us, and seek his guidance on current problems. There was always a Bible reading and short message before prayer and I personally felt that over the years these prayer gatherings welded us together as a family of God perhaps more than anything else.

The Jubilee was marked by the return to the Diocese from Paris of Bishop Chambers, who was to convey greetings from the Archbishop of Canterbury and to preach the sermon on the day. Bishop and Mrs Crabbe came down from Nairobi, and the Bishop of South-West Tanganyika and the Assistant Bishops of Uganda also represented their Dioceses. The Governor of Tanganyika, Sir Edward Twining and Lady Twining were also to be there and present greetings from Her Majesty, Queen Elizabeth II.

The African and European clergy and lay workers in the Diocese processed to their seating and welcomes and greetings were given. The Diocesan welcomed His Excellency the Governor as the Queen's representative. Then after the British National Anthem was sung the Governor read the following message from the Queen:

> I send you my warmest congratulations and share with you and the people of your Diocese the joy which I am sure that you must all feel in the celebration of the twenty-fifth anniversary of the Diocese of Central Tanganyika. I pray that God will preserve and extend the great work which has been accomplished by the Church Missionary Society in Tanganyika during the past 25 years, and that with His help and guidance you and your clergy and all members of the Church in your Diocese may be strengthened and encouraged to continue the devoted labours which have already achieved so much.

After prayers, hymns and thanksgivings, Bishop Chambers gave his address in this Cathedral built during his episcopate. This was translated for non-English speaking folk, the Jubilee offerings were made and the service concluded.

Sir Edward Twining had tried to influence Alf to have the sermon curtailed, partly we think because he and other Government officials were wearing their ceremonial regalia. This was most uncomfortable with tight white breeches and spurs and with shirts buttoned up to the neck, etc. Alf replied that Bishop Chambers had come all the way from Paris to give this one address and in no way would he be asked to curtail it. Alf had the courage, which I'm sure I would have lacked, to stand up to some of the Government administrative officials who often implied by their remarks that the work of the Gospel was not important. On one occasion Sir Edward said to Alf, 'Well! I go to church twice a month, that's good enough isn't it Padre?' Alf answered with humour, 'Fail, sir, that's not even fifty per cent!'.

In the afternoon there was a garden party at Kikuyu in the grounds of the Provost's house for His Excellency and Lady Twining, visiting Bishops and dignitaries and our clergy and missionaries. I also had the ordeal of entertaining the Governor and Lady Twining to dinner. We had to learn the Protocol, such as His Excellency being served before anyone else, and as we never served alcohol or cigarettes, we had to inform their host, the Provincial Commissioner beforehand, that this was our custom.

With so many clergy and diocesan workers, both African and European present for the occasion, many needed to see the Bishop while they were in Dodoma. Some had requests to make and others problems to discuss. To those with problems, maybe disgruntled or out of fellowship with others, Alf would listen and then say without warning, 'Tell me about your prayer life'. Often this would open up the heart of the matter to effective support and counsel. He placed great importance on prayer for a Christian, often saying, 'Most of a Christian's learning is on his knees' shortened to a regular saying, 'you learn on your knees'. He personally favoured above all else the prayer made in private with the door closed. He often told me how easy it is to be diverted from praying. God says to you, 'Go and pray', and then you see a blind that needs adjusting or visitors come before you can get to prayer, and time is used up and your prayer is not prayed.

Alf believed also in the quick short prayer made on the spot. One day in 1954 he was reading the biography of Amy Carmichael, and of how she desired to have the Webb-Peploe brothers join the staff at Dohnavur. She asked God for them and they came. Thinking of his own needs and desires, Alf put his hand in the book to keep his place and asked God, if it were His will, to send him John Denton to be his administrator (he told me this later). He then wrote to John offering him the position, but a letter crossed from John offering to come. We praised the Lord for that.

Later again Alf was praying for an administrative assistant for John and felt God was guiding him to write to the Reverend Douglas Clark of Wood Green in London to enquire whether there was a qualified young lady in his parish willing to be a Diocesan worker. Mr Clark replied that he did not know of anyone to fill that position, so an advertisement was put in the English periodical, *The Life of Faith*. Subsequently, in 1956 when John Denton was in England, he arranged that during this visit he and Kevin Engel should interview Miss Mary Punt who had replied to the advertisement. She was offered the post and accepted it. When John asked her which parish she belonged to, she replied, 'Wood Green'. She came to us the next year and stayed until after we ourselves had left the Diocese, and proved to be a very effective and loyal member of the office team.

When people asked Alf for advice on prayer he often wrote out a prayer for them, asked them to study it and then pray it if they could. This happened with a Swiss girl who sailed on the *Queen Mary* when Alf and two other non-conformist clergymen were on board. They had all talked with her and on the last night aboard Alf was playing chess when she approached him. He took a piece of the ship's stationery, and sensing that she wished to make a commitment to Christ, he wrote out a prayer and said, 'Study it and if you can pray it, then do so'. She did this and next day was radiant with joy in her new found faith. Years later we visited her in Switzerland and she showed us that prayer still kept in her Bible.

Another couple had marital disagreements and when Alf saw them both and spent some time with them he wrote each one a prayer to say daily. They agreed to do this and the marriage was renewed and is firm today.

Many times Alf had proved that 'coincidences happen when we pray'.

CHAPTER 8

TANGANYIKA.
THE UNFOLDING PATTERN

I have been impressed recently, when reading the Bible, at the way in which God appears to begin a new work. The Bible often seems to show us God's chosen leader meeting privately with God in prayer and being given precise details about what he wants his people to be and do. For example:

First — The Communion: Exodus 24:12

> The Lord said to Moses, 'Come up to me on the mountain . . .'
> vv. 15,16: Then Moses went up . . . the cloud covered the mountain.
> v. 18: and Moses was on the mountain forty days and forty nights.

Secondly — The Offering: Exodus 25:1 and 2

> The Lord said to Moses, 'Speak to the people of Israel that they take for me an offering, from every man **whose heart makes him willing** you shall receive the offering for me'.

God then details what He expects the people to give and tells Moses quite precisely how His sanctuary, the tabernacle, is to be constructed.

Thirdly — The Personnel: Exodus 28:3

> 'You shall speak to all who have ability, whom I have endowed with an able mind that they make . . .', *and* (Exodus 31:1-6), The Lord said to Moses, 'See I have called by name Bezalel the son of Uri, son of Hur, of the tribe of Judas: and I have filled him with the Spirit of God, with ability and intelligence, with knowledge and all craftsmanship to devise artistic designs, to work in gold, silver . . . and behold I have appointed with him Oholiab, the son of Ahisamach, of the tribe of Dan; and I have given to all able men ability, that they may make all that I have commanded you.'

It seems to me that this pattern should always apply. If a godly leader seeks God's direction day by day, gifts will be outpoured, capable people will appear and the work will be done to the glory of God. God's work done in God's way (and in His time) will never lack God's supply. Alf's aphorism for this was 'God will always pay for what He orders'.

I have known people to be critical of Alf, who seemed to them always to be talking about money. I, who lived with him, know that he never sought money for any personal end. It was always for God's work that he sought it and, from the above passage, it is clear that a need must first be made known. Moses was told to **tell** the people of the need and then those who were open-hearted and generous would give. So money has to be talked about if it is needed for God's work. Alf said that our stewardship of money itself is an indicator of our character, and we should never worry about anything that could be redeemed by money, for example, to lose one's faith is tragic, but money can be replaced.

So, in the vast work of constructing buildings which Alf was to direct during his twenty years in Tanganyika, he was convinced that he was on God-given grounds when he sought, for example, to provide for blind people and those with leprosy. The pattern was clear — make the need known to the Societies which helped the blind and who provided for leprosy sufferers.

Alf supervised dormitories, classrooms and a new chapel for blind children at Buigiri. He saw a wonderful new Leprosy Settlement come into being, and most of the funds needed underwritten by the Royal Society for the Blind and the Leprosy Mission.

When Alf first came to the diocese, Captain Fred and Mrs Eva Varley of the Church Army were training blind boys to read and write in braille on the verandah of their home. They had very little equipment. It is gratifying to look back now and see the beautiful chapel with its wood carving of the Light of the World skilfully executed by James Mazengo, a lame boy at the school who was taught to carve in order to earn a living; the dormitories built with consideration for the disabilities of the blind, and all sorts of beautiful equipment. Later there was to be a dam and an agricultural project. Then these boys would be trained to grow their own food.

The Leprosy Settlement at Makutupora became quite inadequate for the needs of leprosy patients. For example, the water supply was scanty. Alf approached the Government many times for a suitable plot of land for a new centre, but this was not easy to procure. Where there were settled villages the people did not want sufferers from leprosy to be in their midst. Yet a good supply of water and fertile land was essential so the patients could become self-supporting for food.

The right **timing** for the creation of a new centre occurred when the course of a river, which only flowed during the rainy season, was changed in order to save the east-west road from breaking up during the rains, and was converted into what became quite a large permanent dam at Hombolo.

Alf asked for, and was granted, a large plot of land near the water. Friends from the Geological Department in Dodoma analysed the soil to find if it was suitable for supporting buildings, and the Reverend Geoff Croft and his family came from CMS Sydney and lived at Hombolo in camping style. They built the first house there so that the other anticipated building work could begin.

Eventually it became a beautiful centre with an airy hospital, a dispensary, houses for the patients, staff housing, a chapel and a farm, fruit and vegetable plantations, and later on a fish project. Many able and skilled people brought this into being. Let me name a few. First there was George Hart, a farmer from New Zealand. He had applied to CMS and spent time in training at Moore College, Sydney. In his early days in Tanganyika he was engaged in building at Katoke Teachers' Training Centre in the West, after that at Mvumi at the Girls' School, and also at a Nurses' home for trainee nurses.

Then George built our home, Bishopsbourne, and other projects. He spent his later years building the Hombolo Leprosy Centre and he started the farm there with agriculture and animal husbandry. He kept Ayrshire cows for milk and imported an excellent goat from Pakistan to produce good progeny from the local female goats; he also started poultry keeping. George grew maize and millet, planted fruit trees and other food plants and upgraded the local Zebu cattle so that they were sleek and healthy. In all this work the leprosy patients participated as they could and other Africans were trained in the general farm work. A fine tractor came as a gift from England.

George Hart was one of God's able and skilled workers. But it could have been otherwise, for he had been very ill in his early days at Mvumi. He suffered from ulcerative colitis. Dr Winteler, our friend and the consultant physician in Nairobi, examined him carefully and his advice was that George should return home as Dr Winteler considered he had a poor life expectancy. George asked Alf to anoint him with oil and pray for his healing, taking his request from James 5:14-15 — 'Is any among you sick? Let him call for the elders of the Church and let them pray over him, anointing him with oil in the name of the Lord, and the prayer of faith will save the sick man, and the Lord will raise him up.'

Alf spent some time talking to George. Alf's own stance was that the **sick man himself** must be the one to do the asking, and he, even as his Bishop, would not have suggested it. So an evening was set aside with all our missionary family. George was anointed. We knelt in prayer with much sympathy for George and with a keen desire for his healing.

George returned to Mvumi and in the next few weeks began to feel much better. When he returned to see Dr Winteler, he declared that if he had not examined George personally on the first visit, he would have thought it was a mistaken diagnosis. So George made a good recovery and went on building, including our house, and was married at the end of his tour to Joan Libbey — a great partner for George.

A few years later the illness recurred. This time his guidance was to undergo an operation in Sydney and from then on he was obliged to wear an ileostomy aid. He so mastered this that he carried on all his farming work, even to driving the big tractor. He did a great work for God.

Win Preston, a nurse from Sydney, was another treasure for Hombolo. She had long experience in leprosy work from years spent in Makutupora, and moved to the new centre where she worked until she retired to Australia. She was able to speak Swahili and Gogo and was a good steward of all the available resources, a wonderful asset to the new doctor.

Two more fine qualified people were God's gift to us for Hombolo. They were Dr Guy and Mrs Dawn Timmis. Dawn came to Uganda as a CMS missionary from Western Australia and married Guy, an English doctor in the Ugandan Medical Service. Her mother, formerly Miss M. Barry, had been sent to Uganda by the New South Wales Branch of CMS in 1905. Her father, the Reverend H.A. Brewer from England also arrived in 1905, and after their marriage in 1908, they stayed in Uganda until Mr Brewer died.

When Uganda became independent in 1962, expatriate doctors were replaced by national Ugandan doctors. The Timmis' did not feel they were ready for retirement, so offered to come to our diocese. They went to Mvumi first and then each one, separately, felt that God was calling them to work among sufferers from leprosy. So they found a lovely new hospital waiting for them at Hombolo and did a great work there. Alf and I always felt refreshed after our visits to them.

Every building project became an item on the agenda of Diocesan Council. So when the time was right for a house to be built for the Bishop, Alf explained what he had in mind, adding that he would probably be the only expatriate to live in it since the next Diocesan would be an African. To finance this building he did not want to

Bishopsbourne Chapel, Dodoma.

divert any funds which were given for work in Africa. He suggested that the house owned by the Diocese in King's Road, Windsor in England be sold, as we no longer needed a headquarters there. The Council agreed and the proceeds of the sale were sufficient to build Bishopsbourne and its Chapel.

A good architect, Victor Maddox lived in Mwanza in the West of Tanganyika. He came to Dodoma, saw the plot of land Alf had obtained from the Government authorities and studied the features needed and produced a very good plan. The Chapel was to be fairly large in order to be available for auxiliary services, conferences, retreats, the weekly prayer meeting, etc. On Sundays the Cathedral was busy with services in three languages — English, Gogo and Swahili, so there was no time available there for Family Services where young children could come. The Chapel proved ideal for this purpose.

George Hart built to the specifications with a good labour force whom he had trained. As there were termites everywhere in the soil, the walls were of concrete blocks faced with local coloured stone on the front of the Chapel and on the outer walls of the sitting room. The remainder of the area had a Tyrolean finish, the flooring being of terrazzo tiles, with Mangalore tiles on the roof. Bishopsbourne was built so well, that in the fifteen years we lived in it there was never a repair needed. We moved in in August 1956 and I set about planting trees and shrubs.

Alf envisaged a fine functional building for the Diocesan headquarters, to be built near the Cathedral. The ground floor was to consist of a large bookshop and a chemist's shop. There was no chemist's shop in Dodoma. Medicines were usually sold by the Indians in their shops, and nothing could be dispensed unless obtained through the Government medical services. On the first floor Alf planned a Professional Unit with a doctor and a dentist. (The setting up of a doctor's surgery was a further reason for having a chemist's shop.) The top floor of the building was to house all the diocesan offices and the Bishop's office was to open out on to a balcony from which there was a grand view.

Alf prayed a good deal about this building and as usual he asked God for a 'seal'. He always called this his 'harbinger' and when it came along he began to go ahead with the project. The building took much longer to finance than he had thought, but eventually it was all paid for. Where now, though, was Alf to find the right person to supervise this work? Just at this time Bert Cyster came into our lives. He was an engineer with much experience in building. He had been working in Southern Tanganyika and was experiencing financial difficulties and was in need of engineering or construction work. Alf agreed to hire him, but for wages, while Alf and his staff would do all the costing and order all the materials, etc.

As the building progressed a name was considered for it. 'Mackay House' was chosen, to commemorate the first missionary to spend time in inland Tanganyika.

One of the problems which still troubled Alf was the condition of Mvumi Hospital. He knew that rebuilding it would be very costly and where were the Christian people who could furnish so large an offering? Alf prayed a great deal about this matter but knew that he must wait for God's timing. When it came it certainly was another 'experience of God'. Alf had to attend a conference in Kenya with ecumenical delegates from many countries. He shared a two-bunk cubicle with a small rotund German gentleman with a mild heart condition. Because of this Alf climbed up to the top bunk.

They had good opportunities for conversation and each asked the other who he was and what he represented. Alf's room mate told him that he represented an organisation in West Germany called 'Bread for the World'. On one Sunday every year, a special offering was made in all the churches he represented and it was devoted to special needs in developing countries. 'Do you help hospitals?' asked Alf. 'Why, yes', he replied, 'Do **you** have hospitals which need help?' Then Alf told him about Mvumi and how it needed rebuilding with a good big new ward, an operating theatre and modern equipment. 'How much does it require? Ten thousand pounds or £100,000?', asked the German. Alf said that £100,000 would be enough for the first stage.

So the meeting with this man, whose name now escapes me, not only produced £100,000, but the same sum again for a second stage, and also led to an introduction to other German donor agencies, all wanting to help developing nations. Among these

were the Good Samaritan Foundation, the Christoffel Blinden-
mission and EZE which stood for the Protestant Central Agency for
Development Aid of West Germany. All of these agencies were to
pour much money into the Diocese and so produce lasting buildings. God's people from all over the world were giving from their
hearts to projects that could never be financed by the African
Church.

The German agencies were very efficient and required regular
reports on the buildings. They studied the plans, most of which
were the work of the Bransgrove firm of Dar-es-Salaam. At every
stage Alf costed the work and sent reports. These became the
basis of further grants for other buildings, as the Germans realised
the Diocese was a good steward of their money.

Then under the auspices of the Christian Council of Tanganyika,
a large Conference Centre was built near the Cathedral. This
Council is representative of all the mainline churches and Alf was
Chairman of it for several years. The funds for building the
Conference Centre came from overseas and great developments
were also made at the Alliance Secondary School — large dormitories and fine classroom blocks. Berega and Kilimantinde Hospitals had additional buildings too, theatres, nurses quarters, extra
wards, etc.

The Bible Schools were another wonderful story. The Diocesan
Synod which met just before Alf took home leave in 1960, asked
him to appeal in Australia for money to build Bible Schools for the
training of African evangelists. Alf told the Synod that CMS was
bound to support its mission team on the field but could not be
asked to commit itself to projects which were earmarked, such as
this. However he agreed to put their proposal to the church at
home for consideration, and said he was prepared to appeal for
funds if permitted. Before he reached home he heard that the New
Zealand Church had offered to pay for one school, and on telling of
the need himself, the finance was obtained for the other schools.
By this means Bible Schools were set up quickly at Msalato in the
centre, Morogoro in the East and Kasulu in the West.

Kongwa had long been the centre for Theological training from
its days as a mission station — it commenced in 1904 under the old
Diocese of Mombasa. Runaway slaves from the large slave cara-
vans going down to Bagamoyo often ended up at Kongwa, as it was
well off the route and reasonably safe. There is an enormous
baobab tree there under which the gospel was first preached to the
people, and Canon Westgate from Canada, a missionary of CMS
England, founded St Philip's College there in 1914 — it was called
Huron College in those days. Under Westgate's direction a large
two-storey building was erected. The ground floor became a chapel

and classrooms and the upper floor became living quarters for the college staff. Later, a large house was built for the lady missionaries, and a maternity clinic. Student accommodation was humble, and not far away was a large parish church.

Kongwa station was at the foot of a hill and a long view from the hilltop showed a great flat plain spreading out for miles. This became the site of the great Ground Nut Scheme. After the Second World War, the British Government financed a scheme for producing ground nuts which would be used for edible oils, margarine manufacture, etc. Down from the mission was the small township of Kongwa and here the Ground Nut Scheme built staff houses, a school, a hospital and a system of roads. The surrounding land was totally cleared. The baobab trees were removed and the soil prepared and planted with the nuts. But when the time came to harvest the crop, the soil had baked hard and the nuts could not be extracted. The scheme was a failure and a financial disaster. However it **was** good country for ground nuts, and with hindsight, it was agreed that a small pilot scheme should have been tried initially. The Africans, who grew ground nuts successfully, always left the trees for shade for their crops.

A secondary school for expatriates' children was built at Kongwa, and Bishop Wynn Jones built a beautiful little church on a hill nearby. The dedication of this was his last episcopal act in 1950. In our first years in the diocese, Alf held confirmations there for children from the school. The windows were of clear glass and it was not an uncommon sight to see monkeys peering through the glass during services.

With the failure of the Ground Nut Scheme, the town became deserted and the school moved to Iringa, but the little hospital remained, and Alf closed down the maternity clinic on the Mission Station. As the Ground Nut Scheme was wound up, large public auctions were held for the buildings, equipment and stores. Alf encouraged Max Wiggins, George Pearson, Norman Powys, Norman Gelding, George Hart and Kevin Engel to attend these and to 'buy up' anything useful for the development of the diocese. In this way many of our bush schools received corrugated iron roofing and Mvumi hospital obtained its first electricity generator. Other things purchased were doors, windows, refrigerators, even toilet bowls and two tons of toilet paper (which Kevin Engel sold through the bookshop!).

Bishop Chambers had increased the intake of Kongwa College to forty students in his time, but the need for more clergy to keep pace with church growth, had grown tremendously. The College had a three year course and as most of the ordinands were married men, their wives accompanied them for the second year and courses suitable to their needs were devised. More and more buildings were needed and there was a continuous building programme for class rooms, a Chapel, a common room built in memory of Bishop Chambers, student accommodation, and retaining walls on sloping ground. George Hart's team was well trained, and fashioned the beautiful stone facing which enhanced Kongwa's buildings greatly. A beautiful campus emerged and at the height of the dry season it was aglow with purple bougainvillea and large white frangipani trees.

In 1964, a group of men and women from the Episcopal Church of the USA came with several clergy for a Summer workcamp and built one of the Kongwa classrooms.

In 1965, Alf initiated an additional course called a 'General Knowledge Course', later to be called a 'Pre-Theology Course'. It was for young Africans who had some secondary education and a basic knowledge of English but who, for some reason, were unable to continue higher education. It was a two year course for promising young unmarried students to prepare them for study in English for the ThL Diploma. This course required them to read and understand English theological texts and it covered three years. Jean Meyer, who had been engaged in educational work in the West at Katoke and at Rungwe in Southern Tanganyika and at the Mvumi Girls' School, was asked to be the first Head of this General Knowledge course. Its aim was to reach those who would be likely candidates for theological training in English. This was to be the medium of instruction as it was realised that overseas scholarships would become available to those with some fluency in English. Jean remained at Kongwa, with one or two other shorter assignments in between, until she left the Diocese. Other Kongwa missionaries also lectured to this course.

I think it is a significant fact that three men, all of whom are now African bishops in the Province of Tanzania, started their post-school careers with this course. They are Bishop Gerard Mpango of Western Tanganyika, Bishop Godfrey Mdimi Mhogolo, recently consecrated fifth Bishop of Central Tanganyika, and Bishop Donald Mtetemela, assistant in that Diocese. All these three did post-ordination courses overseas. Jean tells me of others who are now successful in secular careers who likewise attended this course.

The phenomenon of church growth during the twenty years we worked in the Diocese, and the subsequent years under Bishop Yohana Madinda, has frequently been alluded to as 'so many new churches were added each week or fortnight'. I think to Western people a false impression could be conveyed by a statement like this. Most of us equate a 'church' with a building, whereas it would be more correct to say, 'so many new **congregations** were added . . .'. This would in truth mean a gathering of people, perhaps meeting under a tree for some time. A building would be erected later.

Bishop Stephen Neill had a roving commission to evaluate the Church in different lands. He visited East Africa frequently and at one period held the chair of Religious Studies in the University of Nairobi. In a book entitled *Call to Mission*, he referred to Alf and the kind of church growth being experienced in Tanganyika. He wrote:

> Shortly after this a new Bishop, an Australian, was appointed to the Diocese of Central Tanganyika, of which the See city is Dodoma. A missionary of long experience in Africa, he took hold of the situation with driving dynamism, and things began to happen.
>
> Asked in 1964 what he reckoned to be the average increase in the number of Christians in his area, he answered '9 per cent per annum'. The expert mathematician will calculate at once that this means that a church will double itself in seven and a half years. Four years later the Bishop's figure was shown to be almost exactly accurate.
>
> After sixteen years of his episcopate the church in the area was found to have quadrupled itself — from twenty thousand to eighty thousand. If cross-examined as to the causes of this remarkable development, the Bishop would probably lay stress on four factors:
> (a) A powerful and convincing message leading up to a personal surrender to Jesus Christ.
> (b) No spoon feeding. Nothing to be done for African Christians except those things they cannot possibly do for themselves; if they want a church, let them build it themselves by co-operative effort, in the simple style that is suitable to their surroundings.
> (c) The missionary was to keep strictly in the background; responsibility for its own life is to be carried by the African church itself.
> (d) At the earliest possible date, African Christians are to be taught to take up the task of bearing witness to others and so to keep the movement moving.
> What the Bishop would not mention would be admirable and disciplined organisation at the centre, scrupulously careful use of funds, and the encouraging presence of a leader the heart and soul of whose own ministry is the insatiable desire that men and women should be won for Christ.
>
> It is good to be able to add, as an example of international co-operation, that as a result of generous funds made available from Germany, it has been possible to revolutionize the educational work of the Diocese, and so help forward the training of those who in the days to come should be the leaders of the African church.[1]

In the next chapter I want to speak of how Alf envisaged the

[1]*Call to Mission* by Stephen Neill, Fortress Press, Philadelphia, USA, 1970, page 84.

carrying out of Bishop Tucker's[2] definition of what the African Church should be (he advanced these principles set out initially by Henry Venn, a founding member of the Church Missionary Society):

Self-propagating

Self-supporting

Self-governing.

Bishop Tucker succeeded Bishops Hannington and Parker, neither of whom lived to enter Uganda. He had a reasonably long episcopate in Uganda and worked to those principles.

[2]The third Bishop of Uganda, the previous two having died before reaching the diocese.

CHAPTER 9

THE GROWING CHURCH

How does the church grow in Tanganyika? Back in 1844 the first CMS missionary to East Africa, Dr Ludwig Krapf conceived the idea of a chain of mission stations crossing the continent from East to West. Growth would come with the continuous movement westwards. Then by natural means it would be possible to penetrate North and South.

In fact, the history of the Church in East Africa shows that growth was achieved by work begun next to other established work. This has been the normal pioneering method in Tanganyika. New congregations which were formed to worship God through the knowledge of the Lord Jesus Christ reached out naturally to neighbouring villages where he was not known, and a nucleus of groups of believing people were soon incorporated into a parish.

Under both Bishop Chambers and Bishop Wynn Jones the church had grown steadily. In 1927 there were only two clergy. When Alf came in 1951 there were thirty-five. There were eighteen missionaries in 1928 but seventy-seven by 1951 from England, Australia and New Zealand.

At his enthronement Alf said he wanted to see great strides made in the expansion of the Churches of the Diocese. Tanganyika was a developing country and the Church must grow in self-support in both the African congregations and English-speaking chaplaincies. Alf stressed the need to break away from continuing financial support from the countries that sent missionaries and he stressed the need to make greater use of the laity in every branch of the Church's work. He wanted to see work established and continuing among the Asians in Tanganyika. He also mentioned the importance of raising the standard of entrance for the ministry, and giving careful attention to the training of clergy as well as a longer and more efficient training for African evangelists.

So, these were the patterns and goals set by Alf for the coming years. In order to understand the background against which these aims were to be achieved, I want to give a picture of African rural life — it was there that the growth was greatest.

The pattern of an Anglican parish in rural Tanganyika differs greatly from any that we know in the West. There, a parish is the sphere of one pastor but it is common for it to contain ten churches — or congregations — or even more! Even today in Africa, it is doubtful whether one church could ever support its own pastor, except in large townships. The pastor can only be effective by the continuous ministry of a team of evangelists who are really the spearhead of the church. It is they who conduct most of the regular Sunday services, teach literacy to unschooled adults, take classes for baptism and confirmation and support their pastor in any other local duties. The pastor must be a supervisor and itinerate to take the Holy Communion to the churches for which he is responsible — sometimes three or four churches will combine for their regular Communion Service. Each church elects a group of *wazee* (elders) who may be men or women, their counterpart in our system being a Vestry or Parish Council. In Central Tanganyika, there are still today many more baptisms of adults than of children. Throughout the Diocese, the first of November (or the first Sunday in November) is set aside for adult baptisms, after which these people join a confirmation class. The first of November is chosen since it is the Patronal Festival of the Diocese, the day on which it was formed.

The evangelists work for a pittance. Most of them grow their own food and would be likely to be paid a very small cash sum each month by the Church. This does not deter them for volunteering for the work! The majority of African Christians in rural areas are subsistence farmers. A few may plant cash crops depending on the fertility of the soil and rainfall patterns, but the majority depend on crops of maize and millet for their own maintenance perhaps also with ground nuts, sweet potatoes and cassava. The government urges the growing of the root cassava as a famine crop.

In the Central Province of Tanganyika, around Dodoma, the rainfall is low and recurring famines are normal with resultant suffering and loss. Most families keep a few goats and poultry and a few cattle if possible. Where rain water can be conserved, good tomatoes are grown.

As small congregations formed little churches and their numbers grew, an evangelist was appointed to teach them, among many other things, stewardship and their obligation to give to God out of their means. Few people had cash, so the offerings on a Sunday were mostly in kind — maize, millet, eggs, ground nuts, sweet potatoes, and on special occasions hens, sheep and goats. These goods were sold locally. The parish as a whole has to give a stated percentage of its offerings to the Central Church Fund (CCF), and it had to pay its pastor at a rate decided by the Diocesan Council. If a parish was unable to support its pastor it could lose him, though this rarely happened. Especially in famine times the pastor was underpaid — everyone understood the stresses of those times.

The CCF met diocesan costs and expenses and a Provident Fund was established to assist in a pastor's retirement. There are no age pensions in these African countries, so many children in a family are considered the best insurance for old age.

African cultural life is based on an extended family system whereby a child's relationship is based on the brothers and sisters of his *Mama* (Mother) and *Baba* (Father). All his father's brothers he calls *Baba, Baba mkubwa* for an older brother and *Baba mdogo* for a younger brother, and all their children are his brothers and sisters. His mother's sisters are likewise called *Mama mkubwa* or *mdogo* as the case may be, and all their children are also his brothers and sisters. His mother's brothers he calls, uncle and his father's sisters are aunts. This usually means that an African child has a number of relatives who may support him, and in many instances they helped with school fees when their circumstances were better than those of his parents. Because of this wider family life Africans understand community living very well and the Church becomes a strong community of people sharing a similar life-style.

The Gospel of Christ is often carried by a young and keen church to neighbouring villages where as yet there is no witness, and the people are still following tribal and animistic cultural patterns. One parish that I know of decided to make a parish witness to a nearby area where as yet there were no Christians. They asked the residents there if they would receive a group of them for a few days. Africans are naturally hospitable and they were warmly welcomed and fed. As it grew dark a large camp fire was built out in the open, the drums were set nearby to warm so that the stretched skin would soften a little and not be too taut. The host village then entertained the visitors with singing and dancing to the accompaniment of the drums.

Then the visiting Christians responded using a cantor and chorus pattern, singing and dramatizing the Gospel message in easily memorised sentences such as 'God loves us and he sent His Son Jesus to teach us'. The hosts were encouraged to join the chorus after each sentence. This could go on for hours, and each piece of Christian teaching would be repeated and sung again and again. Questions often followed and the hosts would be invited back to the Christians' villages in return and so a bridge would be built. It was likely that 'teachers' would then be invited to teach them about *Yesu Kristo* (Jesus Christ) and the process of evangelism would get under way.

In later years teaching by cassettes proved very popular and it still is today. Cassettes were played on hand-winding machines, by evangelists. Where they encountered other languages, a cassette in that tongue aroused much interest and curiosity and opened the way for further teaching.

When Alf was endeavouring to place well-trained evangelists in areas away from their home, it was necessary to support them financially for two years. By that time it was assumed that they would have built up a body of believers into congregations that would support them. CMS sometimes made decreasing grants for initial church planting of this kind, the grant diminishing each year for approximately five years.

Alf also stressed pioneer evangelism. Pastors of parishes were asked to tell their congregations of the need to send evangelists to unevangelised areas, and to ask them to give regularly towards their support, and many did so. Let me tell you about two such people. The first was an elderly widow. She lived alone in a humble hut and kept a few goats and some hens. She used to walk several miles into Dodoma at regular intervals and make her offering in small sums at the Diocesan Office. Every time she sold a goat or a chicken she put aside a portion for God, and when the sum seemed large enough to her, she would bring it in for pioneer evangelism. She would receive a receipt with the diocesan address on it and return home. When she died, her sons came to collect her few belongings and they found a number of these headed receipts, and not knowing what it meant, they came to see the Bishop who explained that this was what she gave to God to make it possible to send a man to preach the gospel in a pioneer area. Her giving totalled about 4,000/-, a big sum in those days, which would have supported an evangelist for some years. This was devoted and consistent giving out of her love for her Lord.

The second person was a man called Simeoni, a cattle dealer. He was a nominal Christian until he was invited to a series of Revival Fellowship Convention meetings not far from his home. He was convicted of his sins, repented and was soundly converted to Christ. He went home rejoicing in his new found faith saying, 'God has forgiven all my sins!'. He hadn't actually felt convicted of drunkenness yet, so called to his wife to bring him some of her warm home-brewed but potent beer. She did so and he raised the cup to his lips but was unable to drink the beer. He tried several times, and then called to his wife: 'This beer is cold, bring me some more warm beer'. She did so but again he could not get it past his lips. Eventually he put the cup down, realising God was trying to teach him something. He never drank again and repented of the former sin of drunkenness and put his life in order. He decided that every time he sold cattle he would give a generous portion to God for pioneer evangelism. What he gave supported several evangelists for years. Shortly before we left Africa we met him in the local garage. He told us, 'God has blessed me greatly!'. When we asked in what way he said, 'All my children have been accepted for secondary education'. This was indeed great news as the opportunities are few and only those children who do well in the examinations are selected. Truly God is no man's debtor.

As a race Africans are spiritually very perceptive. I do not know whether any African atheists even exist? They are perceptive of both good and evil. In their tribal forms of worship, Satan was worshipped in a placatory way so that he would not harm them. They made him offerings of food and drink. The spirits of their ancestors they felt to be near and they are aware that they themselves have a spiritual nature. They have a great capacity to endure hardship and to 'put up with' a situation which calls for long-suffering. They hang loose to life often with a quite fatalistic attitude. When sorrows or tragedies occur they say it is *Shauri la Mungu* (God's affair).

Most of the African languages have no verb to 'own' or 'possess'. You can only 'be with' something or it is 'with you'. Family members share everything they have with each other. If a visitor comes, even uninvited, he is made welcome and fed, though if he overstays the welcome, he may find a hoe under his bed one morning! They are very perceptive of the Gospel and many become truly radiant Christians. From them we learned much of humility, devotion and enduring service. One African held out the open palm of his hand to Alf and said, 'You must put all you have on the open palm of your hand, so that if God wants it He won't hurt you, but if you grasp things to yourself He may have to hurt you.'

The evangelists were often people of the highest calibre. One day Alf was travelling to a Confirmation service with Archdeacon Meshak Meda. On the way they passed a new *Ujamaa* (communal) village, the type that was brought into being after Independence. New huts were built and others were under construction so Alf asked Meshak, 'Do we have an evangelist here yet?' 'Not yet *Askofu* (Bishop).' 'Why not?' 'It will need a very good man.' 'Do you know of a good man?' 'Yes Askofu, but I don't know whether he is willing to come here.' 'Why not?' 'Well, he has just finished building his house and was recently married, but you will meet him today. He will be at the service and you can ask him yourself.'

After the service Meshak brought this good man to meet Alf who asked him about himself and his work. Would he consider going to this new *Ujamaa* village as an evangelist? The man answered that he would have to go home and discuss it with his wife. He left but

returned quickly with his wife and when Alf asked what decision
had been made, he was told, yes, they were willing to go. Alf was
delighted and said, 'When would you be ready to go?' 'Tomorrow?'
asked the man. This was a humbling reply to Alf to think that the
man and his wife were ready to go at once, at such short notice, to
serve God in a needy area.

As more young Christians passed through Secondary School and
some through Teacher Training Courses both at Katoke and
Rungwe, a few responded to God's call to the ministry. One such
was Yohana Madinda who was born in 1926, just before the
creation of the Diocese of Central Tanganyika. When Alf arrived in
Dodoma in 1951, Yohana was teaching at Kilimatinde. He had been
a pupil at the Alliance Secondary School in Dodoma and had been
trained as a teacher at Rungwe in Southern Tanganyika. He had
married another teacher, Mwendwa, who was at that time a more
committed Christian than he. She persuaded him to start family
prayers with her and the children. When he came to be interviewed
by Alf with a view to the ministry he told of how he had been
reluctant to pray with Mwendwa as he sensed that she would ask
God to make him the kind of man he didn't want to be! He was
much blessed through Revival Fellowship meetings at Kilimatinde,
yielded his life to Christ and felt a call to the ministry.

When Alf had this interview with him the academic year was
about to start and there were no vacant places at Kongwa. Rather
than miss out a year of training, Alf applied for and received a place
for him and Mwendwa at St Paul's College in Limuru, Kenya.
Yohana did the full course and later came on to the staff of the
Cathedral of the Holy Spirit in Dodoma, following ordination.

As political awareness was increasing in the land Alf felt that
it was the time to appoint an African bishop. As yet there was
not a single African bishop in Kenya or Tanganyika, though Uganda
had appointed one. Alf had discussed the matter with the Archbishop of Canterbury. In view of the fact that none of the present
clergy had higher educational qualifications, His Grace's advice was
to choose an able saintly man from among the clergy and he would
consecrate him.

So, the Reverend Yohana Omari of the Cathedral staff was
chosen to be the first African bishop in the whole of Tanganyika.
The Archbishop of Canterbury was willing to come to East Africa
for the consecration. By the time a date was agreed upon, Kenya
had two Africans to be consecrated also. They were a Luyia, the
Reverend Festo Olang' and a Kikuyu, the Reverend Obadiah
Kariuki.

Both were very fine Christians, personally known to us. Also to
be consecrated was the Reverend Canon Daniel Deng Atong of the

Diocese of the Sudan. All four of these men were to be assistant bishops in their dioceses.

The CMS Australia sent warm congratulatory greetings to Yohana, assuring him of their prayers and wishing him God's blessing. Sunday 15th May 1955 was appointed for the Consecration by the Archbishop of Canterbury at St Paul's Cathedral Namirembe, Kampala, Uganda. This was a very fitting setting for the service, as both the dioceses of Mombasa and Central Tanganyika derived from the mother diocese of Eastern Equatorial Africa, centred in Uganda. Great numbers of people from each diocese gathered for the ceremony. Alf and I busied ourselves with outfitting Yohana and his wife Ana. Yohana went ahead of us to a retreat for the Bishops Designate in Kampala. Many of our DCT clergy and missionaries, also lay church members, travelled by train to Mwanza, then by lake steamer to Entebbe and by road to Kampala. Alf and I, with Maxwell and Margaret Wiggins, travelled via Nairobi by car.

Alf had the privilege and joy of acting as Chaplain to the Archbishop and carrying the Primatial Cross in the ceremony. The forms of service for the Ordering of Bishops were printed in three

Abp Geoffrey Fisher and Yohana Omari (on Abp's L.) after Yohana's consecration as the first Tanzanian Bishop at Namirembe Cathedral, Kampala, Uganda, 1955. Alfred Stanway is holding the Primatial Cross of Canterbury. (Photograph: Dept of Information, Kampala)

columns: in English, Luganda and Swahili. The Governor of Uganda and other African Rulers were present including the Kabaka (King) Mutesa of Buganda and his wife, and rulers from the other African kingdoms in Uganda.

Several Holy Tables had been set up in the Cathedral so that all present could take communion. Alf had the privilege of taking communion to Ham Mukasa, now too old and frail to come to the communion rail. He had been a page boy in the court of the Kabaka Mutesa I at the very beginning of the coming of the gospel to Uganda. He escaped the fate of many of his peers who were put to death by the Kabaka because of their Christian stand against Mutesa's immorality. This was a great historical link with the earliest days of Christianity in Uganda. In the afternoon there was a great garden party in the grounds of Makerere University when all the visitors were able to mingle together and share in the joy of the occasion.

On returning to the Diocese of Central Tanganyika, Yohana first went to Mpwapwa, the earliest centre of Christian witness in Tanganyika in 1876. Alf was to leave him there for a few years until the church of the Holy Trinity in Morogoro and two staff houses were built. This was preparing the eastern section of the Diocese to become separate.

Another of Alf's objectives referred to in his enthronement sermon was for ministry to Asians. These people came from many parts of India, but the vast majority were merchants and traders from the Bombay area. From earliest times dhows had sailed between Africa and India following the trade winds. Seasonal winds blew them to India and winds from the reverse quarter blew them back again. Trade between the two countries had a long history. Some of the Tanganyika Asians were Hindus, some Sikhs who were skilled artisans and some Muslims (many of the Ismailia sect, followers of the Aga Khan). The dominant language of the Bombay region was Gujerati and the *lingua franca* was Hindi. Alf started to pray for a Gujerati-speaking clergyman to come to Tanganyika. On one of his overseas trips he was able to meet with Bishop Jacob of the Church of South India and told him of his desire for a godly Gujerati-speaking clergyman. Bishop Jacob said he had a very good man — the only one who could speak Gujerati — called Mathai John. He was one of his best men. 'If that is so, you won't want to lose him,' said Alf. 'No, not so,' said Bishop Jacob, 'My people have been taught that we grow spiritually as we give the best away.'

So, Bishop Jacob sent the Reverend Mathai John, his wife Maryamu and their two little sons to commence work among Asians in Tanganyika. He came first to Dodoma, and accommodation was rented for him in a large Asian multi-storeyed building occupied by Indians. Later he went to Morogoro where he and Bishop Omari lived side by side, Morogoro being close enough to Dar-es-Salaam for him to contact Indians in that city. Another little son, Joseph, was born to them in Dodoma in 1956 and I was privileged to be his sponsor in baptism. Sadly Mathai John was not destined to be with us for long, for while in Morogoro he was operated on for appendicitis. Complications set in after surgery and he died, to our very great sorrow.

A little later another Indian pastor, the Reverend K.T. Thomas, also from South India came to replace Mathai John. He lived first in Morogoro but moved later to Dar-es-Salaam where there were many opportunities for ministry. Many Indians in Tanganyika were very friendly and very helpful to us, but did not convert to Christianity. Sadru Damji, who had a large hardware business in Dodoma was particularly helpful in supplying the Diocese with building materials, etc. — he was a good friend.

At one stage we organised a meeting at our house for a mixed group of men and women who were Aga Khan followers. One of the ladies had asked me previously if I would give a 'lecture' on Christianity. Some of our missionaries, Bishop Omari and Festo Kivengere represented the Christian faith and we agreed to 'witness' to what Christ meant to us personally and not to 'lecture'. Among those who witnessed were Jean Guy (diocesan accountant), Kevin Engel (our bookshop manager), Yohana and Festo. Then the meeting was thrown open to questions. Kevin was given a difficult one to answer — the difference between Roman Catholics and Protestants! He coped very well with this, but a dominant question related to 'sin' — why did we need pardon? Could not a good living man be saved by his good life, etc? We found that most of them had read the New Testament but none would take a step towards baptism. Their religion and their culture are firmly interwoven and conversion to Christianity for them means being an outcast from their community.

In 1957, the diocese was divided into four archdeaconries. Max Wiggins was appointed Archdeacon of Victoria Nyanza, a vast area bordering the Eastern, Southern and Western shores of Lake Victoria Nyanza, with a view to this becoming a future diocese. (It is in fact three dioceses today.) Lionel Bakewell became, at the same time, Archdeacon of the West, which comprised North and South Uha and the towns of Kigoma and Tabora. Archdeacon Cordell continued in the central region with the districts of Kilimatinde, Mpwapwa, Dodoma, Kongwa, Buigiri and Mvumi as his archdeaconry. Archdeacon Daudi Muhando had oversight of the East-Morogoro, Kilosa, Berega and Unguu districts.

On a confirmation tour in the West with Lionel Bakewell, Alf, at

On safari in the West: Marjory and Alfred Stanway with the Rev. Lionel Bakewell.

Bp Yohana Omari, 1955.

Lionel's request, had agreed to go to a remote place called Kivumba to confirm a crippled woman. She had missed previous confirmations which were held at bigger centres because these lay beyond a belt of the tsetse fly country. Owing to her disability she was unable to walk quickly through the tsetse belt and so would be over-exposed to the fly.

This safari took some organising. Lionel was a master of gadgets. It was his task to load up a tent, camp beds, mosquito nets, food, cooking utensils, lamps, etc. From long experience he had safari life very well organised. He arranged to have 'flashes' cut on trees to mark out a route for us since there was no road for the Land Rover to follow and Lionel had to find his way through the bush. Another hazard for the car was the large pot holes caused by elephants as they trampled through the soft muddy soil.

Attached to the Land Rover was a trailer with the camping equipment on board. An African servant travelled with us. On one stage of the journey he calmly said *'behewa imebaki!'* (the trailer has stayed behind!). Lionel pulled up and attached the trailer again. In spite of all the hazards we reached Kivumba safely. As I was the first white woman to visit there I was somewhat of a curiosity. We erected the tent and put up the camp beds. There were distant roars of lions about, so I went around tucking the loose canvas flaps under the legs of the camp beds. Alf was very amused, 'No lion would be deterred by that', he said. He intended to sleep, but in fact we were only able to do so for a few short hours as it became extremely cold, a cold which seemed to come up out of the ground. We piled on all the clothing we could find, and newspapers, but still shivered till daylight. Lionel on his camp bed in the trailer was cold too and even the African servant, in a hut, could not sleep so he got up at 5.00 a.m., made a fire and produced tea for us. We gratefully warmed our hands on the mugs. Once the sun came up the cold disappeared and we had a lovely service in their little mud church. This was an unforgettable experience for Alf and me.

On 11th June 1959, Maxwell Wiggins was consecrated in the Cathedral of the Holy Spirit, Dodoma, as an assistant Bishop in Central Tanganyika. He was consecrated by Alf under mandate from the Archbishop of Canterbury. Maxwell then returned to Mwanza which was to become the See City of the new diocese of Victoria Nyanza (on 16th March 1963) and he its first Bishop.

The Archbishop of Uganda at the time of his consecration was Leslie Brown. He and his wife, Winifred, came to Dodoma, where he conducted a retreat for Max and assisted in the service. Max had been in Tanganyika since 1944, working first at Berega, then as Headmaster of the Alliance Secondary School in Dodoma and Provost of the Cathedral. He was then Principal of Kongwa College before becoming Archdeacon of Victoria Nyanza.

Bishop Yohana Omari diligently visited all the areas under his care at Unguu, Berega, Kilosa and south to the sugar growing area of Kilombero. He took part in many of the Revival Fellowship Conventions in these areas. He attended the Lambeth Conference in 1958 and was accommodated with us (ninety bishops and many of the wives) at Westfield College. He had a wonderful sense of direction and often navigated for Alf when he was driving out of London. Yohana told us of the impact of Western materialism on him. As he saw the great shops of London he saw many things he would have liked to buy for his family. He told of how God had spoken to him from John 4:14, 'Whoever drinks of the water that I shall give him will never thirst; the water that I shall give him will become in him a spring of water welling up to eternal life.' He said his thirst for 'things' was taken away and Jesus satisfied him. After the 1958 Lambeth Conference, Alf sent him to Australia with Festo Kivengere where he made a great impression for his Lord.

In May 1960, The Archbishop of York, Michael Ramsay, accompanied by his Chaplain, Martin Kaye, spent a weekend with us. The object of his visit to Tanganyika was the celebration of a hundred years of the work of the Universities' Mission to Central Africa. He had visited the Diocese of Masasi and South West Tanganyika and then flew up to us via Iringa. He arrived on the Saturday morning. At that time John Denton had returned from leave, but as Shirley had not yet joined him he was staying with us and proved a great help in looking after the Archbishop. It was a hectic week-end for me, four men staying in the house, nine people to lunch and a garden party for 500 in our grounds that afternoon. All the African clergy came to Dodoma for the occasion. They met His Grace at the airport all clad in cassocks. This was a deliberate ruling as many of them were quite poor and did not have good clothing, but all had cassocks.

Diocesan officials, clergy, missionaries and Government officials and their wives comprised the group at the party. The African clergy handed round tea and food — sandwiches and cakes — in large open African baskets. That night our house party all had dinner at the home of the Provincial Commissioner. Next day His Grace attended all the services in the Cathedral. He preached at night from 1 Peter 2:5, '... and like living stones be yourselves built up into a spiritual house'.

The Archbishop of Canterbury and Mrs Fisher were also our guests at the end of July, 1960, along with Michael Adie, the chaplain. His visit to Tanganyika was to inaugurate the Province of East Africa in Dar-es-Salaam. Once again all our clergy gathered at the Dodoma airport. There was a large luncheon party, but the garden party was at the school at Kikuyu. I remember one humorous touch in the Archbishop's talk at the party when he said, 'My wife and I always travel around in double harness', and we locals all waited to see what Lionel Bakewell would say in translation before many people who had never seen a horse in their lives!

Next day Archbishop Fisher preached at all the services and was duly presented with African shields, spears, etc. After evensong we had a reception for the visitors with the Cathedral Congregation in Mackay House. The next day, Monday, was August Bank Holiday. Archbishop and Mrs Fisher had expected to fly to Dar-es-Salaam after breakfast but a message came from Government House to say that the plane was not able to reach Dodoma before 2.00 p.m. We had nothing scheduled for that morning but as members of our Diocese were to play cricket against Government officials, Alf invited the Fishers to go across to the Club and watch the match. His Grace said he might have been watching cricket in England on August Bank Holiday! I organised lunch and after they had left by plane, Alf and I had to scurry off by car to make Dar-es-Salaam for the celebrations the next day. We stayed at Berega overnight and reached Dar-es-Salaam in time for the Garden Party organised as part of the celebrations. On 3rd August 1960, the Province of East Africa was inaugurated and the Right Reverend L.J. Beecher was installed as Archbishop in the Church of St Alban, Dar-es-Salaam, by his Grace the Archbishop of Canterbury. This meant that the Archbishop of Canterbury then yielded up his metropolitical jurisdiction in East Africa — I remember feeling a sense of loss as we no longer prayed for 'Geoffrey our Archbishop' each Sunday.

Alf now felt that the Church was becoming more self-governing.

As he was moved to make each new appointment he consulted with the Diocesan Council, asking each member, in a secret ballot, to show which candidate he favoured.

Thus when Max Wiggins was appointed as Bishop of Victoria Nyanza their preference coincided with Alf's. Once again there was need to get the Western Archdeaconry ready for self-government. This time the Council, with Alf concurring, suggested the Reverend Musa Kahurananga be appointed the first bishop of that area. He was a Muha from that region, and in 1962 he was consecrated at Kasulu by Archbishop Beecher as Assistant Bishop in Central Tanganyika, for service in what had been the Western Archdeaconry. Alf's photographs showed an enormous out-of-door 'church' built just for the occasion, consisting of upright poles and a thatching of dried grass to give protection from the sun. There were multitudes present. Now Alf had three assistant bishops of whom two were Africans.

To our great sorrow Bishop Omari died very suddenly in 1963. He had been at Berega for several days taking part in a big convention with the 'Jesus satisfies' theme. He was kept on the 'go' for hours at a time and when driving back home to Morogoro afterwards he felt unwell and pulled into the home of Pastor Ephraim Madimilo to rest a while. He had just seated himself in a chair when he died from a coronary attack. When the news reached Morogoro early that evening, Ted Newing, the resident chaplain at Morogoro, phoned us at Bishopsbourne with the news. Alf was six miles away taking a mission address at the Msalato Girls' School, so I collected Margaret McKechnie for company, and drove out to tell Alf the news. He came home quickly, contacted Radio Tanganyika in Dar-es-Salaam to put out the information on their late news session, and left early the next morning for Morogoro where he conducted the funeral service. Yohana was buried in the grounds of his church at Holy Trinity and was deeply mourned by his friends and colleagues. Christian friends made themselves responsible for building a little house in Morogoro for Ana where she still lives today.

In 1963 the first division of the Diocese of Central Tanganyika took place with the formation of the Diocese of Victoria Nyanza. Alf and I travelled to Mwanza for the ceremony and celebrations and said goodbye to the Christians of Mwanza. Then Robert Glen, a New Zealand clergyman, drove us to Tarime, for a farewell visit near the Kenya border, after which we travelled by plane to Ngara to say goodbye to our mission centre at Murgwanza. So Victoria Nyanza became the first viable unit separated from the mother Diocese of Central Tanganyika.

In 1964 Yohana Madinda, who had been serving in the Cathedral parish in Dodoma, was consecrated in Morogoro by Archbishop Beecher and for a short time replaced Bishop Omari there as Assistant Bishop. In 1965 Morogoro was now ready for division from the Diocese of Central Tanganyika. Two names were submitted for election, Bishop Yohana Madinda and the Reverend Gresford Chitemo. Gresford had been trained at Moore College, Sydney and was a native of Ukaguru. He asked for his name to be withdrawn, but so did Yohana, since each felt the other to be the right choice! The committee proceeded with the election and Gresford was chosen and consecrated by Archbishop Beecher at Holy Trinity, Morogoro in 1965. Now there were three assistant bishops, all Africans, and the division of the diocese went forward that same year with Gresford becoming the Bishop of Morogoro. Alf recalled Bishop Yohana Madinda to work with him in the central region. In 1966 Western Tanganyika was divided off with Kasulu as its See city and Musa Kahurananga as its Diocesan.

So Central Tanganyika had divided into four dioceses with three African and two European bishops. Self-government in the church was well established, Bible Schools for the training of evangelists were functioning, and nearly 1000 evangelists and their pastors — now over one hundred in the Central area alone, were continuing the thrust of evangelism and building up self-support. Central Church Funds were reassessed and percentages of offerings fixed to new levels.

One of the structures Alf introduced during his episcopate was the formation of rural deaneries. Archdeaconries had been formed during the early days when the numbers of clergy and churches were much fewer, but with rapid growth in the extensive area of the diocese, it was not possible for the Archdeacons to oversee the administration of the parishes. There were just over twenty rural deaneries when Alf left Dodoma, two had seven parishes, two had six, five had five, nine had four and five had three parishes. When it is remembered that a parish consists of ten or more churches, a deanery was certainly large enough to have its own overseer — a Rural Dean. In fact these men succeeded so well in their oversight of the work that some years later Archdeacons were not reappointed, though the present Bishop is considering restoring this office.

Chaplaincy work over this period was carried on mainly with missionary clergy, and a few under the auspices of the Commonwealth and Continental Church Society. But two retired clergymen, one from Australia and one from England were a great asset to the work. The Reverend Nigel Backhouse from Sydney, the father of one of our missionary doctors, Juliet Backhouse, came out in 1957 and did a complete tour serving in the Tabora Chaplaincy.

He was greatly loved and appreciated. There were two Secondary Schools in Tabora and he related well to the students. Then a Government educational officer, a member of the Cathedral parish in Dodoma, put Alf in touch with his father-in-law who came out from England on a visit. Alf invited the Reverend Frank Read to take a chaplaincy post at Moshi, at the foot of Mount Kilimanjaro. He gladly accepted. There was a temporary church-cum-vicarage there and during Mr Read's tenure he raised the money to build the beautiful new church of St Margaret's. He was a widower and not a very well man but he did a wonderful work in Moshi. The story is told of him visiting all the wealthy coffee-planters who were members of his church and asking for donations towards St Margaret's. A bag of coffee was a very valuable donation. One very wealthy man, on being asked what he would contribute to the fund replied, 'I'll give what I can afford! Whereupon Mr Read raised his hat and said, 'Thank God, the church is built.'

Mr Read stayed until ill-health forced him to retire to England. In 1959 Bishop and Mrs Chambers, by arrangement with Alf, came back to Tanganyika and he became chaplain at Iringa until he left for Australia in February, 1962 by which time he was 84 years old. Mrs Chambers declared that she made a good 'curate'. She did all the office work and their service was greatly appreciated by the expatriates in the Iringa district.

In Arusha one of the longest-serving wardens at Christ Church was Anstis Bewes, who with his wife Beatrice became great friends to us. He was the son of a clergyman and the brother of another (Cecil). He managed the large Ford agency of Riddoch's in Arusha and Alf purchased most of the diocesan fleet of cars through him. Alf financed a scheme for cars which were needed for our work. They were kept on the road by a system of paying mileage through the institution by which they were used, and any personal mileage was paid for by the user. Out of this fund repairs were financed and a capital sum put aside for new vehicles. Any credits in Diocesan bank accounts were put into fixed deposit to earn interest.

All moneys donated to the Diocese were published in a monthly statement and distributed to all diocesan staff, African and European. It showed the origin of the donation, its amount with conversion to Tanzanian shillings and its intended destination. This provided confidence in the administration of the Diocese. There was a very competent loyal office and administrative staff who assisted Alf in this task.

By the time Independence had come to the country in 1961 and it became a Republic in 1962, the Church was well on the way to almost complete Africanisation. Top posts were filled by Africans and many former missionary jobs were under-studied and later filled by Africans.

In 1964 there was a revolution on the island of Zanzibar with the dominant African political party succeeding in ousting the Arab rulers who had held sway for more than a century. It was a possibility that the island could become a communist outpost, with the ultra-socialist government which took over. Dr Julius Nyerere, the President of Tanganyika at the time, himself a socialist but not a communist, was able to initiate a union between the two countries. Zanzibar and Tanganyika became that year the United Republic of Tanzania, a name formed from both their names.

In 1969, the Provincial Synod of East Africa met in Dodoma. It decided that the Province of East Africa should become the two provinces of Tanzania and Kenya. So on 5th July 1970, the Church of the Province of Tanzania was inaugurated at the Cathedral Church of St Nicholas and African Martyrs at Ilala, in Dar-es-Salaam. Archbishop Beecher installed the Right Reverend John Sepeku, then Bishop of Dar-es-Salaam as its first Archbishop. With an African Archbishop, the Church in Tanzania was now truly self-governing.

CHAPTER 10

COMINGS AND GOINGS — IN AND OUT OF AFRICA — 1953–1960

Alf spent most of 1953 in the diocese working with a good office team, among whom were Mary Bolitho, Dulcie McLeish and Genevieve Cutler. He carried out his round of confirmations, planned for the future of the ministry and the placements of staff. During the year he had a visit from the Reverend Edward Carlile, the Executive Head of the Church Army. This body had sent some splendid and well-trained workers to Tanganyika, among whom were Captain John Ball and his wife Dorothy who were stationed at Kilimatinde. Some years later John was chosen to be the founding Principal of a Church Army Training Institution in Nairobi, Kenya. Captain John (Jack) Bennett and his wife, Ethel worked in the West of Tanganyika for many years and were to continue on during our time. In the late 1950s Jack was elected to the Legislative Assembly of the Tanganyika Government and was also working in Dar-es-Salaam. Sister Lesley Bangham, another Church Army officer, had a well established work at a maternity clinic at Nkalinzi in Uha country. She and other Church Army workers such as Rebecca Thrush, Gertrude Cloudsdale and Dorothy Almond gave very valuable service, Rebecca in the nursing field, Gertrude in pastoral work, and Dorothy Almond in teaching at St Philip's College, Kongwa and the Msalato Bible School.

Other visitors to Tanganyika included Alf's old friend Cecil Bewes who was now Africa Secretary of the CMS UK. He came with Lt Col. George Grimshaw who was the representative of the Society in East Africa.

Early in 1953, Mary Bolitho and Norman Powys, a CMS missionary doctor, were married in Dodoma. Mary's mother came out for the wedding, but just a few days before that date her husband died suddenly in Melbourne. It was decided to carry on with the ceremony in the Cathedral at which Alf officiated — a reception was held in the grounds of our house.

The Archbishop of Canterbury made it possible for Alf to attend the Anglican World Congress in Minneapolis in 1954, followed by the General Assembly of the World Council of Churches in Evanston. Mrs Bolitho had decided to visit family in England before going back to Australia, so she invited me to make a base with her in London while Alf went to Minneapolis and Evanston.

I left for England by sea and Alf followed by plane. He spent a short time in England then crossed to the USA by sea. He found the Congress stimulating, more for the fellowship it provided and the meeting with other church leaders, than for the actual content of the meetings.

During this time Margaret McKechnie was in England. She had cared for her mother in Melbourne, but on her mother's death she decided to go overseas, and in her thoughts was the desire to help in the missionary situation. She had arranged with Alf to come to Tanganyika as a diocesan worker. She, with Alf and myself, had a week touring in Scotland which we all enjoyed. Then Alf flew back to East Africa while Margaret and I, with two new recruits, went by sea.

Other missionaries who joined the team in 1954 were the Reverend Kevin and Dorothy Engel, the Reverend Max and Valda Corbett, the Reverend Kenneth (later Bishop) and Gloria Short and Sister Enid Stahl. Kevin Engel told me that he was lined up for work in the bookshop the very next day after his arrival! The bookshop was then a very small affair compared with what it was to become. Alf already had great ideas for the future in literature.

Many years later I heard Dorothy Engel speak at a meeting in Melbourne. She said that in their early days in Dodoma the Engels' day started with three B's — Breakfast, Bishop and Bookshop! The Engels lived close to the then Diocesan Offices, so Alf would spin off his over-night ideas on Kevin on his way to the office.

John Denton came to us as a CMS missionary early in 1955, to be an administrative secretary for the Diocese. He was to take a big load off Alf, who handed over to him much of the detail of administration together with his confidence and trust. Margaret McKechnie settled into the secretarial work and Jean Guy, from the CMS Melbourne into the Accounts department.

In August, Alf and I went to Mwanza and stayed with the Reverend Hugh Thompson and his wife Margaret from New Zealand. He was the chaplain at St Nicholas Church and had oversight of the African work south of Lake Victoria. This included the Gold Mining scheme at Geita. Hugh took us to the site of the graves of Bishop Parker (the second bishop of Eastern Equatorial Africa, successor to Hannington) and his colleagues. They had died from illness in March 1888, before reaching their goal of Uganda.

We then set off to visit churches in the South Mwanza area but the car gave a lot of trouble, mainly with its springs. Hugh tied them up with wire and string and we finally caught the ferry to Mwanza with only minutes to spare. The next day we left in a small four-passenger Rapide plane for Tororo in Uganda. This proved a very hazardous flight. We were booked for Tororo but when we landed at Kisumu — the stop before Tororo — Alf was uneasy and decided not to go ahead by plane. He hired a car in Kisumu, a town which we knew from our Maseno days, and we travelled the last 105 miles to Kitale in north-west Kenya, where Alf was due to give a series of addresses at the Keswick Convention. The committee had sent a car to Tororo to meet us and were very puzzled when told that no plane had arrived that day. We entered the meeting hall just as the chairman was saying, 'I don't know what has happened to Bishop Stanway'. Alf then related what had happened and we all gave thanks for journeying mercies. We found the days at Kitale refreshing and spiritually challenging.

In December 1955, Frank and Margery Sellwood, BCMS representatives in Nairobi, came to visit other BCMS missionaries in our diocese. Alf drove them to the mission stations where their workers lived. The rains had broken that month, and the roads were in bad condition. One night they could not get home because several lorries were bogged ahead of them on the road. Alf left his car for the Sellwoods to try to sleep in, and he climbed up on one of the bogged lorries and lay down on some sacks of maize meal. He slept, but the next week succumbed to a very bad attack of malaria.

These days saw the arrival of many new workers. Dr Joseph and Joan Taylor had come to us from Northern Kenya where they had worked at Marsabit, supported by BCMS. Their early days in our diocese were spent at Lwande building their home and starting medical work — a pioneering situation. Later they came to Mvumi. Who could have foreseen in those days what a great work Joe Taylor was to do in the medical field during the next thirty years!

In August 1956, we moved into our new home Bishopsbourne. Although the house was ready for occupation, the chapel floor still needed to be tiled and a few other jobs needed to be done. A pile of planks were stacked on one side of the chapel. One evening a party of five Americans whom we knew, asked if we could put them up for the night. As our guest rooms were occupied, we said they could set up their camp beds in the chapel and we would feed them. We had to go out that night, and when we came home one of the Americans showed us a huge puff-adder which he had killed. When they moved the planks to set up their beds they had disturbed it. How glad we were to get rid of such a dangerous occupant!

We were due to leave Dodoma by train on Sunday evening, 9th

September, to take a ship from Dar-es-Salaam to Bombay, the first stage of our journey home to Australia. That date also happened to be Alf's birthday. On 8th September, John Denton was married to Shirley Wise, a nursing sister who had recently arrived in Tanganyika. Alf performed the ceremony in the Cathedral and the reception was held in the Bishopsbourne grounds. It was a happy occasion and, of course, we knew the weather would be good since no rains could be expected at that time of the year. John and Shirley were to caretake Bishopsbourne while we were away.

Next day I had forgotten that it was Alf's birthday, though I had made a cake for the occasion. Alf did not remind me. We attended the early communion service and later the baptism of the Indian pastor's son, and somewhere about lunch time I remembered to wish him a happy birthday! My role as packer-in-chief had completely filled my mind as we had to be at the railway station by 5.00 p.m. that evening.

When we arrived in Dar-es-Salaam the next morning, we were told that owing to the closure of the Suez Canal, the ship we had expected to board in Bombay (the P&O *Iberia*) would now be going via Capetown and we must board her there. We had a very rough passage. The further south we went the rougher it became.

Alf was never a good sailor and did not enjoy the trip. However, the journey from the Cape to Melbourne was good and we were happy to be back in Melbourne after five years away.

During this leave Alf visited all the States and spoke at the Belgrave Heights Convention and CMS Summer Schools, where he told of the situation in Central Tanganyika. He renewed his friendship with Marcus and Patricia Loane. By this time Marcus had been the Principal of Moore Theological College in Sydney for some years and was already a noted author of several devotional and biographical books. He had generously and regularly sent Alf a copy of each of these, which afforded Alf and me much pleasure. *The Man of Sorrows*, published in 1953 was dedicated to Alf — 'in token of friendship'.

In April, 1957 Alf was speaking at several meetings and conferences in Adelaide and the Hills, when he was told of the sudden death of Dr Norman Powys in Sydney, leaving his wife, Mary, with two small boys and another baby on the way. Alf was very upset by the news and flew from Adelaide to Sydney to be with Mary and assure her of the love and support of their colleagues on the field.

We began our new tour in June, 1957. We sailed to Bombay and from there Alf flew on to Africa and I followed by sea. Alf was eager to get back into the thick of things, to see how the current building work was progressing and to meet the team again. Also going to Africa was for Alf and me by this time going 'home'.

Alf's next sortie was a very complicated one. He and one of his clergy, Daniel Lungwa, were going to an All Africa Conference of Churches at Accra in Ghana. They first travelled by train to Kigoma then across Lake Tanganyika to Albertville by steamer. They arrived there on 17th December , but did not reach their destination until 10th January, 1958. They spent a fortnight in Accra at the conference and were able to get a quicker return via Nairobi where I was staying.

The one memorable thing about the Accra visit was Alf's attitude to frustration. Several times he quoted to me, 'God will forgive us our frustrations'. Someone at the Conference had given an address with this message in it. From that time Alf formed a 'habit' (as he was wont to call it) never to let himself get frustrated and another aphorism joined his list: 'No future in frustration', and, allied to that, 'no future in grumbling'.

During our time in Australia, Marcus Loane had been preparing for his consecration as a coadjutor Bishop of Sydney. He was consecrated in St Andrew's Cathedral, Sydney by Archbishop Mowll on the feast of St Matthias, 24th February, 1958. Alf, of course, was delighted and there were now prospects of them meeting at the Lambeth Conference later that year.

We left Dodoma on 24th May for London. This was an occasion when we both travelled together by air. Alf had arranged with the Colonial (later Commonwealth) and Continental Church Society to fill a summer chaplaincy at Interlaken in Switzerland for six weeks at the conclusion of the Lambeth Conference. Through Riddoch's Ford agency in Arusha, he had ordered a new car which met us at Heathrow Airport, the agreement being that when we left England it would be reclaimed and shipped back to Tanganyika.

A special train ran to Canterbury for the opening ceremony of the Lambeth Conference in the Cathedral. Bishop Omari, Alf and I were accommodated in Westfield College with a group of Bishops from different countries and some of their wives. Mrs William Temple, the widow of the great Archbishop William Temple, was our hostess — we all loved her.

I met Marcus Loane on the train on the way to the Opening Ceremony of Lambeth. Alf and Bishop Omari had travelled down by car a few days earlier to attend a gathering of bishops from Africa so they met us at the station. Scholars from the King's School also met the train and helped the bishops with their cases. To us, the service was very inspiring, dignified and impressive. One could sense the weight of history connected with Canterbury and the long tradition of the Church in England.

In 1958, the Conference meetings were still held in the Great Hall at Lambeth. A large marquee was set up in the Palace grounds for communal lunches. During all the plenary sessions, Alf and Marcus sat side by side and every lunch-hour they walked round and round the large lawn where the marquee was pitched. Some of the wives of the bishops, especially those from America, very much longed to eat in that marquee, so the Archbishop agreed that at the conclusion of the Conference they be invited for a Communion Service in the Lambeth Chapel followed by breakfast in the marquee.

On the afternoon of the day when the Bishops were to attend Buckingham Palace to pay their homage to the Queen, the Lord Chancellor, by the gracious permission of Her Majesty, invited the wives to be present. They were not at the ceremony but they lined a long gallery-type room through which the Queen walked on her way to the ceremony. When the doors opened and she entered the room, she stopped first and spoke to Mrs Fisher and Mrs Ramsey. She then said in a clear audible voice, 'I've had such fun, I have been watching the Bishops arriving through my binoculars!' This broke the ice, and she slowly proceeded down the lines of ladies, speaking to one or other of the wives as she progressed. She looked most regal in a gold lamé frock.

One other enjoyable social event was an evening cruise down the Thames from Westminster to Greenwich. To our amazement on approaching the Tower Bridge, the Bridge opened, as was usual for larger craft, and our launch, certainly not in that class, passed through. Alf took some very good photographs of the salute to the bishops by the Tower Bridge.

When Alf had time in London he grasped every opportunity to visit societies and agencies which supported the Diocese. These included CMS, BCMS, Mothers' Union, Colonial and Continental Church Society, Church Army, and a meeting was arranged for Central Tanganyika Diocesan Association supporters. Two other large Sunday Services were held during Lambeth, a Holy Communion in St Paul's Cathedral, and the concluding Holy Communion service in Westminster Abbey. Both of these services were inspiring and impressive. Alf very much enjoyed meeting fellow bishops from all over the world and especially the African bishops from Kenya and Uganda.

At the conclusion of the Lambeth Conference we prepared for our six weeks in the Switzerland chaplaincy with eager anticipation. I had been told by an English friend that I would understand more of the meaning of glory, by the grandeur of the Swiss Alps! Marcus joined us for the first part of the journey as he had to be in Geneva by a given date. We had booked on the Air Ferry which took off at Lydd on the Kentish coast. Our car was packed with our suitcases and everything else needed for the journey, then it and other cars were driven up a ramp into the large 'nose' of the plane and we entered the passenger compartment.

It was a very quick trip to Le Touquet, and from there we drove to Arras. Then we travelled across Germany to the Austrian countryside, spending a little while in Berchtesgarten to reflect on the past war. Marcus was all for going up to the 'Eagle's eyrie', but Alf recognised this teasing effort!

I have a vivid memory of them both sitting beside a beautiful mountain stream and skimming stones across the water. We travelled on to Salzburg hoping to spend the night there, but as the Mozart Festival was being held we were obliged to go on further and find accommodation for the night. Marcus had been asked to look out for a notice saying *'Zimmer frei'*. For a while we could not see one and Marcus commented 'not a glimmer of a zimmer' as the sun was going down.

In Geneva, we parted from Marcus and then travelled on to Interlaken which was to be our base. We were booked into the Victoria-Jungfrau, a very prestigious hotel, by the chaplaincy agents. After unpacking, we set out along the Hoheweg to visit the two ladies, Ida Baumann and Gertrud Stahel, who took responsibility for all the chaplaincy matters. Alf discovered that his main responsibility was to conduct the English Sunday services and to be available for counselling and any emergency, such as a funeral, should it occur.

What to us then was a most unexpected joy, was to meet Dr John Winteler of Nairobi in the street! John had a Swiss father, and every year on his annual holidays, spent some time in Switzerland. It was great to have a friend to share our time in Interlaken. John had no car, so Alf now had an assistant driver who knew all the country so well. John also knew all the best cafés in the town and after dinner in the evenings, he would take us to one or other where we could drink coffee and listen to the musicians.

The day after our arrival John took us to visit a medical friend, Dr Sheila Davidson, who was staying with her sister Grace in a chalet near one of the lakes. This was the beginning of an ongoing friendship with Sheila, and later her husband Arthur, which endured until the end of Alf's life and is still continuing with me today. We were able to make up picnic parties to places suggested by John who had now become our driver. The Sunday services were held in the Swiss Reformed Church — one end of it was designed for Swiss worship and the other for Anglican services. We were surprised by the size of the congregations. It seemed to be a British custom to go to church on Sundays when holidaying abroad.

While John was with us, he and his Auntie May accompanied Alf and me to an evening service at Wilderswil in the mountains near

Interlaken. There was a big old church there with a pipe organ but no organist, so John played for us, which added to the pleasure of the occasion.

The 9th of September came round again and this time I was ready for Alf's birthday. He was going to be 50, and according to him 'the best age to be' (in fact he said this every birthday up to and including his 70th and since I was never at the age he was, his was always the best!). At breakfast time the Hotel Manager had a delicious chocolate cake, decorated with fresh aster flowers, delivered to our table. This was arranged by our chaplaincy ladies. How would you imagine Alf spent the day? We drove to Gstaad and met Paul Feuter and Clare, his wife, Moravian missionary friends from the Southern Highlands of Tanganyika. We took a chair lift up to the surrounding mountains where Paul and Alf played chess and Alf left it on record that he won, 5-0! Meanwhile we ladies enjoyed looking at the wide panorama of beautiful scenery.

That night our chaplaincy ladies had arranged a small party at their home. The Swiss pastor and his wife came and an American couple staying at our hotel. The chocolate cake was mounted on a revolving musical-box cake stand which played 'Happy birthday to you'. Alf had received a cablegram from 'his slaves' (their word) in Dodoma with a suitable greeting and this pleased him immensely. He then showed slides of Tanganyika which were of great interest to Gertrud Stahel who was a professional photographer, and shared with Ida in a photographer's studio.

She was intensely interested in the African 'light' effects saying how 'white' the snow looked on Kilimanjaro, and as reflected in the white surplices of the clergy. She was able to give Alf some excellent hints on photography during our stay. Our hotel room looked out to the three famous mountains, the Eiger (eagle), Monck (monk) and Jungfrau (young lady) so Alf was able to take very good photographs of them. Our time in Switzerland was the best holiday we had ever had, and left us with enduring happy memories.

On our return to England Alf drove the car to London. He had to make a turn near Covent Garden and asked a worker there, 'Can I go this way?' 'Guv', came the answer, 'with a car like that you can go anywhere!'

On our return to Dodoma, Alf settled down to a very busy period. There was a great deal of building work going on, and, as always in Dodoma, the comings and goings of missionaries going on leave and new workers arriving. Len and Flo Straw, Church Army workers, were settled at Mpwapwa where Len worked with George Pearson as his archdeacon. Later he and Flo were to go to

Bushubi country in the far West, a rather isolated area, where there were many refugees from Ruanda.

Alf had been invited by members of the African Inland Mission at Rethi, in the Belgian Congo (now Zaire), to take a series of Bible Studies for their missionary personnel. It was a troubled time in the Congo, with great unrest and the missionaries were uneasy. Alf had chosen to speak from John's Gospel, Chapters 13, 14 and 15 which speak of persecution and trial. He said to me that he thought the choice of subject was apposite as riots followed and within two years many people were massacred by the Simba rebels.

A few months later some refugees from Albertville fled across Lake Tanganyika to Kigoma, where they caught a train bound for Dar-es-Salaam. They had been taken by surprise, as the rebels attacked their town suddenly, and they had fled without waiting to pick up any necessities — even mothers with babies had no personal effects. The government alerted us in Dodoma, as the train was on its way, to be ready to help. We were asked to boil up drinking water and bottle large quantities of it to supply the travellers on the long journey to Dar-es-Salaam. Meanwhile in Dodoma we were encouraged to take groups of them to our houses to bathe and be fed, and then get them back to the station by a stated time. Among those I assisted were a Mr Ray and Mrs Emma Williams of Sydney and four Belgian ladies. This party reached Dar-es-Salaam safely and KLM Airlines flew them back to Belgium.

In the latter half of 1959, discussions were held in Dodoma about the formation of a Province of East Africa. Bishops, Archdeacons and other clerical and lay members of the Synods of Kenya and Tanganyika met in Conference for this purpose and it was unanimously agreed to go ahead. For us in Tanganyika, our diocese and the dioceses formed through the work of the Universities' Mission to Central Africa, were to join with the existing Kenya dioceses to form this Province.

The building of Mackay House, our Diocesan Headquarters was proceeding well and was completed early in 1960. Bishop and Mrs Chambers, engaged in chaplaincy work at Iringa, came up for the opening on 24th February and Bishop Chambers dedicated the building before a large crowd. These headquarters were to prove a great asset and before long the move was effected from the old offices, and the big new bookshop was fitted out, likewise the chemist's shop. Chemists who worked there in our time were Barry Bryant, Martyn Linton (relieving from Mvumi) and Stanley Kerr. Dr Robin Smith, whom Alf had recruited from England, was the first doctor in the Professional Unit. He came with Elizabeth, his wife.

Mackay House, Headquarters for the Diocese of Central Tanganyika, Dodoma, opened 1960.

Alf at his desk at Mackay House.

Chemist Shop, Mackay House.

James Charlwood, our first dentist, whom Alf had interviewed in England, came with his wife, Lenore. Modern dental equipment was ordered from England and installed. Now we had dental care in Dodoma for the very first time — a great boon to us all. James was followed by Christine Shepherd, also from England. She worked with us till her marriage to Denis Osborne who was lecturing in the Physics faculty in the University of Dar-es-Salaam. He and Christine returned to England where he was working with the British Government. Today they are in Lilongwe in Malawi where he is High Commissioner for Britain.

In Mackay House, together with our expatriate team, was a cheerful young African office worker, among several others, called Godfrey Mhogolo. None of us at that time could have imagined that one day he was to be the fifth Bishop of Central Tanganyika! Downstairs in Mackay House, Kevin Engel and his bookshop team were doing well. Gillian Smith of BCMS England had joined the team as did Joan Rice from Melbourne and John Burnett from Scotland, a former Comet pilot who served for a few years before going back to Scotland for training in the Presbyterian ministry. He now ministers at Dollar, not far from Edinburgh. In the bookshop, school supplies came with regularity, Bibles, New Testaments and Hymn books in Swahili and Gogo were ordered, delivered and sold very quickly, and other Christian literature and stationery supplies were available.

From 17th–19th May 1960, a committee met in Dodoma for a review of the Swahili Prayer Book. Our diocese had been using the 1662 Book translated by Bishop Steere in the Kiunguja dialect, but standardised Swahili had altered the orthography somewhat. For example, double consonants had been removed, so alterations were necessary. In Kenya they had used several books in the Kimvita dialect and then later standard Swahili, so now it was necessary to have a book which would meet the needs of most dioceses of the Province. The Reverend Kenneth Stovold represented Kenya at this review, with African delegates as well. The Tanganyika delegates met with them and all parties agreed for the revision to be completed by the Reverend Dick Feuerheerd, a noted Swahili scholar and then on the staff of St Philip's Theological College, Kongwa. His work was completed in 1962 and the Prayer Book published in 1964 by SPCK for the Province of East Africa.

From 3rd–6th June, a residential conference for CMS missionaries was held at Mvumi. This was arranged through a request from the Federal Council of CMS Australia, and the Reverend Geoffrey Fletcher, the then General Secretary of the New South Wales branch of CMS, came out to represent the Home Society to the missionaries. Alf was unhappy about an all-expatriate missionaries' conference. He felt the time had come when we should no longer have conferences in Africa which excluded the participation of Africans. Also in the Diocese, there were many non-Australian missionaries and diocesan workers. It seemed unfair to exclude them from the fellowship that such a conference could give.

There had been criticism from some CMS folk at home, unaware of the political situation in Africa, that Alf was Africanizing much too fast, to which his reply always was, 'History will prove that I was not fast enough'. So he decided to invite a group of English speaking Africans to attend the Conference sessions and they eagerly responded.

Bishop and Mrs Chambers came up from Iringa, and with the assistance of a driver for their car, came out to attend the morning sessions while returning to sleep at Bishopsbourne. The missionary staff at Mvumi nobly responded to the great influx of visitors, while Mary Newell and her helpers from the Girls' School staff, together with Sister Enid Stahl and other helpers, did a valiant job as the caterers, managing all the logistics of feeding such a crowd.

Alf was to take daily Bible Readings from 1 Peter, an epistle he found very helpful personally. Unfortunately, on the second day of the conference he had a very sore throat, and had to miss his session. Dr Juliet Backhouse assisted him with effective medication and he recovered quickly and was able to attend the remainder of the meetings. Stanley Giltrap from Ireland, who had worked as a CMS UK missionary in the Sudan and was now the CMS Secretary of the Kenya mission in Nairobi, gave an address about reaching Muslims. He produced a small book published by the United Society for Christian Literature (the Lutterworth Press) entitled *Explaining the Gospel to Muslims*, which he felt ought to be made available in Swahili. I volunteered to do the translation if Dick Feuerheerd would be kind enough to edit it. He gladly agreed and the booklet was ready before we went on home leave.

The Reverend Geoffrey Fletcher addressed the conference on behalf of the Australian CMS and was available to answer questions. Most of us enjoyed the fellowship and the opportunity to get up-to-date with one another, since many of the missionaries lived so far from our centre in Dodoma. There were about sixty of us present. There was never another conference of this type but Keswick Conventions were held yearly in the diocese from 1962 onwards, and so provided for the need for a wider fellowship and spiritual refreshment, in which Africans and Europeans could meet on an equal footing.

In March 1959, Dr Wellesley Hannah of Mvumi, by African nomination, became a member of the Legislative Assembly of Parliament, as did Captain John Bennett of the Church Army. At the time of the above conference at Mvumi, Dr Julius Nyerere, then the leader of the Tanganyika African National Union (TANU) was visiting Gogo country. Wellesley invited him to come and meet our people which he was happy to do. When asked to address us, he said he would prefer that we should ask him questions. Many such were asked and he answered them graciously and without hesitation. Wellesley Hannah kept his seat in the Assembly until he left Tanganyika in June, 1960 to return to Australia.

CHAPTER 11

A NEW ERA. TANGANYIKA — TANZANIA 1961–1967

Throughout the 1950s political awareness had been growing among young educated Africans, especially those with tertiary training who had travelled overseas. On 7th July, 1954 a political party was founded in Dodoma called TANU (Tanganyika African National Union), of which Julius Nyerere was the President. This day was to become the National Day in the years ahead and was called *Saba Saba Day* (= seven seven, i.e. 7.7.54).

Julius Nyerere was born into a very small tribe on the north-eastern side of Lake Victoria. As a youth he joined the Roman Catholic Church and had the opportunity to study in Edinburgh where he took a Master's degree. On his return home he taught in Roman Catholic schools, but as his political activity increased he gave himself full-time to TANU. He travelled all over the country promoting the call to *Uhuru* (freedom), advocating that the mandate administered by Britain be annulled and the country achieve its independence from Britain. There had been much political activity in Uganda and Kenya, but both of these countries had to wait a little longer to achieve their independence.

Alf frequently met with Dr Nyerere in his travels and always found him friendly and open. *Uhuru* was granted in December 1961. In preparation for the celebrations, TANU had adopted the African National Congress (South Africa) song as their national anthem, by changing the words a little; it became 'God bless Tanganyika' (later Tanzania) and was sung to the same melody.

A new flag was designed. The overall ground colour was green with a horizontal gold-edged black stripe running across the centre. The symbolism was green for the land, black for the people and gold for the mineral wealth. So one night early in December 1961, all over the land, people of all races gathered on open arenas. At midnight the Union Jack was lowered and the new flag raised amid great rejoicing. We expatriates were glad for the Africans but apprehensive as to how intelligent but inexperienced people would be able to handle government. Dr Nyerere became Prime Minister and chose his Cabinet. He was an idealist and a visionary. He intended to make Tanganyika a socialist but not communist country, with a one-party government. He stirred up his fellow Africans to fight the common enemies: Poverty, Ignorance and Disease. On 9th December 1962, Tanganyika was declared a Republic (*Jamhuri*) and Nyerere became its first President. The following year, 1963, the Afro-Shirazi Party in Zanzibar won Government of the Island, but the next year there was a revolution (January 1964) when the Arabs, who had ruled the Island for more than a century, were overthrown. The Sultan fled to exile in Britain and many Arabs left Zanzibar for good. This new government in Zanzibar leaned heavily to the communist world and accepted aid from East Germany. Negotiations with Nyerere resulted in the United Republic of Tanzania being formed in April 1964. The flag was changed. Now the gold-edged black stripe ran across the ground diagonally. The upper quarter was green for the land, and the lower quarter blue for the sea.

TANU now set about educating the populace in its doctrines. Watchwords were coined such as *usiwe kupe*, meaning 'don't be a tick' (parasite), challenging people to work hard and produce more food. Luxury cars were frowned upon and the word for a capitalist was *mbenzi* (meaning the owner of a Mercedes car).

Not long into Nyerere's leadership there was an attempted coup, organised by Oscar Kambona, who had once been on the staff of our Alliance School and a friend of Nyerere. We, in Dodoma, heard this news over the BBC 9.00 p.m. news service! The coup failed and Kambona fled to England. Various Africans were 'detained' in prison including Oscar's brother. Oscar wrote to Alf asking him to visit his brother in prison and pray with him. Alf wrote to Nyerere for official permission to make such a visit and this was granted. Kingsley Green, one of our teaching staff at the Alliance school, used to visit the prison regularly and was very surprised that there was no objection to his visiting political prisoners.

Fortunately for us, the new government approved of religion and religious teaching in schools. During this time our diocesan schools had been growing in numbers and had advanced to higher levels. We needed a secondary school for girls. There was no more room to extend the buildings at Mvumi, so a new site had to be found.

Alf had always enjoyed going out to the Mvumi school, especially to confirm the girls. Avis Richardson, their headmistress, had been there since 1932, and a fine tradition had grown up. The girls were always very well prepared for confirmation. Some of the teaching staff in the late fifties were Beryl Evenett, Mary Newell, Jean Meyer and Elisabeth Knox, Mary and Elisabeth being qualified to teach in Secondary Schools.

Alf, with others, inspected a plot of land at Msalato, about six miles north of Dodoma, off the Great North Road. It was scrub or bush land, but as there was piped water coming into Dodoma close at hand, it made a suitable site for a girls' school. He was granted the land, leasehold, and in 1960 the building work began with a view to its being completed for the next academic year. Staff houses had to be built also but all was ready by early 1961. Miss Mary Newell was the new Headmistress. In her own words:

> In 1959 plans were made to develop coeducational teacher training colleges. It was decided that Miss Richardson and Miss Jean Meyer should go to Katoke in Western Tanganyika to the teacher training college there with the senior girls from Mvumi, and help establish the new coeducational college. This move left space in the Mvumi Girls' School, and I was asked if I would begin a Secondary School, even though I hadn't seen a Secondary School for 16 years. We did this in 1960. The bulk of the girls that year were from Moravian, Lutheran and Mvumi schools, about a third from each. Basically they were all Christian girls and all from Protestant Missions.
>
> At the beginning of 1961 I went with that group and another intake of Form I to Msalato to start the new school there. The beginnings of the school had their excitements, not the least of these being problems caused by the heavy rains which prevented the lorries from bringing the furniture from Mvumi. As a result we began with very little in these new beautiful school buildings.[1]

While the school buildings were taking shape, the first Bible School was being built at Msalato nearer to the road. There was a single staff house, dormitories, a dining room, store and a classroom and these were added to later as the school grew. Alf appointed the Reverend Kenneth Short as its first Principal, and he became Chaplain to the school also, while Gloria, his wife, led its Christian Union. At this stage, neither the Girls' School nor the Bible School had chapels, though they were to be built in the near future. The Bible School was opened in June 1961 by the Federal Secretary of the CMS in Australia, the Reverend Canon (later Bishop) Jack Dain.

Meanwhile at the Alliance School, plans were being drawn up for some necessary extensions, and once more Alf was able to have the total project financed by a German Agency. In the final stages,

---

[1]*Three CMS Missionaries in East Africa*, Keith Cole and Dick Pethybridge. Keith Cole Publications, 1986, page 82.

there were to be several double storey classrooms and science blocks, large double storey dormitory units, an assembly hall and a beautiful chapel. Headmasters at this school, following Max Wiggins, were a dual headship of Jack Shellard and Noel Bythell (later to be ordained). They were followed by an honorary worker from England, Alex Dick, who remained at the school until an African Headmaster was appointed.

With what seemed later as prophetic insight, Alf saw clearly that the African Government in the future would take over all schools in the country and put in their own men as Heads. So he forestalled this by asking the Government to choose for him a good man to take over from our expatriate Headmaster. The Government agreed, and sent him Richard Juma a very good man indeed and a fine Christian. The name of the school was changed to the Mazengo Secondary School, after the Paramount Chief of the Gogo tribe.

Bible School messenger.

Mazengo was the last of the Paramount Chiefs in Tanganyika. He was Chief of the Gogo people and lived quite near the Mvumi Mission Station which he had observed throughout its history. He was well acquainted with all that happened there. He exercised the authority of his office even after paramount chiefs were phased out by the new African Government. He had not become a Christian because he continued to be a polygamist. He had four wives and was not prepared to give them up by becoming a Christian. However, by the age of eighty years, he decided he could manage with one wife and, having made arrangements for the other three, he asked to be baptised. Alf baptised him with the name of Daudi (David) and President Nyerere added to this Sulemani (Solomon). Not long after this Mazengo died and Alf buried him in a great ceremony.

In Dodoma itself, missionary staff had run a day primary school for many years called Stockley Road School. It was an English-medium school, educating the many expatriate children in the town. Following the new trend to exchange European names for African ones, the school was re-named the Canon Andrea Mwaka School — a name chosen by our Christian Africans.

Andrea Mwaka's father was a chief, and he himself had been offered a chieftainship to follow his father, under the German Government prior to World War I. He declined saying that it would interfere with his service for God. He was one of the only two clergy in the land when Bishop Chambers arrived in 1927, and he was made a Canon when the Cathedral of the Holy Spirit was consecrated in Dodoma. He had died in Mvumi Hospital after a long illness. In writing about him Avis Richardson said:

> I have heard him spoken of as the greatest of the Wagogo. During the funeral service in the church and at the cemetery there was a solemn strange beating of the drum used only when a chief dies, a few slow beats, a few rapid beats, sudden silence for a space, then the same again.[2]

A Diocesan School in Arusha was started in 1932, when the need arose for the education of European children in the Diocese, and Bishop Chambers sent the Reverend William Wynn Jones to found the school. A farmhouse was lent to the Diocese, and it was adapted to provide classrooms, dormitories, a dining room, and home for the Headmaster. The school grew and the Governor, at the time — Sir Stewart Symes — offered Bishop Chambers £10,000 for a new school and all expenses paid, if the Diocese would allow Wynn Jones to be the first Headmaster. This was

[2]*Hold High the Torch.* Avis Richardson MBE, p. 51.

agreed to and he continued at the school until his consecration as Assistant Bishop to Bishop Chambers in 1946. The school functioned with Diocesan staff until it was taken over by the Government as a boarding school, for European children in the Northern Province. The good traditions of the school carried over and it enrolled multi-racial pupils after Independence. President Nyerere sent one of his sons there to be educated.

A further, not unexpected move of the Government when it took over all the schools in the land, was to change their ethos. No longer could parents decide where to send their children to school. Children were zoned to schools so we found our diocesan schools obliged to take in Muslim children as well as Christians and other groups. European-medium schools as such ceased to be.

The teaching medium was Swahili, but as far as our Diocese was concerned there were to be the two international schools: the Canon Andrea Mwaka School, these days offering secondary training, and the International School at Moshi, where English was maintained as the medium.

For boarding pupils problems soon arose. Muslims insisted that meat be killed only by Muslim butchers, and this created catering problems. On the other hand, there were opportunities to allow Muslim children to mix with Christian children. In our diocese, one of the most outstanding converts was the Reverend Alpha (now Bishop) Mohamed. He was called Abdullah and was born in a Muslim home not far from Dodoma. He was the only boy in his family and his father doted on his heir. Abdullah attended a school for the study of the Koran and was well instructed in the faith of Islam, learning to read portions of the Koran. He was a diligent student, much praised as a fine child, obedient and respectful to his elders.

He was zoned to go to the Mazengo Secondary School and his teachers thought he had a good character. However, in a tract which he wrote for Muslims some years later, he said that if one could have seen into his heart, it wasn't like that at all, but full of evil. Although he was seen as a God-fearer, his religion gave him no victory — he was a defeated person and he had given up all ambition and saw no reason for living, and had no expectations in this life.

One day a friend gave him a 'certain little book' which he very carefully read, especially the words which said, 'I know your deeds, that you are neither cold nor hot. So, because you are lukewarm I shall spew you out of my mouth.' These words, spoken by the Lord Jesus Christ in the Book of Revelation, penetrated his inner being — he found out what he was really like and saw that he needed help. He longed for true comfort. There was a great heaviness in his spirit and he looked for someone to give him peace of heart. As time went on, the longing increased. He was helped further by being shown another reading concerning Jesus, 'Nor is there salvation in anyone else at all, for there is no other name under heaven given to mankind by which to be saved'. Here, he said, he began to experience the wonder of God. Although he was troubled, unclean, and saw no profit in living, God still loved him, and he read the Gospel of John where Jesus said, 'I am the way, the truth and the life, no man comes to the Father but by me.'

Again he read those great words which said, 'For this reason, God so loved the world that he sent His only Son, so that everyone who believes in him is not lost but has eternal life'. This verse drew him and he decided to follow Jesus Christ. Christ saved him. It was a wonder, and Christ filled him with the expectation of life, after leaving this wicked world so full of confusion, fear and trouble. Christ gave him faith and joy such as this world cannot give. When Abdullah left Mazengo he saw that it behoved him to serve this wonderful Lord Jesus, since all that he did for him was wonderful. Abdullah, in this tract, went on to exhort Muslims to seek this way of joy and peace through Christ, the life-giver.

If he had not gone to Mazengo school and shared in a dormitory with Christian boys, he may have missed meeting with the Lord. He was baptised, and instead of Abdullah became 'Alpha'.

Alfred Stanway with his first three Assistant Bishops (L. to R.) — Maxwell Wiggins, Musa Kahurananga and Yohana Omari at consecration of Bp Kahurananga, 1962. (Photograph: Diocese of Central Tanganyika)

One Sunday morning, Alpha attended the Cathedral for a School Service in Swahili. Alf was preaching on the verse from Romans 10:14-15, 'But how are men to call upon Him in whom they have not believed? And how are they to believe in Him of whom they have never heard? And how are they to hear without a preacher? And how can men preach unless they are sent? As it is written, 'How beautiful are the feet of those who preach good news.' That day God called Alpha to serve him in the ordained ministry and, after leaving school, he went to St Philip's College Kongwa for training.

So, although Christian schools as such no longer existed, the opportunities for witness were many and Christian Unions were established in the schools without hindrance. John (Jack) Shellard, a CMS missionary from Sydney, spent a short time at the Alliance School and then went up to Musoma in the East Lake area to Head a secondary school there. Missionary teachers are still welcome where vacancies exist, and many teach in Bible Schools. Gerald Clarke, a CMS New Zealand missionary, went to Kigoma to found Livingstone College, another secondary school, and Ian Pearce taught at Mazengo for many years. Kigoma is the port on Lake Tanganyika, just a few miles from Ujiji where Livingstone and Stanley met.

In 1961, Ken Short asked me if I would help with some teaching

Alfred with three Tanzanian Bishops — Madinda, Kahurananga and Chitemo, 1962.
(Photograph by H.A. Steyn, Missionary Aviation Fellowship, Nairobi)

at the Msalato Bible School. I was thrilled to be asked and it seemed to me to be 'real' missionary work — though Alf always emphasized that 'real' missionary work entailed many mundane chores. I used to go out on Fridays and teach the morning periods. The students, mostly older men evangelists, were very responsive and a joy to teach. I continued at Msalato each Friday, first under Ken's, then under the Reverend Peter Dawson's Principalship.

Towards the end of 1962, the Reverend Campbell Begbie was appointed as the CMS Representative in Tanganyika. There had always been a representative, usually one of the senior missionaries on the field. Mr Begbie remained in this post until 1968 when he and Mrs Begbie returned home and the Reverend Max Corbett succeeded him. Later two CMS missionaries were to act for the four dioceses.

Archdeacon and Mrs Cordell were living and working in Kenya during the 1960s. He was engaged in educational work and checking the proofs of the Gogo Bible — he had done a great deal of translation work especially in the Gogo language. When the Bible was published and arrived in East Africa, the Cordells with Mr and Mrs Ashley of the British and Foreign Bible Society, and also their African representative, Mr John T. Mpaayei, came to Dodoma. A special celebratory Gogo Service was held in the Cathedral in August 1962 to mark the event. The British and Foreign Bible Society van was outside the Cathedral, packed with Gogo bibles for sale after the service and there was great rejoicing to have a complete bible in this language for the first time.

During August and September in 1963, Robert Loane, Marcus' son and Alf's godson, spent some time with us. He was on vacation from Cambridge and Alf was able to arrange for him to go out to Mvumi and see some medical work (as he was studying medicine) and we had a trip with him to Manyara, a game park in the north of the country.

Also in 1963, I helped Lionel Bakewell with a language school at Mvumi. He helped the quick learners and I took the slower ones. He and his wife, Chris, were to go to Nairobi to start a Language School there for new missionary recruits. They remained there until the end of their service in East Africa.

All missionaries in our diocese were required to sit for lower and higher Swahili examinations. In Kenya, other vernaculars were studied at the school.

In October 1963, we went home to Australia on leave. We were involved in the usual round of deputations, summer schools and the Belgrave Heights Convention at which Alf spoke. Alf left by sea early in March 1964, to return to Dodoma. He flew from Karachi to Nairobi for the last leg of the journey. I had accumulated some needed household replacements, and left early in April 1964 on a Dutch cargo ship. All the officers on board were interested in stamp collecting and soon we four passengers became involved too. I hoped to be back in Dodoma for 3rd June, our silver wedding anniversary.

Before I arrived, Alf heard of the visits to Dodoma of several important people, so he asked Dawn and Guy Timmis if they would come to Dodoma to act as host and hostess in Bishopsbourne. They were with him from 24th March to 10th April. The first visitor was Bishop Geoffrey Sambell, at that time coadjutor Bishop of Melbourne and later to be Archbishop of Perth. He was followed from 2nd to 4th April by Archbishop Hugh Gough of Sydney and then by Leonard and Jane Buck of Melbourne. Leonard was a longtime friend and a Christian businessman from Melbourne.

When our ship came in to Beira, there was a letter from Alf giving dates when he would be coming to Dar-es-Salaam for meetings of the Christian Council of Tanzania. He advised me, if the need arose, to fly from Zanzibar to Dar-es-Salaam. I had understood that after Beira that we would berth in Dar, but instead we went to Zanzibar and from there the ship went on to Mombasa, then Tanga then Dar. I knew that would not get me to Dodoma by 3rd June. I asked the purser to obtain permission for me to land in Zanzibar. I was very apprehensive, since the revolution was not long over. I was given a twenty-four hour only pass, and had to leave all my baggage with the customs while I tried to get an air passage. Fortunately I secured a ticket for a midday flight. I then went to the post office and bought all the stamps 5/- and under which had *Jamhuri* (republic) printed over the Sultan's head.

I arrived safely in Dar and the African customs officer asked 'What are you smuggling?' When I looked surprised he smiled and said, 'How's the Bishop?' He was one of our Christians from the west. He allowed me to use his office phone to speak to Alf who said, 'Where are you?' since I could have been in any East African port. I said, 'At the Dar airport'. 'Right', he said, 'I'm coming'. He left in the middle of his lunch and collected me and the baggage.

We travelled back to Dodoma by car with a few days in hand. I had a cousin in England who was a silversmith, and he designed and made a hand beaten silver chalice and paten and matching alms dish for us, to be our silver jubilee gift for the Chapel at Bishopsbourne. On 3rd June we had a lovely service with our guests in the Chapel, when these gifts were dedicated. We then had a dinner party with some Melbourne friends present, Margaret McKechnie, Mary Newell and Jean Meyer, also the Begbies, some senior Africans and visiting Lutheran missionaries.

Alf was very surprised by my stamp collecting. He now began to collect for me, but I soon tired of it and he carried it on which was good as it was to prove an absorbing hobby during the years of his illness.

In August 1964, a Keswick Convention was held at Msalato and the Reverend David MacInnes (the son of the then Archbishop of Jerusalem) and Clare, his wife, came to stay with us and to be one of the speakers. The chapel at the Msalato Girls' School had been built with money set aside by Miss Richardson for a chapel at Mvumi which had not eventuated. It was a large, beautiful airy building and used for conventions, missions and synods in the days ahead, as well as the daily school services.

WESTONARIA MISSION

In November 1964, Alf was asked to conduct a mission in an Anglican church in Westonaria, a suburb of Johannesburg. On Alf's arrival in Salisbury en route to Johannesburg, he had a free day which he spent in preparation, and on arrival in Johannesburg itself, he had another free day to prepare. On the Friday evening, a meeting for young people was held and 120 came and 35 of these bought booklets, especially John Stott's *Becoming a Christian*. During the week attendances averaged 145, the largest being 211. Alf reported,

> Each night there was a very deep sense of God's presence and on the Wednesday evening all were very conscious of this. Some had never experienced anything like it before and I have seldom known such an amazing sense of God's presence and power.
>
> Only twice during the mission did I ask anybody to remain behind for counselling. Six of those who remained were members of the Church Council.
>
> There is a lot of giving of oneself in a mission, and though I was tired at the end of each day, I was always fresh the next day. A very real work of grace was accomplished in many hearts. I returned to my tasks here (in Dodoma) glad that I went and grateful to God for his abundant grace.

Alf had been asked to return the next year to another Anglican Church in a Johannesburg suburb called Bezhuidenhout Valley (locally known as Bez Valley) and I was able to go as well. Almost every night there were conversions. One such was the church secretary, Peggy Gibbs, who came into blessing and has kept in touch with us ever since. Another interesting incident concerned an Afrikaans woman who came to be counselled by Alf. She was very bitter and tearful. She earned her living selling clothing from door to door. Many years before she had lent her sister £100 and although she had asked for its repayment, the sister rebuffed her rudely and gave no indication of when she intended to repay her.

Alf tried to help the woman get a spiritual perspective and asked her if peace with God was worth more to her than £100? He said he could sense her fighting the suggestion but finally she gave in and said it was. Alf then advised her to write to her sister and say that she was sorry the debt was not repaid but would never ask for it again. In the days which followed it was obvious that she had found peace.

The Vicar's wife had problems too. She had been nagging her husband to buy a certain piece of farm land which she coveted. The Vicar wanted to please her but knew it would be wrong. Alf advised her to go down on her knees and pray to be delivered from hankering after something which was obviously not for her. Just last year we had a letter from her reminding us of the incident, and telling us the end of the story, that the Government soon afterwards pushed a road through that property so it would never have been of any value to her.

After Bez Valley we went to Mowbray, a suburb of Capetown, where Alf took another mission. There were many conversions here. One night he felt led to speak about the woman from Bez Valley and the £100. After the meeting a woman approached him and said, 'I also am like that woman, I also lent my sister £100 and I haven't forgiven her for not repaying it.' Alf counselled her to make peace with God and her sister, and she went off determined to straighten out the situation.

From the days when we were stationed in Nairobi, Alf had become involved in Christian literature and in its publication and distribution world-wide. He had an English colleague, Charles Richards, with whom he worked in Nairobi, who became Director of the Literature Bureau of East Africa. They were both associated with the Christian Literature Fund, a world-wide movement of which they were both to become members, often travelling overseas for joint meetings with similar bodies. Charles eventually left Nairobi to be based in Lausanne, Switzerland.

In 1965, Synod met in January. Alf then left for Dar-es-Salaam and from there flew to Holland for literature meetings, and then on to Denmark and Sweden. He was away for a month and I was left with a large empty house. So I arranged a live-in course for five clergy wives (I had five spare beds). This was a very blessed time as we all came to know one another better and to share our concerns.

In early August, Alf and I set out for the Murchison Falls Park along the Nile River in Uganda. We spent our first night at our old mission station at Maseno, then next day arrived at Paraa in the Murchison Park. Road notices informed us that 'Elephants have right of way'. At one stage, Alf was photographing an elephant right in front of him and we had to urge him to get back in the car, as another elephant was approaching from his rear! On the road it is not possible to hear them walking as they have a very silent footfall.

At this time a friend gave Alf a sum of money for his personal use. He was asked to buy himself a very good camera and to upgrade my car. This meant I sold my Fiat and bought a Ford Anglia which had a low mileage and was in good condition. We also purchased a Persian carpet in Nairobi. When all our disbursements were made, Alf decided that we should invest the remainder in Australia for use in our future retirement. This was the first time we had invested anything for ourselves. We let all the dividends be reinvested and this was the beginning of a fund set aside for our future.

Towards the end of the year (1965) in mid-December, Alf left on another long literature trip which was to take him to Japan, Canada and the United States of America. He was able so to arrange the flights, at no extra cost, to take in Australia. He met up with Marcus Loane and then he went to Melbourne and married my nephew Max and Evelyn at Christ Church, Hawthorn. From there Alf went to Borneo (now Sabah) and Malaysia for the Borneo Evangelical Mission. In Sarawak on 1st February, he spoke to the missionaries on preparing for political changes in the country. He also visited the CMS work in Jesselton and Tawau, then went up the river by canoe to visit some of the CMS missionaries. In March he visited Canada and the USA and then returned to Dodoma via England.

In July, Alf and I with Bishop Madinda drove to our first mission station at Kaloleni, where Alf and Yohana were to conduct a mission, at the request of Dr David Milton-Thompson. There were quite a few conversions and encouragements, including an African godson of mine then in his twenties. On the last day of the mission, five African girls came one after another to see Alf, and he led them one by one to the Saviour.

On 21st July 1966, we had the joy of hearing that Marcus had been elected Archbishop of Sydney, the first Australian born Archbishop. John Reid, who had come to speak at our Keswick at Msalato and later at a Kenya Keswick, had been present at the ceremony of enthronement and had shown Alf photographs and press cuttings, as well as giving us a first-hand report of the event. At Msalato, John had given four morning bible readings and one evening address, which were very much appreciated. Alf had hoped that Marcus could have come for this Keswick, but as he was unable to do so, he had sent John Reid to 'substitute' for him. One comment Alf heard, was that John's addresses reached the standard of English Keswick teaching. John was also very much appreciated in Kenya, where we heard he had spoken on the 'liberty of the sons' from Romans 14. There was a big crowd at those meetings.

Alf attended the World Congress on Evangelism later that year in Berlin, which he found most stimulating, and gave him the opportunity to renew fellowship with many Australian delegates. John Reid, Alf and Geoff Fletcher managed to visit East Berlin, where they endeavoured, unsuccessfully, to communicate with an East German pastor. They had no common language but they valued the experience.

In August 1966, the Reverend Donald (later Bishop) and Rosemary Cameron came to stay. He was then the Federal Secretary of the CMS Australia and Alf arranged for all the Central Province missionaries to come in to Dodoma to talk with Donald. I remember that he gave us a very good thought-provoking address, but delivered at great speed!

Alf reported that a mission had been planned in late December 1966 for students of the University of Dar-es-Salaam. Its theme was to be 'Moments of Truth'. The five meetings were to have as their topics:

1. Who is this?   Based on Peter and covering the subject of *the person of Christ*.
2. Conflict.   Based on Paul, covering the subject of *conversion*.
3. Death.   Based on our Lord and the thief on the Cross, the subject being *faith*.
4. Morality.   Based on David, the subject of *sin and its consequences*.
5. Life.   Based on the Rich Young Ruler, the subject of *decision*.

However, between the planning and the mission itself, several hundred of the students took part in a demonstration against the Tanzanian Government over the question of national service. As a result 300 or so of them were sent down and were not allowed to return for two years. We decided to go on with the mission even though it would mean reduced numbers, the number of students remaining in the University being around 400.

Quite a number of these students were Muslims, Sikhs, Hindus and Parsees. The University had a Chaplain provided by the Lutheran Church assisted by a committee of students and staff. For the number of staff in the University an unusual number were keen Christians — including four Professors. Not only did the latter support the mission by attendances, they and other members of staff threw open their homes for receptions, coffee parties and question times. The publicity was good. There was a general poster and one which was changed each day on all the University notice boards.

Personal invitations were sent out to all students, coffee parties covered the five halls and receptions covered the various faculties by years.

I was ably assisted by the Reverend David Gitari (later to be Bishop of Mount Kenya East), then a Chaplain at the University of Nairobi, Miss Barbara Jeays in charge of the music, Miss Christine Shepherd, our dental surgeon from Dodoma and Archdeacon Naftali Lusinde, as well as Mr E. Kibera, the Regional Education Officer for the Coast and Miss Glennice Allen, a school teacher.

Prayers were answered in that expected opposition did not really arise except perhaps in question times, and we averaged over 200 a night at the meetings. A large amount of literature was available, and many came for booklets such as *How I can be sure I am a Christian* or *Becoming a Christian*. No appeals were made and it is difficult to say what real results have taken place.

It is obvious that many Christians were helped — this came out in our interviews. On the very last night as I came out, a second year student told me he had been converted at the Saturday night meeting. All the team were greatly encouraged by many evidences of God's answers to our prayers.

The attendances alone were a great evidence of God's blessing, as in one way or another we must have contacted three-quarters of the total of the students of the university. We would be glad of your prayers for the follow-up and particularly when I return to the University for some days in February.

Before the end of 1966 Alf encouraged Dick and Shirley Feuer-heerd to advance their home-going to Australia with their three daughters in order to spend Christmas with Erica, their third daughter who had been at school in Ballarat. They were leaving Iringa in Tanzania for good to make their future home in Australia. They arrived in time to spend Christmas as a family together, but shortly afterwards Dick died from leukaemia which developed very suddenly. On 23rd February 1967, Alf went down to Iringa to install the Reverend Barry Skellett as Chaplain and to hold a Thanksgiving Service in memory of Dick who had had a happy and blessed ministry as the Chaplain of Iringa.

On 11th May 1967 we went home on leave. This was to be our last home leave, though of course we did not realise it at the time. Also it was to be our first winter for twenty years! Alf had now completed just over 30 years with CMS and relatives at home began to ask, 'When are you coming home for good?' It was something Alf began to think about from this time forward.

CHAPTER 12

LITERATURE AND LITERACY

The field of literature held Alf's interest throughout his life. I think it was first stimulated when he was working with the Lawrence Publishing Company prior to his entering Ridley College. He was interested in the production and presentation of books and tracts, but particularly in their spiritual content.

During his time in Africa he promoted literacy campaigns which were designed to get adult Africans reading for themselves. Many older Africans had not had the opportunity to go to school. Both Government and Mission Agencies were advocating literacy as a priority. From the earliest days, Missions had concentrated on teaching people to read, and it was an obligatory part of the preparation for baptism. Africans were required to be able to read before they were baptised. They attended baptism classes for up to a year or more. Of course baptism depended on their public confession of faith in Christ as Lord and Saviour, but it was seen as necessary to growth in faith to be able to read their bibles for themselves. In the early days, no Christian literature was available except the Gospels, and most older people learned to read from these. If a person was unable to cope with learning to read, he would be accepted for baptism on his confession of faith.

Miss Beryl Long, who first went to Tanganyika in 1944 as a CMS missionary, was a trained teacher. She taught in several schools including the Mvumi Girls' School and for a while she was engaged full time in running literacy campaigns. She had studied the Laubach method and was able to relate other literacy campaigns to what suited the needs of Tanganyika. Later she was engaged in pastoral work in Western Tanganyika, and became the Principal of the Kasulu Bible School.

When Independence came to Tanganyika, the new Government had as an important priority, the promotion of education so that all children would have a primary education. Of course this could only advance as fast as teachers could be trained and the economy meet the extra costs, but great and commendable progress was made.

During Alf's earlier service in Nairobi, he thoroughly reorganised the CMS Bookshop and made it profitable. He also initiated a Publishing Department which continued to be a workable proposition. Alf was able to cooperate with Charles Richards from England, who was to become the Director of the East African Literature Bureau. Alf learned of what was happening on the international front in the promotion of Christian literature in developing countries, and was thus able to assist with the publication of needed literature.

When Alf first arrived in Dodoma, he found a small bookshop which became a base to build on. However, the bigger scheme of a large centre to produce and publish Christian literature, had to await the timing of available finance. Alf wrote an article about two years ago which explained the situation:

> Literature is required wherever the Gospel is preached, and when Christians need the bible and simple teaching arising from their new found faith. Many people know that the quickest way to poverty is an unsuccessful publication, and the average missionary has no skills, beyond the simplest, for publishing. On looking back to the fifties, then a post-war period, this era was alive with difficulty.
>
> Like many other missionary societies, ours (CMS) decided to publish some needed literature. Everywhere in Africa attempts were being made to get the literature by seconding staff and allocating funds from all too heavily committed expenditure budgets. Concerned World Christian bodies decided to launch a million-dollar fund to set the work forward.
>
> The set-up in Europe, and to a lesser degree in the USA, was to set aside enough money to print the required books. Publishing takes time and needs skilled workers. It was not long before many centres needed books priced beyond the money people were prepared to pay. Our mission had three literature secretaries, and the help of those local people who had the linguistic knowledge and were occupying important educational posts. Further sums were raised and a Christian Literature Fund was started. Before long mission funds were available for the publication of the known needed literature. There was no real line of survey of the field and a secretary was not able to manage a retail job selling books, checking manuscripts and finding how best to sell such books.
>
> The church was locked into the Missionary Societies and had to make arrangements to carry on the work when the initial capital was all spent. Further sums were raised and a committee chosen. The committee consisted of missionary leaders from around the world and those already in the battle for Christian Literature.
>
> To see the thing whole was a puzzle to be solved. The hindrances to progress were the lack of channels of communication because of

the multiplicity of tribal languages in the third world, and a struggling church looking to the Society which planted the Gospel and which was not wanting to take the next step.

I was appointed Chairman of the new International Committee and given support. We discussed new ways of approach and tried to rationalise the priorities. It was agreed that Literature Agencies would discuss the budgets with other Societies which signified their willingness to look at the needs of the whole field, and set in motion the whole process of publication and distribution through viable bookshops, and seek to play their part in joint exercises.

The European Societies had years of cooperation behind them and discussed the plan with goodwill. Christians who were thinking in new terms were not prepared to subsidize work that offered no chance of success, and were eager to join and cooperate in new schemes.

The immediate result was the appointing of nationals to key posts and there was better cooperation at local levels. Broadcasting and radio work lent itself to inter-regional and international action, and literature work followed that pattern.

This statement by Alf was important as these ideas influenced the work which he founded in Australia when he returned to live there in 1971, i.e. the formation of the Australian Christian Literature Society.

With the arrival in Dodoma of CMS missionaries, the Reverend Kevin Engel and his wife, Dorothy, Alf began to promote his ideas more widely. There were constant discussions with Kevin. Dorothy was a trained nurse but prior to that, had worked at bookbinding and this skill was a valuable asset. Most of the existing bookshop work was taken over by Kevin, and he and Alf anticipated that literature work would be extended with the construction of the new Diocesan Headquarters at Mackay House and the large Bookshop to be set up there. They also looked forward to a large new centre where publication and printing processes could be initiated.

When Mackay House was built, expatriate staff were joined by Africans trained to work in the store and despatch department. Small bookshops had been established, or were soon to be set up, in all the large mission centres.

In February 1955, on returning to Tanganyika from Uganda, Alf visited Nairobi for consultations about bookshop matters. He then visited Moshi, where he was joined by Kevin Engel, and they took over control of the CMS Bookshop there, from Nairobi.

In 1958, the 80th anniversary of the beginning of missionary work at Mpwapwa by Alexander Mackay (in 1878) was celebrated. Celebrations commenced with a large convention. A tent was erected, and the meetings commenced on Wednesday, 8th October and continued until Saturday midday. Special speakers were Bishop Omari and Messrs Jacobs (Mennonite Mission), Johanson

(Lutheran Mission), Festo Kivengere from Dodoma and the Reverend Erisafati Matovu from Kasulu. Captain Len and Mrs Florence Straw of the Church Army, who were stationed at Mpwapwa, organised the celebrations. At the Saturday morning meeting Alf spoke from John's Gospel, Chapter 8, and after this meeting Pastor Daniel Lungwa's wife, Tiriza, met Alf and told him she was rejoicing in a new sense of forgiveness of sins. Other people were blessed too and we were conscious of the power of God's Spirit at work.

At 3.00 p.m., Alf laid the foundation stone of a new bookshop to mark this special occasion and it has since served the literature needs of Mpwapwa. On the Sunday morning Alf preached at the tent meeting with a Jubilee message, and quite a number of expatriate Government Officials were present.

After the Girls' School and the Bible School were established at Msalato, the building of the Literature and Christian Education Centre was commenced. It was close to the Bible School and these two institutions worked in harmony with each other. The Reverend Kevin Engel was appointed as the first Director of the Literature Centre in 1964. In 1959, Miss Betty Durham, who had been on the Home Staff of the Sydney CMS, came to Tanganyika. Alf had interviewed her on his last home leave, and realised she had the potential for work in the field of literature, as well as skills in youth work. She attended a special training course at the African Literature Centre at Kitwe in Zambia, to widen her experience. Some years later, in 1978 and 1979, she also went to Fiji to work in publishing, and then later in Papua New Guinea (1980-84). This was followed by a period back in Sydney in the Home Office until 1987, but she is now back at Msalato with a greatly widened experience.

The Reverend Petro Hango, a Tanzanian with special gifts in mass literacy teaching, joined the Msalato team. He spent much of his time training literacy teachers and supervisors, and visiting literacy classes in session. Other teachers who came to the Centre in its early years were Miss Nancy Collett, ThL from Sydney. She was trained in Religious Education and was skilled in Sunday School work. She prepared a great deal of curriculum material for various Sunday Schools in the country, and was an expert in the field of audio-visual aids. Nancy and Kevin co-authored a book on that subject.

Also from Sydney came Miss Patricia McIntosh, a trained commercial artist from the advertising world. She was an excellent illustrator. She prepared publicity for the publishing programme, covers and illustrations for books and youth manuals, and for the primers to be used in community literacy campaigns.

The Central Tanganyika Press was thus set up at Msalato. Two African girls were recruited for the literature work, on completion of their secondary education at the Girls' School. They were Miss Merion Ng'onja, who married the Reverend John Kilalo, a former theology student at Moore College in Sydney, and Miss Mary Harnaa, who married Dr Bura, a paediatrician who did post-graduate studies in England, and who had been educated at Mazengo School. The former helped in the training courses and in Swahili translation, and the latter in general office routine.

Miss Janet Wyatt from Sydney, came in 1963. She had a first class ThL qualification and became a good linguist. She worked with Kevin Engel in the literature field, producing very helpful books when she returned to Australia. She worked in Canberra with the Government Printing Department, and was attached to the Acorn Press until her death.

Miss Jeanette Boyd came in 1965, from CMS Sydney, a trained teacher with a first class ThL qualification. She spent much time in the Bible School and in Women's and Lay Training, and also in field work in a rural parish near Dodoma.

The first buildings at the Literature Centre consisted of a two-storey Literature and Christian Education block, providing living accommodation for three staff members and incorporating an Art Studio, offices and a lecture room. In 1965, two residences were built, one of them by an international team of volunteer students from the USA, England and Tanzania under the leadership of Kevin Engel. The next building was a three-storey block with accommo-dation for twelve women (in residence for courses) and two staff workers. Then came a print workshop with facilities for offset printing.

A yet later addition was a recording studio, where cassette messages were recorded for Radio Tanzania and for FEBA (the Far East Broadcasting Association) which beams its messages from the Seychelles Islands. These broadcasts are heard over the Middle East, Iran, Africa, etc. Mrs Marie Dawson was involved in the early stages of this project, as was also Stone Senyagwa, who had joined the staff earlier as a printer. Today Stone still supervises this work. Gospel messages in several languages were prepared on tapes to be used by itinerant evangelists and those working in pioneer areas. These tapes are played back to listeners on hand-winding cassettephones. With the use of the offset press, it became possible for written materials, art work and teaching posters to be prepared for use with the tapes, and kits of this equipment could be supplied in several centres.

Writing workshops were held at intervals, to encourage Africans in this field and to gather ideas for future commentaries and other reading needs. Our diocese, through Alf, became associated with African Christian Press, which was based in Ghana and there was mutual exchange of productions. Some of their material in English, which would suit our needs, Alf had translated into Swahili, by various members of his staff.

As the Literature and Education Centre grew and developed it became a well-known name throughout East and Central Africa and other countries. It was to have two future African Directors. The major publishing lines were theological text books, children's books and other material for children, also general books for youth groups, adult literacy, Home Care, etc. Much interest in buying Central Tanganyika Press books has been shown by booksellers in Malawi, Zambia and Ethiopia, and there has been an increase in the number of titles which have been produced each year. The most mammoth task attempted so far has been the Swahili Concordance of the Bible. This has been in preparation for over twenty years, but is nearing completion. Delays in obtaining stationery and printing supplies, because of severe restrictions on imports into Tanzania, have hindered progress severely.[1]

The Msalato Literature Centre serves the whole Province of Tanzania and the Christian Council of Tanzania. There is no such centre anywhere else in Tanzania, or indeed in East Africa.

It came into being through the vision and expertise of Alf and Kevin, with financial support and advice from Christian Literature World Agencies. Both Alf and Kevin were to travel around the world for many years, giving and taking advice to and from bodies such as the Christian Literature Fund, JACLO (Joint Action on Christian Literature Organisation), and WACC (World Association for Christian Communication), of which Kevin is now the World Treasurer. Alf was planning and advising on Christian Literature to the end of his life.

Alf often had ideas for books himself, but apart from a small booklet called *Now I am a Christian*, which he prepared for newly converted Christians, and especially for use following Missions to universities in East Africa, he wrote nothing else. This booklet was published in 1970 by the Central Tanganyika Press, and reprinted in 1976 by the Inland Press at Mwanza. It was translated into Swahili and Amharic (for Ethiopia) and one of the Sudanese languages. For quite a long time, Alf worked away at a book on prayer, for which he left all the material to be edited and put into shape by a friend. His growing disabilities prevented him from

---

[1]Since this MS was submitted the Concordance was completed and launched at a special service in the Dodoma Cathedral in 1990. The first edition sold out quickly.

bringing this to a conclusion by himself (It has now been published by Acorn Press, Canberra.)

At this point I should mention that on three occasions Alf was involved in Missions to the Nairobi University. Some years previously, he and David Gitari (now Bishop of Mount Kenya East) were the two missioners. Alf went up to the next mission at Kenyatta College, in September 1968. He said it was encouraging, with a few conversions. There were no public appeals but quite a number of commitments to Christ were made. Attendances averaged 450-500 each night, and there were fifteen smaller meetings by invitation. Alf had a deep sense of God's help.

The third mission took place from 8th to 15th November 1970. I will write of this in the next chapter.

Bibles, Prayer Books, Hymn Books and Gospels in several languages were distributed by the Literature Centre out to the rural bookshops, and to missionaries and evangelists visiting areas where no books could be bought locally. Many stories are told of Africans and their early adventures with books. One concerns a young Maasai warrior. The Maasai are a pastoral nomadic people who graze their large herds of cattle over a wide area of Kenya and Tanzania. They have a very simple life style. The men are usually naked, their bodies are greased and coated with red ochre, and their hair is likewise coated and drawn back, with the addition of string, into long fat pigtails. They wear a blanket draped over one shoulder and are seldom seen without a spear. Many stories are told of their prowess in fighting wild animals, in particular lion.

One day, a young Maasai came to Alf to buy a gospel. Alf asked him if he knew how to read and he said that he did. So Alf selected a gospel and opening it asked him to read the passage next to his finger. The man took the book, looked at it for a minute then turned it upside down. 'No', said Alf, turning it the right way up. The man looked mystified, then again turned it upside down and began to read. It seemed that he had learned to read by sharing a book with two others. They sat on the ground and from where he sat he could only see the print distinctly, upside down, and had learned to read it that way. I never heard whether he was re-educated to read correctly, but he bought the gospel and went off with it quite happily.

Many of the Gogo people likewise used to ochre their bodies in the same way as the Maasai. But after Independence, if they came into Dodoma coated in ochre they could be fined. The Government brought in this ruling in order to encourage them to read. When adorned with ochre, it came off on books or anything else they touched, especially hospital sheets!

Miss Avis Richardson spent her last years in Tanzania as a

Diocesan Literature Secretary, before retiring in 1964. She was awarded an MBE for her work in education and on returning to Australia became Assistant Warden of the CMS Federal Training Centre, St Andrew's Hall in Melbourne, from 1964 to 1969.

The output of Christian Literature from Msalato has steadily increased year by year, with dedicated and well-trained personnel in management.

The Reverend Kevin Engel enlarges on what has already been written:

SOME REFLECTIONS ON VARIOUS ASPECTS OF THE MINISTRY AND INTERESTS OF ALFRED STANWAY

Central Tanganyika Press

Two nights after I arrived in Dodoma in late April 1954, Alf Stanway took me into the old Diocesan Office and said, 'We must set up the accounts for Central Tanganyika Press'. I knew something about printing and accountancy but nothing about publishing. However, from this evening CTP came into being.

The first titles were nine literacy readers in Cigogo produced with the help of the Laubach Foundation and one unusual title — *Pains in the Back and Neck*. This book in English was an instant success as a doctor friend of Alf's in Nairobi bought the entire print run!

Over the next few years, new titles were added as needs arose in the life of the church. The main thrust began when CTP moved to Morogoro in 1960 and Betty Durham joined the staff. Sunday School materials, books for lay workers, women's books and revisions of service books started to roll off the presses. About this time the Diocese of Central Tanganyika undertook to be the Literature Secretariat for the Christian Council of Tanganyika of which Alf was the chairman for many years.

When Avis Richardson retired as headmistress of the Mvumi Girls' School she was asked to establish a literature office for the Provincial Church — first of East Africa and later when it was formed, the Province of Tanganyika (later Tanzania). CTP moved back to Dodoma in 1963 and then to Msalato in 1965 where it found a permanent home.

Alf was always actively involved in every new publication. He helped to raise funds for capital and buildings. He became a familiar figure to such organisations as SPCK London, Joint Action for Christian Literature, Feed the Minds and organisations in America. When I visited these institutions on behalf of CTP, I found that they were very willing to listen to new proposals as they had confidence in the Diocese because of Alf Stanway's leadership and the track record that had already been established. Starting from nothing, CTP grew into an international publishing house producing books on a wide range of subjects and in several languages.

Msalato Literature and Christian Education Centre

It is difficult to separate one work from another as they were often closely intertwined. When the Diocese applied for land to build a new Girls' School to replace Mvumi (see Bible Schools), it also applied for land for what the colonial government at that stage could only grant as 'a mission station'. The Diocese had moved well beyond this type of thinking and a wide range of activities was planned but the government was still back in the early years of colonial rule.

One of the ideas was that there should be a lay training centre which would train men and women in a wide range of skills which the growing church needed. Three immediate goals were set. First, to train Africans in all the processes and methods needed in writing, design and publishing. Next, to train African women in modern areas of health care, child nurture, dressmaking, and at the same time giving them an introduction to bible study and leadership, especially in the field of Christian Education and Sunday School work. Thirdly, there was a dream that one day a residential centre might be built where men and women would come to write and edit the theological and other books which a new nation would require.

Plans were drawn for the first building but there were no funds available. Alf said, 'God will give us a clear sign when the time is right'. One Sunday afternoon, three Indian Christian ladies came to our house and gave my wife a gift of two hundred shillings, 'towards the work you told us about for a special place to produce Sunday School books'. When I took this to Alf at the time of our regular Sunday evening time of prayer which preceded the evening church service, he said, 'This is the harbinger of spring, boy. You can let the contract tomorrow.' So the next day on the basis of a gift of ten pounds a contract was given for six thousand pounds! So the first two storey building rose above the thorn bush at Msalato. All the rest followed as agencies abroad saw what had happened and supported this venture, funds came from England and Germany. A printing press was given by clergy attending a prayer breakfast in the States at which Alf spoke. Staff from several overseas countries were recruited and local men and women joined and were trained. Outstanding amongst these was Alexander Chibehe who became involved while still a schoolboy at the old Alliance Secondary School, and who went on to become a graduate and was Director of the Centre and CTP Manager when he was tragically killed in a car accident.

Alf was always prepared to encourage young men and women to branch out even when, as in those early days, there were few prospects of lifetime careers in such fields.

Bible Schools

From the beginning of the missionary work in East Africa, there had been a strong emphasis on training the catechists and lay evangelists who were at the forefront of the church's growth. However, this usually took the form of a day's teaching once a month when the men (and some women) came in from outlying parts.

In 1956 while the Reverend Max Corbett was District Superintendent at Kilimatinde and I was responsible for the Dodoma District we decided on an experiment. We would bring together all the pastors and evangelists from the two areas at a midway point and have a three weeks' extended time of teaching. Alf encouraged us in our planning and promised some financial help.

Several times he himself came to give teaching and also visited at night when filmstrips were shown running off the bishop's car battery. On the last of these evenings a special meal was prepared with the appropriate speeches that were always part of such occasions. The late Canon Jonathani Songolo had been appointed spokesman by the group of almost a hundred 'students'. In a humorous yet impassioned talk full of little historical anecdotes he asked Alf if the Diocese would establish a permanent place — a school where the pastors could send their men and women for deeper training and teaching.

Alf was very moved and gave a solemn undertaking to do so even though he had no prospects of funding or staffing for such a place.

Shortly after that he met with the Diocesan Council and put before them the idea of a number of Bible Schools; one to be near Dodoma, another in the West and the third to serve Morogoro. Following this he felt that he could ask CMS in Australia to provide the basic funds to put up some very simple buildings serving each of these areas. It was quite a break with CMS's policy at the time when they agreed to provide building capital and this was due to the strong conviction that Alf had that the Church in Tanganyika needed all the trained men and women that they could recruit.

Obtaining the site at Msalato — about seven miles to the north of Dodoma — was in itself another remarkable story.

There was a road maintenance camp at what was called Seven Mile by the PWD (Public Works Department) and Msalato by the local Wagogo. Right next to this on a fairly level area was some thorn bush country which had been worked over years before as small planting places but abandoned because of the poor soil. Also there were some large gravel pits from which road building materials had been extracted. There was however another significant factor about this point. It was the place to which water in the main pipeline that passed from Makutupora to Dodoma flowed back when the pumps stopped.

The Bishop, Archdeacon Naftali Lusinde and I went out to walk through the bush. At the highest point there was a small tree growing out of an ant hill. On the Bishop's instructions I climbed this while he and the Archdeacon provided their hands and shoulders to hold me aloft. I relayed answers to questions from below about the slope on the land, whether there were any huts or *shambas* (cultivated plots) on it and a decision was made. We would apply for this site.

The next day I went to see the District Commissioner, who at that time was an English Officer. I thought that there would be a long formal process with appropriate forms to fill. Instead the officer passed me a writing pad and asked for a rough sketch of the area. Not having any accurate measurements I drew a rough rectangle facing the great North Road and put arrows indicating a frontage of 'a quarter of a mile by three quarters of a mile'. 'That should be fine' was the response and after checking with the local chief and people the Diocese very quickly acquired a formal title to two areas: one for the Girls' School, and for what they called a 'Mission Site', which became the Bible School and the Msalato Centre.

Missionary Aviation Fellowship (MAF)

It was only through the long and persistent representation of Alf Stanway that MAF agreed to establish a base in Dodoma. There was considerable doubt as to whether there would be enough flying. Could the Diocese supply a house for the pilot who would also require to be a certified engineer? Were there enough airstrips serving the key centres? Alf gave positive responses to all these questions and set about organising with missionaries, pastors and local chiefs, the clearing and construction of fairly rough airstrips at Mvumi, Kilimatinde, Berega and several places in the West of the Diocese. The first Cessna 186 arrived. Hennie Steyne was the pilot and lived in what had been the 'old' bishop's house. A simple hangar was erected and the plane was in constant use.

Chaplaincies

Although the majority of services were held in either Swahili or the local tribal languages throughout the Diocese, Alf Stanway was concerned that all races should have the opportunity of worshipping and hearing God's Word in their own tongue. Consequently he built on the earlier chaplaincy work established by Bishop George Chambers, but where there had been irregular, periodic visits, these now became permanent bases for ministry with resident staff. In the years since, several of these places such as Arusha, Tabora, Iringa and Morogoro have become the headquarters of new Dioceses.

In the early days of his episcopate, Alf tried to reach the expatriate Europeans through these ministries but later he became convinced that an outreach to the Asian members of the town communities was needed and so he recruited Indian ministers from South India to travel, teach and minister to the Malayalam, Gujerati and Hindi speaking people.

Odd Notes

Travel with Alf was an experience. These journeys were often used for 'thinking aloud' through some issue, opportunity or crisis which was before the Diocese. When driving with him he had a simple rule. We would change every hour or every fifty miles, whichever came up first. There were always stops at strategic places to greet missionaries or pastors or to look at a new area of possible outreach. There were games to play to relieve the tension of driving over very difficult roads. Spotting wild animals with a fixed point score depending on the animal's rarity was a favourite. Playing chess at the camp in the evening was a required discipline for all young missionaries.

Flying with Alf was another experience. He had a host of tales of near disasters and a flight in a canvas covered Caspair plane over Lake Victoria with him was another tale to be told when we almost ditched in the Lake just off Bukoba. (The chess game was abandoned by mutual consent.)

CHAPTER 13

THE CLOSING SCENE IN AFRICA — MAY 1967–JULY 1971

We flew home to Australia via Mauritius to spend our first few days with Alf's sister Grace and her husband in Gosford. They had started to build in Paynesville, a fishing township on the Gippsland lakes (where a number of Stanway cousins lived) and were shortly to move there. We went to Sydney and after a weekend with Marcus and Patricia Loane flew to Melbourne and moved into a CMS flat in East Malvern.

Alf now started a very busy deputation programme which took him to most of the Australian States. We were only to be home for five months and planned a short holiday in September, with deputations and other meetings filling up the rest of the time. During our holiday period Alf had accepted Marcus' invitation to speak at a clergy school for the Sydney Diocese on 5th, 6th and 7th September, from 2 Corinthians, chapters 4, 5 and 6. Later Marcus commented that 'the insights and the practical and spiritual bearing on the text of chapter 5 was exceptionally helpful'. Alf's comment to me was that this was the chapter he found the most difficult to prepare!

The Scotchmers came to Australia and stayed with us in East Malvern. Alf had borrowed a car and we drove to Canberra. We spent the first night in Bairnsdale where there was a supper party with the local Stanway cousins. Alf was particularly pleased to meet up with them after many years.

The next day we set out for Cooma and a tour of the Snowy Mountains. There was a fresh snow storm on the mountains and we four East Africans shivered. We drove to Canberra where Spring had arrived with a wonderful display of cherry blossom. For the last part of our leave Alf was moving from one State to another and I stayed with my sister in Hawthorn. During this leave, one event which Alf enjoyed was laying the foundation stone of a new residential hall for Ridley College (called Aickin) on 10th September, 1967.

Early in October 1967, we returned to Tanzania, having flown by Constellation via the Cocos Islands to Mauritius. The diocesan team in Dodoma had set up a novel welcome home for us. When our plane touched down on the Dodoma airstrip there was quite a crowd to welcome us back. A strip of red carpet was rushed out and four helmeted Msalato ladies on Honda motor-cycles acted as outriders to our car back to Bishopsbourne.

Once again life moved into its busy pace. Just a week after arriving back we had a visit from the German Ambassador and his wife. From now on Alf was to find how much easier it was to administer a much smaller diocese. Communication was simpler and confirmations and diocesan meetings less difficult to plan.

For some time, a committee had been planning a mission to the Nairobi Colleges which were to become the University in the near future. Alf wrote to his praying friends in October 1967, concerning this mission, which was to be held in November:

> Judging by human standards there has never been a successful mission at an East African or Central African University, that is if one is to count success in terms of obvious response such as has been seen in some of the missions in West Africa. However God's call has come and there is no reason why past experience should lower expectations and hinder our faith. God is able to work in the midst of all classes of persons at all times, and there are indications that the present time may be opportune for such a mission at a university. I would be glad of your prayers for the student body which is organising the mission, for the missioners and others who will speak. It is going to cost about £500. We expect to bring a missioner from India for the Asian students. I hope all this doesn't sound too cold and factual, but you are my friends, you know what I believe and what I will seek to make clear and I shall be grateful for your prayers from now until then.
>
> On Sunday, 19th November I preach at the University service for the opening of the mission on the text, 'A man came running'. This service is to be broadcast, though it may not be heard until later in the programme. I will then speak each night at the mission as well as preach on the following Sunday morning. The topics are:

Tuesday 21st	What is man?
Wednesday 22nd	Who is Christ Jesus?
Thursday 23rd	Why did Christ die?
Friday 24th	What does God require?
Saturday 25th	What does it cost?
Sunday 26th	Where does it end?

After the mission concluded Alf wrote:

> There is so much for which we must praise God. When I arrived in

Nairobi the Committee told me that the full budget of £500 had been received and two students were converted in the week prior to the mission. All of this put us in good heart.

The service on the Sunday was the largest university service ever in Nairobi. More than 250 came. We had hired a tent capable of seating 240 which with extending flaps could seat extra. We filled the tent every night and had to use the flaps. After the first night the numbers were 300 and stayed there. We invited members of the Senior Common Room to a lunch and expected 20 or 30 replies but 60 came. It was a great meeting and I felt tremendously encouraged both by the way the message was given to me and help in answering questions. During the mission there were 40 subsidiary meetings. Sixty-five students met Professor Osborne of the Physics Department of the Dar-es-Salaam University. I spoke to 45 commerce students on the subject 'Money Matters' and it was one of my best meetings. There was a meeting for Hindus, at their request, but only four attended. There was also a big gathering for Muslims at their invitation at which Dr Wilfrid Stott spoke on 'Mohammed's view of Christ'. This led to a good discussion and opened the way for further talks. I met with the Roman Catholic Chaplains and twenty members of the Newman Society and they all came to the main meeting afterwards. We also sold quantities of the type of Christian book which would be most helpful.

Dr George Kinoti, an African who is a lecturer in Zoology at Makerere (Uganda University) was most helpful with students troubled about the difference between science and religion, and Professor Osborne's address on the point that the 'incomprehensible is not necessarily untrue and the comprehensible is not independent of God', plus a fine personal testimony, was a tremendous introduction on Thursday night.

We had a fine team. As well as the others already mentioned there was Joseph Masembe and David Gitari, both graduates of the College, the former engaged in education curriculum work and the latter secretary of the Pan African Students' Fellowship. Then there was Dr Wilfrid Stott and the Reverend Ted Newing of St Paul's Theological College and Miss Christine Shepherd, our dentist from Dodoma, who as well as speaking illustrated her message by singing with her guitar. We made no appeals for decisions but made our purpose plain and had many opportunities for meeting with students.

By Friday we had the first one coming to say he had really decided for Christ. This was followed by others. The pattern seemed to be — a talk — a going away — and then a returning to say the decision had been taken and they had told their friends. There were 11 such clear cut decisions that we know of. Many others were greatly helped, and a large number were seriously considering the messages.

What none of us could escape was the tremendous friendliness, so different from the past, and the obvious willingness of the audience not only to listen but to go along with the speaker, and even those who were finding it difficult to come to grips with the Christian faith treated us very much as their friends. To say I was helped in speaking would be much less than the truth. I was tremendously conscious of help, both in the preparation and in the delivery, and all the subjects which had been chosen for me by the committee seemed to be right when the time came. In many smaller ways there was great evidence of answered prayer, and although there were gaps in the organisation there were no serious hitches.

One of the most encouraging things was the obvious growth in stature of many Christians during the week, and the joy that some of them radiated as obvious blessing began to come.

During February 1968, Festo Kivengere came to visit the Diocese of Central Tanganyika. He ran a series of missions in our Second-ary Schools. He was now an ordained Anglican priest with a BD qualification. Arthur Scotchmer spent some time in Zambia, so Sheila came to us for a few days. From 13th–18th January 1968, Mary and Henry Young from Geelong in Victoria, with their children Stephen and Angela, came to stay with us. Mary's brother, Dr David Milton-Thompson, worked at Kaloleni and they had come to us after visiting them. Once Alf had hoped that Mary might work as his Secretary but Henry claimed her first! One day we took them to visit Hombolo and we were caught in a torrential rain storm. We travelled cautiously but became stuck in the mud with the rain pouring down and obliterating our view of the road. It was too wet to get out of the car. Little Stephen seemed fearful. How were we to get unstuck? Alf assured him that God would send help to us. Not long after that Stephen Cyster came by in a Land Rover and was able to tow us out of the mud.

Early in March Alf travelled to Bonn in West Germany for a quick visit to confer with the EZE Agency (for development aid) about the Mazengo School buildings now under construction. He returned via England where he saw agents of the Automobile Association to arrange for a car for our use during the Lambeth period later this year. When he arrived home he said that he thought we would receive £160,000 for the school buildings and further help for the Mvumi Hospital buildings which was a tremen-dous encouragement.

Although Alf was extremely happy in all that he was doing he was trying to be sensitive about the future. He wanted to stay in Africa as long as possible but wanted to be sure of what was God's plan for him. Dr Leon Morris of Ridley College, Melbourne, had asked him to consider anything Ridley had to offer by way of a future posting and Alf said he would give this offer his first consideration.

Over quite a number of years Alf had developed a morning habit, usually after his Quiet Time and before breakfast, of humming a six-note tune (not very tuneful) and singing over and over 'I'm on the rising tide, I'm on the rising tide'!

This only happened in my presence or in front of family. If visitors were with us, he engaged them in conversation, but this little song portrayed his early morning mood. He was always cheerful first thing in the morning and wanting to 'get at' his work. He also believed in a good breakfast, not all that much to eat, but something sustaining. He called this 'laying a base'. By this time he had completed more than thirty years with CMS and was keeping everything, including the future, constantly under review.

In early March of 1968, Eric Stockton, a longtime personal friend, came to visit us and see the work. He had been Treasurer of CMS Melbourne for many years and was to work with the Bible Society. He was able to see several of our centres. Alf and Marcus Loane had been corresponding over a period about our meeting in England during Lambeth. Patricia was to accompany Marcus, and he and Alf were now planning a trip on the continent after the conclusion of Lambeth, for all four of us. When the time came for us to leave Dodoma, the planning included a trip to Greece and the Holy Land prior to the Conference, with no extra cost on air tickets.

By this time, Alf had another conference to attend in Geneva to act as chairman of the Reviewing Committee of the Christian Literature Fund. With his ability to make every situation fit into his pattern, he arranged a meeting for Directors of the Dar-es-Salaam Bookshop on 23rd May, and on our way out to Europe he stayed on for a night with the Australian High Commissioner and Mrs Bullock at the Embassy while I flew on to Nairobi and stayed with the Sansoms. Alf followed a day later by Comet and flew to Geneva on the 26th where he met up with John Winteler who was on the first stage of his annual holiday in Switzerland. After the meeting they flew together to Athens.

I left on 30th May on a VC10 and arrived very early in the morning at Athens and took a taxi to our hotel where I met Alf at the door on his way to meet me. John had booked a day tour for us. We crossed over the Corinth Canal to Corinth and saw all the historic buildings and the Agora with the Bema (judgement seat) where Paul was arraigned before Gallio. After lunch we travelled around the Peloponnesian Peninsula to see the famous ancient Lion Gate at Mycenae and other historic sites. Next day we visited the Acropolis with its famous buildings, notably the Parthenon. We noticed the relationship of Mars Hill to the Acropolis and thought once more of Paul. After seeing something of the ancient buildings in Athens itself, we left in the afternoon of 1st June for the Holy Land.

John Winteler had been stationed in Baghdad as a Medical Officer during World War II and had had frequent trips to the Holy Land and became familiar with every aspect of the country. As well he was a good Bible scholar. He had planned this trip very carefully for us. It was a special time to arrive in the Land because it was Pentecost Sabbath as we landed at Lod (Lydda) and went on to Tel Aviv. Everywhere was very quiet and there were few movements in the street. John had arranged with us to stay with a Mrs Irma Lambie, a personal friend. She was an American, the widow of a doctor who had served in Ethiopia as a missionary, and had come to the Holy Land to take charge of a hospital for Arab refugees suffering from tuberculosis. Her husband had died some years back but she had continued working at the hospital which was in the Baraka Valley, or Ein Arroub (the place of springs), a few miles south of Bethlehem.

Next day was the Christian Pentecost Sunday. We travelled to Jerusalem and entered the city by way of the Allenby Memorial commemorating the handing over of the keys to General Allenby by the Turks in 1917, and his entry into Jerusalem on foot. He would not ride in mounted as a conqueror. To him the victorious entry belonged to Christ. We joined in a service in the garden surrounding the Garden Tomb, then went to Gethsemane, then to St George's to meet Archbishop and Mrs McInnes. We travelled with Arab drivers down the Baraka Valley to Mrs Lambie's home, passing King Solomon's pools. During the next few days we travelled around Mt Zion, saw the pool of Siloam, the Dome of the Rock — a Muslim shrine built around the stone altar from Solomon's Temple, visited the El Aksa mosque where Muslims worship, saw the extent of the former Temple site and went down to the Bursa or Wailing Wall. As it was just after their Pentecost, there were still many Hasidic Jews swaying, praying and reciting there. We were told that the book of Ruth was recited there at Pentecost.

We were most impressed by the remains of the Roman Pavement under the Ecce Homo Church, no doubt the Gabbatha of the gospels.

That same afternoon we went to Emmaus, a moving experience, and Alf and I walked down the Roman road where Christ and the two others walked and listened to Him expounding the scripture. The church nearby has a rose window over the Holy Table depicting our Lord breaking the bread before a man and a woman.

On 4th June we were driven up the Mount of Olives and over the top to Bethphage and down to Bethany, then down, down into the Judean wilderness, and what a wilderness! There was a burnt out tank there, a memorial to the Six Day War. The 5th of June was to be the first anniversary of this war. We were startled and pleased to see an old Druse shepherd with his staff and leathern bucket leading his black-faced sheep up a hill — just as in scripture with the shepherd leading and the sheep following in a single line.

Descending further down towards Jericho, suddenly we saw water flowing down the side of a hill in this barren, dry land and were told it was the brook Cherith where Elijah was fed by the ravens. It was very hot in Jericho as we were now below sea level. When we descended to the Dead Sea we were 1300 ft below sea level. Alf and John swam in the Sea telling me how easy it was to stay afloat because of the dense mineral property of the water. It did not appeal to me! We were intensely interested in the excavations of an ancient Essene monastery near the Sea and seeing up above us the caves in which the Dead Sea Scrolls had been discovered. Later we went to the Museum of the scrolls, which is built in the shape of the clay jars in which the writings were sealed. Now the writings are spread on a wall and covered with perspex. This Museum is not far from the Knesset — the present Israeli Parliament buildings.

On 5th June, the first anniversary of the Six Day War, we took the coast road to Galilee, not attempting to go through Samaria (now West Bank country) where there are heavy concentrations of anti-Israeli Arabs. We were most interested in the historic relics at Caesarea, then went north to Haifa, a modern city, and up to Mt Carmel from where we could look north to the Bay of Acre and the town of Tyre. From Carmel we travelled east to Nazareth and then on to Cana and down to Tiberias to stay at the Scottish Hospice. The Sea of Galilee here is 800 ft below sea level. Next day we drove north to Ein Tabha, where there are the remains of a Byzantine mosaic floor of a church depicting a basket containing two fishes and five loaves. We saw several coves down near the lake, from which our Lord could have preached to the crowds. We stood on the Mount of Beatitudes and then visited Capernaum with a well-excavated synagogue site. On returning to Tiberias we went out on the lake in a speed boat and after dinner at night, saw little boys fishing from the edge of the lake. They were catching what is locally called 'Peter's fish', but to us resembled the Tilapia of East African lakes. Next day on our return journey we saw the south of the lake where the waters narrow and feed into the Jordan River. We passed by Gerizim and Ebal to Nablus (the ancient Shechem) where Jacob's well is, and by the roadside not far off, the tomb of Joseph, where his embalmed body was interred after being carried back from Egypt. Further south we saw the ruins of ancient Shiloh and had to go through a road check before passing by Jerusalem.

The next day we visited Hebron, a most ancient city and fiercely Arab. Mrs Lambie was well-known and respected, and our drivers were Arabs so we were secure. To get there we passed through the fertile valley of Eshkol, with great vines and plump grapes forming. Before coming into Hebron, we came to Mamre where there is a large well and we remembered Abraham and his sojourn here. We were permitted to enter the Mosque of Abraham in Hebron. John told us that before the Six Day War, any Christian or Jew entering that mosque risked his life.

The Arab custodian of the mosque told us his family had been custodians there since the sixteenth century AD. He guided us through, showed us the large foundation stone of the fortress Herod had built over the cave of Machpelah, purchased from the Hittites by Abraham where Sarah was buried. Also buried there were Abraham, Isaac, Rebecca, Jacob and Leah. There were Hebrew inscriptions over their shrines which Alf could read for us. The cave was below the floor of the fortress, about 12 ft down we were told. The Byzantines built a church over the fortress in the fourth century AD and the Ottoman Muslims a mosque over that and it was possible to see the four architectural remains towering over us. There is an enormous pool in the town. Hebron was among the most impressive of the Holy Land sights. The town looked very ancient and we visited a potter sitting with his feet over the edge of a pit in which was the treadle and he worked away at small clay pots. Another place of interest was where the famous Hebron blue glass was made. The glass-blowers still made it and many glass objects were moulded in that colour.

On our way back to Baraka we passed the Herodion, Herod's summer palace, and we went on to Bethlehem, passing several burnt out tanks en route. We visited the Church of the Nativity and saw David's well, discovered in 1960 by a man boring for water. It is huge with an enormous quantity of water. Also discovered were 150 cave tombs, some of which we saw. The two Christian Arab drivers took us to their Bethlehem home for tea and coffee and traditional round Arab bread. We had to be back at Baraka by 7 p.m. because there was a curfew on account of the hospital refugees. Next day we walked about in the walled city of Jerusalem and now felt we had stored up a lifetime of memories which would come to mind when we met these names in the Bible. We were astonished by the small geographical size of the Holy Land and the fact that Bethlehem and Jerusalem were close enough to see the one from the other. Our views were brought into perspective and the small scale of the country helped us to encompass it in our minds. Marcus had quoted to Alf, 'The land throws light on the Book, then the Book throws more light on the Lord'. He passed this saying on to everyone whom he heard was going to the Holy Land. This was a visit we had always hoped to make but did not know how it could be accomplished, and now it had come to pass at no extra travel cost plus the careful arrangements and planning made by John.

We left Israel for London on 9th June and stayed overnight at Wimbledon with the Scott family. Mary Scott had met us in Tanganyika when she was visiting friends. Alf was able to drive her from Mbulu in the north to Dodoma where she stayed with us before going on to Morogoro. This had been the beginning of another long enduring friendship. The following day Alf obtained the car he had ordered and we drove to Grace and Stuart Laurie-Walker's home in Surrey, collected Arthur and Sheila Scotchmer and we all crossed by air ferry to Le Touquet and motored across France, Luxembourg and the Tyrol to Innsbruck, from there to St Moritz, then to Lakes Como and Maggiore in Italy and back to Interlaken where we met the two chaplaincy representatives of ten years ago, Misses Baumann and Stahel. We then went to Basle, Strasbourg and across France to Le Touquet and so back to our base.

It was a time of fellowship and interest. Alf and I, now back in England, spent this pre-Lambeth period with John Blandford, a widower, and his daughter Maureen at their home in East Molesey. He had been our bank manager in Dodoma and had lived next door to us. In the next few days we visited old friends, Alex and Valerie Dick at Torquay and Jim and Lesley Harris on a farm near Tiverton. Jim had been the last British Provincial Commissioner in Dodoma, and had had to leave after Independence when the Province became a Region. and an African Regional Commissioner had taken his place. They had been regular attenders at our Cathedral services. On 5th July, friends took us to see the Men's Singles finals on the Centre Court at Wimbledon.

Every Sunday when Alf was free from Lambeth meetings he preached in various English churches. On this first Sunday, 31st July, he preached on 'Say the Word' in a village church near Romsey. The next Sunday found us in Paris, with Alf preaching at the British Embassy Church for two services, on the work in Tanzania. They supported our Diocese. There were various discussion groups, one being attended by thirty young people. Then Alf had a two day visit to Stockholm to chair another Literature Committee. On 10th July there was a very well attended Central Tanganyika Diocesan Association 'get together' at the Church Army Headquarters with Bishop Madinda speaking as well as Alf.

After this, we went north to Middleton in Lancashire, where Len and Flo Straw were working and joined in a parish weekend for overseas missionary work. There was a walk of witness through the town after the morning service at which Alf preached, and that evening he spoke at Cheadle Hulme. Another interesting gathering was in a village in Oxfordshire where Alf spoke to a group of seventy people on the theme, 'Christian faith in the world of today'.

We visited cousins of mine in Essex, and met Colonel and Mrs Upton who were to visit us in Tanzania in 1970. Rosemary Upton was a well-known ornithologist and we were intrigued to see hundreds of budgerigars nesting in trees in their gardens. They were all imported birds, but thrived in this environment.

On 18th July, we moved to Blackheath to stay with Jack and Ethel Bennett, and to be closer to Westminster. Next day Alf went to Church House in Westminster for pre-Lambeth consultations. On 20th July, we visited ex-Dodoma friends near Royston and then went to Cockfosters to the Reverend Kenneth and Mrs Hooker. Next day Alf preached at the two morning services where a number of his friends came along for the day, and that night we went to Oakhill Theological College when Marcus preached at Evensong. We now stayed at the College and joined in an EFAC Conference (Evangelical Fellowship in the Anglican Communion). The Reverend Dr John Stott led Bible Studies from 2 Timothy, Chapters 1 and 2.

We left for Canterbury on 24th July and stayed overnight with friends; then we joined in the great opening Celebration at Canterbury Cathedral, a wonderful and inspiring service with Archbishop Michael Ramsey preaching. Then followed a series of Lambeth Conference sessions for the Bishops, with receptions at Lambeth and Buckingham Palaces and a Lord Mayor's Reception at the Guildhall. On Sunday 28th, a service of Holy Communion was held in Westminster Abbey which was televised and Leonard Beecher, the Archbishop of East Africa, preached. It was a very long service lasting from 10.30 a.m.–1.15 p.m. The next weekend, Alf collected Bishop Madinda and we went to Leicester where he preached for the Reverend Edward Wilson Carlile of the Church Army, and in the evening at Symon Beesley's Church. Symon had been on the staff of Kongwa College for a few years and his wife's parents had been colleagues of ours in Kenya. It was good to meet them again. Archbishop Ramsey gave a most inspiring lecture to the wives on 'Jesus is God'. He also answered questions we asked of him.

During the following week I went to several events arranged for the Bishops' wives in Winchester, then came back to accompany Alf to Durham for what was participation in the 'Lambeth Walk'. Durham itself was a most interesting place, with a massive Cathedral on a prominent site above the river, dating back to the twelfth century. The home of the Bishop of Durham, Auckland Castle, was also very old and impressive. We had evensong and dinner there on 16th August and Alf and I went to Bishopwearmouth to stay. Next morning Alf met with the deanery clergy, and in the afternoon there was a large combined service in Durham Cathedral, where the tombs of St Cuthbert and the Venerable

Bede are to be seen. Alf preached next morning in the ancient (883 AD) church of Chester-le-Street.

On returning to London, Alf and I went one evening to Lambeth Palace for evensong and dinner.

The following Sunday, the closing service of the Conference was a sung eucharist in St Paul's Cathedral, when the preacher was the Metropolitan of India, Pakistan, Burma and Ceylon. By this time, our stamina was flagging and we were looking forward to a few days with Patricia and Marcus on the Continent. Before we left, Alf booked tickets at the famous old Mermaid Theatre near the Thames to see the play *Hadrian VII*. He planned to take our friends the Scott family of Wimbledon, on his birthday, 9th September.

Alf collected our picnic equipment, and we called for Patricia and Marcus at Betchworth, and again set out for Lydd and crossed to Ostend in Belgium by air-ferry. We followed a route from Liege along the Rhine, seeing the old historic castles on either side and stopping to see the Luther memorial group of statuary in Worms. The next day saw us going south and east through Stuttgart and Munich, and by autobahn to Salzburg and Berchtesgarten, and south to Hallein.

On 29th August we arrived in Vienna. We had seen beautiful scenery en route and enjoyed picnic meals. In one picnic area, Marcus found some wild scented cyclamen growing. In Vienna we visited St Stefan's Cathedral, saw the Vienna Boys' Choir setting out from there in fiacres, and drove around the city past the Opera House and other historic public buildings. The 'blue' Danube at Vienna seemed small, and as muddy as our Yarra River and only half as wide! We realised we were close to the Czech border, but turned back west again, travelling next day through green valleys and by clear running streams. We then followed south to Venice and did all the 'touristy things', taking a gondola to the Grand Canal and the Rialto Bridge and then by smaller canals to the glass factory. It was fascinating to watch the glass blowers at work, shaping little horses as we watched. We then went to the famous Byzantine Cathedral of St Mark and climbed up to stand by the noted St Mark's horses; and to sit in the great Square.

We left Venice via Padua and Verona and travelled to Lake Como. On Sunday we sat by the lake shore for prayer together and Marcus spoke to us of our Lord's use of the word 'Father'. The next day we travelled to Menaggio on the western shore of Como, then on to Lake Lugano and north to Switzerland via the St Gothard and Furka Passes. We walked through an 'Ice Palace' carved in the Rhone Glacier, before travelling on to Interlaken, and once again visited our chaplaincy ladies and had coffee with them.

On 4th September, we crossed through Montreux to Geneva

and walked to the famous Reformation Monument, built on an impressive scale, and also saw Calvin's church, the Cathedral of St Peter. We continued to travel across France to Troyes, Soissons and Compiegne where we visited Le Clairiere de L'Armistice, where the signing of the armistice took place at the conclusion of the 1914-1918 war. The railway tracks are preserved there and the sites of the German plenipotentiaries, and Marshal Foch's carriage. One could inspect these by payment of a fee in French currency — no German currency was accepted. There was enough French coinage in our possession for Marcus and Alf to go inside — Patricia and I were not as interested as they. Later we visited the beautiful Cathedral at Amiens and stayed the night in Le Touquet. Alf and I visited Canon and Mrs Harland there. He was on the staff of the Commonwealth and Continental Church Society, and had worked at Moshi in our Diocese for a few years.

On 6th September we were back in Lydd, and drove to Bexhill to see Mrs Crabbe, the widow of our dear Bishop Crabbe of Kenya days. Then we travelled to Sevenoaks to leave Patricia and Marcus with friends. We were sad to say goodbye after so many days of fellowship together. We went on to Kingswood in Surrey to Grace and Stuart Laurie-Walker's home where we stayed until the time came to return to Dodoma. We saw the play *Hadrian VII* and enjoyed it immensely. By 13th September we were back home to what was to seem 'a quiet life' after the last few months in Europe.

Alf was now sixty years old and began to review his career and pray about his future. Thirteen years later (in 1981) he revealed that in 1968 he had asked God to grant him another ten years of effective ministry. 'They were', he said, 'the best years of my life'.

Alf wrote to his friends, asking them to pray for a Mission to Kenyatta College in Nairobi in October 1968, on the theme of 'Becoming a free man'. He said he would be assisted by Canon and Mrs Corbett and a group of African graduates from Kenya. The Chaplain of the College was the Reverend Ronald Dain, brother of Bishop A.J. Dain of Sydney. There were 937 students and 683 teacher trainees at the College. The report of this mission appears to have been lost.

The BCMS in England sent the Reverend Edward Whitmore and his wife, Janet, to Central Tanganyika for pastoral work, in the sixties. He was located to St Philip's College, Kongwa for his first years, lecturing at the College and becoming proficient in Swahili. Then Alf transferred him to Dodoma to initiate Theological Education by Extension (TEE), a programme to assist the ministry of a fast growing church.

It was a programmed course which spread gradually through many parts of Africa in the mid-sixties. Phenomenal church growth

President Julius Nyerere (on Alfred Stanway's R.) inspects early building additions at Mazengo Secondary School, Dodoma, 1968.

in which the ministry could not keep pace with rapid increase in the number of Christians requiring shepherding, called for a drastic and immediate remedy. There were too many Christians for too few pastors. TEE was designed to help meet the challenge of this situation. It educated a person where he lived and most of the course was carried out by correspondence lessons. The student who enrolled did systematic study by himself, whilst being involved in the local church. He had a tutor who arranged regular seminars with other students, and they had open discussions about the assignments set. Some seminars were for a few hours weekly or of two-day duration once a month and were essential to the success of the method.

Alf was increasingly impressed at how well the Diocesan team was coping. Day by day, now he was making important decisions and influential visitors were arriving to see the work. The first of these was Ernst Mogler from the German EZE (aid agency) who came to see progress on the Mazengo School buildings, now moving into their final stages. The Reverend Francis Foulkes, the Principal of St Andrew's Hall, the CMS Training College in Melbourne, came to visit graduates of St Andrew's in their field situations, and Charles Richards came representing the Christian Literature Fund's Swiss Headquarters. The Reverend Alan Neech of the BCMS also came, as did John Wilson from the Common-wealth Society for the Blind. All of these visits were interesting, encouraging and fruitful.

In March 1969, Alf led a course in Dodoma on Administration for bishops and archdeacons. He wrote, 'One of the principles I have been advocating, which most books on administration suggest, is that you concentrate on those places where a change will make a good deal of difference, rather than on solving the problem.' He also used to advise people over the years not to organise their lives on the basis of extreme busyness, but to leave margins. Some-times the margins would have to be taken up, but that was why they were there. The way in which he did this himself was, whenever possible (usually most days), to rest for about half an hour on his bed after lunch. He started this habit on the tropical coast of Mombasa, and insisted that I did the same. He invariably slept at this time, though I usually read. He liked to have some time of recreation between 5.00 and 7.00 p.m., and when it was possible he went to bed as early as 9.30 p.m.. He did not like to read in bed. Reading was always done in his study or the sitting room. He was a fast reader with a good retentive memory, and covered a wide range of books, often having several on hand at once — he seemed able to go from one to another without losing the sense of their themes.

On two occasions during the Dodoma years, he was asked to review and advise on accounts in other dioceses, once in the Upper Nile, and once for Archbishop Leslie Brown in Kampala. This was an area where he seemed to have a flair for spotting mistakes, and for seeing combinations of figures which suggested mistakes.

Some said that figures 'talked' to him! Another of his observa-tions was that leaders get criticized most for their best decisions and wisest judgments. 'This', he said, 'is simply because as the leader is one step ahead of others, he does the unexpected'.

Alf continued to keep in touch with Dr Leon Morris during 1969. The door to Ridley was open but Alf wanted to be sure that the door was closing in Africa before he made any move. He said, 'every month helps the Diocese forward, so the Africans gather experience and the Diocese gathers strength'. President Nyerere continued to pass through Dodoma frequently and on one such occasion at a small reception, they both discussed leadership, and Alf said he had a good book on the subject called *Spiritual Leader-ship* by Oswald Sanders, and would the President care to have a copy? Dr Nyerere said that he would and when next they met Alf asked had he read it? He said he had but added, 'Remember I am a politician!'

Alf thought our possible next leave in Australia should be in

1971. That year there was to be an Australia-wide NEAC (National Evangelical Anglican Conference) in Melbourne to which he wished to go. Margaret McKechnie was due for leave at the end of September 1969, and Alf asked CMS Australia for a missionary secretary whom he could train to work for his successor. The latter would be an African, therefore Alf wanted the new secretary to do language study when she first came out, so that she would be fully equipped. CMS arranged to send Joan Thornton the following year. She did language study, worked with Alf and then carried on for the new bishop after Alf had gone.

In August 1969 Alf said, 'I could be coming home for good in 1971. It is difficult to say but so far my plans do not point in that direction'. By October he was saying, 'I feel at peace in remaining now, and feel undue speculation would only be disturbing. Better to plan the next steps as they come, knowing that God will keep me in the way as He has done in the past. God would not leave me idle in Australia. I doubt if, with the many people there, I could add a great deal except in a few specific fields, whereas here I can add what only a person of long experience in Africa can add and there are fewer and fewer of those in the land. I continually take comfort from Paul's words, 'I make it my ambition to please Him in all things', and I know that the prayers made for me will be that the peace I have on the matter will remain. There have always been two reasons why I would like to come back to Australia. One is to try and pass on to the new generation something of the truths that I feel are the most important ones for young people to hold. The second is I would have liked to have been a catalyst to see that some large scale reforms were instituted in missionary societies. The old order must give way to the new if anything worthwhile is to be achieved in the future.'

In September, we took six days of our annual holiday to fit in with Colonel and Mrs Upton's desire to visit one of the Game Parks of Tanzania. As Rosemary Upton was an experienced ornithologist she had been advised to go to the Ruaha Park in South West Tanzania. On writing to us about this possibility, we realised it was utterly impossible for them, as complete strangers to East Africa, to do such a trip alone. For one thing, Ruaha was rather remote and one had to take a stove, cooking utensils and all the food needed for six days and a knowledge of Swahili was essential for conversing with Park Guides.

Alf invited Max and Val Corbett to come with us. Max was needed to drive the Diocesan Land Rover, which we hired for travelling in the Park and for conveying our stove, food and equipment. Alf left two days ahead of us with the visitors, whom he settled into the White Horse Inn in Iringa, while he stayed with the

Reverend Daniel Lungwa at the Chaplaincy House. Next day, Sunday, Alf preached at the English and Swahili services at St George's. Max, Val and I loaded up the Land Rover and joined them on the Monday, and after lunch we travelled west along the Ruaha River to the Park. There we were accommodated in three rondavel huts near the river, where there was a stand of 'whistling' thorn trees. These bear long seed pods which 'whistle' in the breeze. There was an open *banda* (a thatched hut with walls half-way, then open to the roof) where netted safes were provided for our food. There were tables, forms and dish-washing equipment supplied. Max, Val and I were camp cooks and managers, while Alf looked after our visitors.

The African camp scouts came and lit large bonfires at night outside the banda. This was to keep the elephants from investigating our food. One evening they came all around us as we were eating. The bonfire kept them at a distance but we could not leave the banda to go to our huts until they moved away. They loved the 'whistling' seed-pods and reached up with their trunks to pull them off. Another night when we were in bed, some of them rested their bodies against the walls of the rondavels. Rosemary said she could have put her hand through the window and have touched them. We were very close to nature!

We had very good views of the water birds of all varieties, and particularly the large handsome fish eagle with its haunting cries. In all, we saw and recorded forty-two species. One day, we took tea in our thermoses and biscuits for an afternoon picnic, and after touring around and seeing various species of animals, we stopped in a clearing under a huge shady baobab tree. We could easily spot anything coming near us and hop back into the Land Rover if necessary. I spread out the cups on the bonnet of the Land Rover and poured out the tea. Max climbed up on the car to get a long view, to see if we were safe. Just as I handed Val a cup of tea, Max shouted 'bees!'. He had been attacked and started to run, and the bees came after us (African bees are noted for their savage attacking instincts). Val said, 'What will I do with the tea?' 'Put it down', said Alf as he proceeded to beat off the bees from her with his hat. She promptly threw the cup on the ground and ran! We all took to our heels. Max had the most stings on his face which swelled up. After a while we crept back, packed up and moved off. We called this our 'stinging' (not swinging!!) safari'. We collected a few tsetse bites also, but no harm came from those. We enjoyed this safari though there were too many elephants for our liking!

Jan Lamb, who had come from Sydney to relieve Margaret McKechnie, continued to work on for Alf and enjoyed her time in Tanzania. In late November we had a visit from Noel Davey of

SPCK London, who visited our Literature Centre. During early 1970 there was a severe famine in the land. The 1969 rains had been scanty and the crops very poor. President Nyerere had decided not to go begging from Britain now that the country was independent, but in truth the food resources were very limited. There was much sickness locally and some people were collapsing in the streets. The most affected area was our Central Region. On writing of this time Alf said, 'We've been able to meet all the needs we have seen, but the Government folk are very tender on the question of famine and like to do all the relief work themselves. However, they have neither the staff, the transport nor the food to cover everything. You have to be careful what you say or you'd be out on the next plane! I have been able to get quite a lot done through the local member of Parliament, and by other ways. We've been helping such as are our special responsibility and any needy ones we find. As the recent rains have been good the prospects for a harvest for 1970 (around August) are good. CMS Australia gave a special gift to relieve famine sufferers and I was able to send some of this to Bishop Gresford Chitemo for one region in his diocese, and asked that it be used to buy food for the pastors and evangelists in that area.'

Margaret McKechnie became the financial secretary of what was called the Inter-Diocesan Committee. She dealt with a whole range of financial matters relating to missionaries in the four dioceses which evolved from the original DCT, i.e. their salaries, leave travelling, medical expenses, etc. When the time came for an African to be Diocesan Bishop, his office would be relieved of these matters concerning expatriate workers.

The Reverend Donald Cameron, the Australian Federal Secretary of CMS, came once more to the Diocese (in 1970) and met with many of the missionaries and Diocesan workers in the CCT Conference Centre. It was a valuable conference. Alf and I went to Dar-es-Salaam with Bishop Madinda and other diocesan representatives for the inauguration of the new Anglican Province of Tanzania and the installation of the Right Reverend John Sepeku as its first Archbishop on 5th July. This was held at Ilala in the grounds of the Cathedral Church of St Nicholas and African Martyrs. There was a good congregation consisting of delegates from all the dioceses of Tanzania.

It became clearer now to Alf that the time had come for him to consider leaving Africa. With the appointment of an African Archbishop he felt the next step should be for an African to succeed him before too long and he began to ask for prayer that his successor be prepared for the task. He also decided to accept Dr Morris' invitation to join the staff of his old college, Ridley.

The Christian Union of the University of Nairobi invited Alf to lead another mission on their campus in November 1970, the theme of which was to be *Live Issues*. It was two years since Alf had led a mission there, so they produced a brochure to advertise the meetings with a photograph of Alf, and beneath it this message from him:

> I appreciate the opportunity of being asked again to come and speak at Nairobi, now a University in its own right. The subjects I have chosen relate to the questions being asked all over the world today by thinking people, and I trust as one who in his thirty-three years in East Africa has grown to love this land and its people, I may be enabled to say things that may prove useful to many and which will be relevant to us all in the nineteen seventies.

The programme was advertised as a Series of Evening Talks at 8.00 p.m. in the tent on the Chaplaincy lawn. The subjects were listed as:

Monday	TRUTH
Tuesday	SEX
Wednesday	LIFE
Thursday	DEATH
Friday	FAITH
Saturday	?

On the back of the brochure were the names and academic qualifications of the team members, and the hall or place where they could be found. Four of the team were from DCT, Mrs Marion Glen, Mrs Christine Osborne, Miss Jeanette Boyd and the Reverend Ron Taylor. The Reverend Tom Houston and two other Europeans and six graduate Africans completed the team. They were available to help during the week and could be found in the Halls indicated.

In writing to a friend about the Mission Alf said:

> It was a first-class mission. Attendances were good. At the two Sunday morning services there were 350 and 500 present respectively. The first night of the mission we had 265 present but there were College elections on the same night. The next night 550 were present for the subject of 'Sex', the following nights were 390, 390 and 450 respectively. On the last Saturday when many were away 350 attended. We had at least 25 conversions. There were some during the training course which preceded the mission, six were converted in the coffee parties held each night, one was converted by the singing, and others at the meetings. Some came to see us afterwards. I had a great Saturday morning with five coming to see

me. Two of them to tell of their conversion on the night before, and three who wanted to accept Christ just there and then. The receptivity was marvellous and the results were better than the team had expected!

After we returned from Nairobi, President Nyerere was in Dodoma for meetings of the TANU Executive. Thought was already being given to Dodoma becoming the Capital of Tanzania, because of its centrality. The Colonial Government had considered moving the capital from Dar-es-Salaam many times, on account of the coastal heat. Dodoma they knew would have a problem in increasing its water supply. They tackled the problem of Dar-es-Salaam's climate by changing the working-day hours from 7.00 a.m.–2.00 p.m. but this had not proved as helpful as anticipated. They also considered Morogoro as a possible capital and Tabora.

Some long term missionaries were now returning to Australia because of the educational needs of their children. We had lost the Corbetts and early in December the Engels were to leave. Alf himself left early in December for more consultations on literature in Switzerland, and was to make a visit to England in March–April, then to New York in early May 1971 for a World Literature consultation.

In the middle of January 1971, Alf represented the Anglican Province of Tanzania at the Anglican Consultative Council meetings in Nairobi. He recorded that fifty-five delegates attended the meetings and among those present were the former Archbishop of Uganda, Leslie Brown, and Professor Norman Anderson, both acquaintances of his. He returned with Archbishop Sir Frank Woods of Melbourne. They drove from Nairobi, stopping at different centres in our Diocese to view the work. Alf took the Archbishop to visit St Philip's College, Kongwa, where the Archbishop opened the new building in which Miss Mary Newell would be training wives of students. He was also shown the complex of Bible Schools, Literature Centre and Girls' School at Msalato and other near areas of work. We held a Garden Party for him to meet our Diocesan Staff, both African and European, and Dodoma residents. By this time Archbishop Woods knew that Alf was returning to Australia to take up a post at Ridley College and he warmly welcomed him back to the Melbourne Diocese.

Archbishop John Sepeku then visited us, his first visit since being installed in the office of Metropolitan. He was followed by Bishop David Hand from Papua New Guinea, who brought a Papuan pastor with him. The Africans were intrigued and mystified that this man was not an African! He looked like one! When they spoke to him in Swahili he did not respond. Through interpretation they asked him how his ancestors came to leave Africa and go to his land? When he mingled with Africans it was impossible to discern that he was racially different!

Bishop Hand was to be the last visitor in our Dodoma home. He left us on 12th March, and a few days later we both left for England, stopping en route at the Hague, where the British Chaplaincy supported our Diocese. They had specially helped with bicycles for pastors. Alf preached on the Sunday for them and then went to other meetings in the Netherlands, before crossing to England. After a few days there at Reigate, Alf went across to America for meetings of the Christian Literature Fund in several centres in the States. In New York, Alf was greatly encouraged by a large gift for the Diocese just as he was leaving.

Before leaving Dodoma, I had completed most of the packing up of our goods. Alf had given away most of his books, leaving a skeleton selection to build on at home. Some books in the Africana range, notably language books now out of print, we had sold to the University in Nairobi. I disposed of the accretions of 34 years in East Africa, by bonfires in a forty gallon drum. We were to return to Dodoma in mid-May for our last few weeks in Africa.

THE BISHOP AND HIS OFFICE TEAM
By Margaret McKechnie, Bishop's Secretary 1954-69

The Mackay House team was a happy united group. We all appreciated the Bishop and he drew out our maximum response to the work, partly because of his infectious enthusiasm about everything. We commenced the day at 8.00 a.m. with prayers in the Bishop's office. As soon as prayers were over he liked to get on to correspondence with his secretary. He would have come to the office with his basket of letters all sorted and ready to be answered. There were no interviews until his secretary had enough work to keep her busy for most of the day.

When I was working with the Bishop I always felt that he was a leader who had his finger on the pulse of the whole Diocese though it was so huge. It stretched in the north and west to the borders of Tanganyika and to the south and east nearly two hundred miles from Dodoma. There was also a large number of missionary colleagues with whom he regularly kept in touch. Sometimes he was away from Dodoma for quite a long period when he was on confirmation safaris, which were long, slow, car or train journeys, but even then he liked to hear from the centre by receiving regular letters.

If there was no-one waiting for an interview when he had finished dictation with his secretary, he was off to one of the other offices to see how his staff was getting on and what information they had for him. He visited the bookshop and chemist shop daily, and called in on the doctor and dentist in the Professional Unit. He liked to know the financial situation each day so the Accounts Department was an important place. The receipt of certain monies often meant an answer to prayer, or progress in needy areas. Some people did not understand the Bishop's interest in finance, but it was often important because of its spiritual implications for the work.

The planning of new buildings, with all the work this entailed, was attended to in the office of the Administrative Secretary and his Assistant, and much prayer went into this because for most of the twenty years that Alfred was Bishop, new buildings were going up somewhere within his huge Diocese. The Diocesan Secretary would come to see the Bishop with interesting or encouraging reports about the pastors and their work. The Bishop took close interest in all aspects of the administration, and gave encouragement to all by enquiring regularly about how things were going.

Letters were important to him. Sometimes they came by train, sometimes by air, and the messenger was off to the post office to get the mail at the earliest opportunity. Occasionally the train was late and that really delayed our work. Sometimes it was the plane that did not arrive on time. He never lost his interest in the mail and all his letters were answered.

When he was on safari in East Africa the mail — or a precis of it — was sent on to him so that he could keep up to date and not have everything awaiting his return. If he were abroad we had a numbering system, and a precis of letters would be sent to him. A reply would come back just ticking items to show they had been noted, or instructions as to what answer to send. In this way he was able to keep in touch even though he might be thousands of miles away. Just before leaving on an overseas trip, he would say enthusiastically, 'I've emptied my basket, everything's dealt with and I'm ready to go!'

He enjoyed his safaris and worked hard beforehand to get all the important work out of the way before going off. When he came back he would take his letters home to read and sort into categories, then come in the next day saying what was the total to be answered, and he would work away until they were all done.

Every person in the team felt his or her work was important because there was a leader who led by example and made everyone feel that the job he or she was doing was very worthwhile even though it might seem like routine in its way. The monthly newsletter, composed by the Bishop's Secretary, kept all our workers informed about happenings in the Diocese, and it included a list of the Bishop's coming engagements. This was specially important for those who lived a long way from the centre.

We all felt we were working for the cause of the Gospel in a team under God's appointed leader.

CHAPTER 14

THE LAST DAYS IN AFRICA — MAY TO AUGUST 1971

Our last few weeks in the Diocese were very busy. On the home front we had crates made for trans-shipping our household goods. By the laws then current in Tanzania, we were obliged to leave open our crates and suitcases — all twenty-nine of them! — for a final customs inspection. (This was to guard against artefacts being taken out of the country.) We had to have jewellery valued and were permitted to take only a limited amount of money. These regulations caused us no concern. When the young Christian Customs officer came to the house for the final inspection, it was obvious that he disliked what he had to do. All the crates were sealed with a customs tag, and we produced six typed forms of a Table of Contents. Fortunately I was allowed to keep one copy, which proved helpful on entering Australia.

A Tanzania-wide Pastors' Conference met in Dodoma in May. It was sponsored by World Vision. Its leader was Paul Rees, and it was held in the now completed Mazengo Assembly Hall. Alf chaired the Conference and hundreds of clergy were present. The Reverend Festo Kivengere came as a speaker and one of our young clergymen, Simon Chiwanga, did a fine piece of organising work. President Nyerere came for the opening meeting and addressed the assembly, and later honoured the School by performing the opening ceremony of the complex of buildings. This was most meaningful for the school and demonstrated the good relationship the Diocese had maintained with Government in educational affairs.

Our farewell service was arranged to take place in the Cathedral on the afternoon of Sunday, 20th June, and as all the clergy from the DCT, together with many from the daughter dioceses, were to be present, Alf arranged a Refresher Course for them at Msalato.

He led a series of Bible Studies on 1 Peter each day and Bishop Gresford Chitemo led the Evening Devotions. Topics such as Christian Marriage, Christian Service, Literature, Bible Schools and Politics were discussed and Saturday, 19th June was set apart for Convention Meetings. Pastors' wives now joined their husbands and parish representatives were welcome to attend.

On that Saturday afternoon, which was the tenth anniversary of the opening of the Bible School, Alf laid the foundation stone of its Chapel. There was enough money in hand to complete the first stage, to pour the concrete for the floor and to build the Vestry and the Principal's office. The rest of the building would follow as the money came in — there was some money already set aside for Chapel furniture. The finished Chapel would seat 150 students. At this stage there were 72 in residence, forty of whom were reading for the three months' course and thirty-two for the nine months' course. This was a memorable service, with all the clergy and bishops robed and a great sense of thanksgiving for what God had done for the Church in those past ten years.

Sunday afternoon saw a packed Cathedral for our farewell service to be followed by a tea-party with speeches and gifts. I quote now from the Diocesan Newsletter of those days.

As Bishop of the Diocese of Central Tanganyika, Alfred presents the Rev. Canon L.J. Bakewell (Principal of the CMS Language School, Nairobi, and former member of the Diocese) with Diocesan crests for his clerical robes, at Alfred's farewell service on 20.6.71.

At 2.00 p.m. in the Cathedral, all the Pastors and visitors from the parishes gathered for the farewell service for the Bishop and Mrs Stanway. People came from near and far and this was a special time for all concerned — a time of sadness and joy, as people remembered with gratitude and thankfulness before God, the twenty years during which Bishop Stanway had been our Diocesan. Bishop Stanway preached and hearts were blessed. Following the service there was an informal gathering for tea in the Conference Centre when presentations were made.

Lionel and Chris Bakewell came down specially from Nairobi for this event. They themselves were retiring from their work in the Nairobi Language School, after forty-two years of service in East Africa. During the Cathedral Service Alf presented Lionel with two woven badges of the Diocesan Coat of Arms, to wear on his scarf.

Bishop Madinda led the service, which opened with the hymn, 'Lord you are my portion'. This was followed by a bidding prayer acknowledging and giving thanks for Alf's leadership over the years. A Litany of Thanksgiving succeeded this, and Canon Chidosa, who had been the first archdeacon appointed by Alf, read the lesson from Ephesians 1:3-14, after which the hymn 'Rock of Ages' was sung and Alf preached. After singing 'Stand up, stand up for Jesus', Bishop Madinda led in prayer for Alf and for me in our

Clergy of the Diocese of Central Tanganyika together with Alfred and Marjory Stanway (C.) after the farewell service in the Cathedral of the Holy Spirit, Dodoma, 20.6.71.

future work. Alf then gave the Blessing followed by the singing of
'God be with you till we meet again', which is a hymn I always find
upsetting on occasions like this.

We assembled for a photograph with all the clergy immediately
on coming out of the Cathedral. Then we gathered in the Conference Centre nearby for the tea party and the speeches and gifts.
Canon Chidosa opened this session with prayer and three choirs
from the Cathedral, Dodoma parish and the Matumbulu Church
sang to us. Many loving gifts were presented to us, baskets,
beads, walking sticks, cloths, even a Swahili Bible! (We were
giving our own away!!) Then there was an enormous and heavy
mahogany shield with the Diocesan Coat of Arms painted on it.
(I flinched inwardly as I realised it would not fit into any of our
pieces of luggage and I would have to carry it home!) Each
presentation came with a gracious little speech and usually a
written record of what was said, for us to keep.

The Mothers' Union made a speech for me, followed by Bishop
Madinda's address on behalf of the Diocese. I am going to quote
much of what he said, as I feel it demonstrates the fulfilment of
what Alf had hoped to achieve when he preached on his hopes and
expectations at his enthronement· service. As is the African custom, we were presented with a copy of his speech from which I
now translate.

*Mr A. Kanyamala presents a replica of the Diocesan coat-of-arms to Alfred and
Marjory at a farewell gathering, 20.6.71. Far R.: The Rt Rev. Y. Madinda and Mrs
Madinda.*

It is not easy to try and compose an address which is fitting for our dear parents Baba Askofu and Mama Stanway in a brief time like this, and it is not easy to find the thoughts, expression and language to build a speech which is able to be listened to attentively by a great crowd like this, nor to draw the attention they deserve.

Baba and Mama, this occasion will be thought of for a long time and it is no wonder to think its like will not be seen again, it is like a man who is looking at a ship sailing out of a harbour. All of it is seen at first, afterwards just the mast then smoke and finally it disappears.

This is a sad time when we think of our past years of living together, getting to know one another and then to think in no time at all this will come to an end, although our fellowship in the Spirit will remain till that day when we meet again in heaven with Jesus for ever as the well-known hymn says . . .

I think you will agree with me when I say, when we consider your zeal in the Lord's work and your fellowship with us through all the years you have been with us, many thoughts come flooding over us like an overflowing river, it is difficult to know what to say and what not to say? . . . Undoubtedly Baba Askofu, it must be said that after taking up the heavy load of DCT you began to investigate and read the existing files about the work of the Diocese, left by Bishop Wynn Jones . . . the thing that was new to us was the alteration you made of the title 'Missionary-in-Charge' to be District Superintendent, in order that in the future there would be no difficulty when you were to give nationals, who were not missionaries, the responsibility of the work. Also another change you made was to remove the letters 'CMS' and to replace them by DCT, because there were other expatriate workers, not from CMS, who were working in the Diocese.

You brought great progress in strengthening Chaplaincy ministries. It used to be the custom to send visiting chaplains at certain times such as Christmas and Easter to take services. You continued to appoint chaplains to live in towns such as Morogoro, Kilosa, Arusha, Moshi, Iringa, Tabora, Mwanza and Kalinzi (from where they ministered to Kigoma), and you helped them with the equipment to perform their work such as motor cars, etc., and people were ministered to more often than in the past.

You began to share out and give authority to nationals by appointing them Rural Deans and Archdeacons. You stressed the importance of self-support through the Central Church Fund, step by step until you reached 20% of the offerings, and even now some parishes have already begun to increase their CCF to 21%. This was the open door to the progress of our Diocese by making use of overseas aid for other projects and not clergy salaries.

Another important thing you did was to appoint Assistant Bishops. In 1955 Bishop Yohana Omari was consecrated as Assistant Bishop, the first African Bishop in the whole of Tanganyika. In 1959 Bishop Maxwell Wiggins was consecrated as Assistant Bishop of the Lake Region. In 1962 Bishop Musa Kahurananga was consecrated Bishop of the Western Region and after the death of Bishop Omari, Bishop Yohana Madinda was consecrated in 1964 to be an Assistant Bishop in DCT.

Because of the great size of the Diocese you began to think about dividing it, and took these steps:

1963 — The Diocese of Lake Victoria Nyanza with Bishop Wiggins

1965 — Bishop Gresford Chitemo was consecrated for Morogoro and it was cut off.

1966 — You divided off the West under Bishop Musa.

Other things were important buildings in our Diocese such as the beautiful and spacious buildings at Mvumi, Hombolo and Kilimatinde Hospitals. Impressive and beautiful buildings were erected at the Mazengo Secondary School and the Msalato Girls' Secondary School, the Msalato Bible School and the Literature and Christian Education Centre, also the Central Tanganyika Press.

New and beautiful buildings rose up at Kongwa College, Bishops-bourne and missionaries' houses were built, Mwaka House, the Christian Council of Tanzania Conference Centre, and you even gave us 'eyes' when the Buigiri School for Blind Boys was built.

You will remember when you took over the Diocese there were very few clergy and only a few missionaries, but if you look around the clergy who have come forward from your ministry they are the crowd you see here now! Even when you leave us Baba Askofu, we are a complete group which will go on fighting for the church of Christ and defending it during this time of change in our land of Tanzania, and make our requests to our President Mwalimu (Teacher) Julius Nyerere and the leaders of our Government, also our political party TANU in its new leadership, that the purpose of the church of Christ is to do the work of spreading the Gospel of His Kingdom in the hearts of people and live in peace and quietness.

But as well as the increase in the clergy, I must, Baba, mention another thing; there are some pastors who, because of your foresight of the days to come, you sent overseas for clergy training and some who experienced western parish life in England and Australia. Our African bishops have been enabled to go to America.

As I said earlier, if we consider all your years among us and the blessing of Almighty God which has come to our Diocese because of your ministry many thoughts come rushing upon us like the overflowing river and it is difficult to decide what to say and what to leave. For example, when listening to a preacher such as I, it seems as though he is about to finish his address and lo! and behold! he keeps on going!

However I must say your ministry wasn't only in our Diocese but even to other churches united in the CCT (Christian Council of Tanzania). Since you were chairman of the CCT there has come much good progress, such as advocating educational advance for all schools controlled by churches, and to bring a good relationship between Government teachers and our church teachers, especially concerning the difference in their salaries and other such matters. Also you set forward medical matters concerning doctors and hospitals and adult literacy.

CCT has united the churches to have one voice before the Government for their needs and is listened to carefully. You have given a great deal of help in other dioceses with their financial concerns. If my memory is right you went to Uganda to help with their money management. Then there have been your journeys almost to the ends of the world to meetings and discussions concerning Christian literature.

You had confidence and trust in all the ideas you put forward and they have come to pass. All that God entrusted to you, you used in our Diocese, and by your carefulness you have developed the Diocese and you leave it in the state you now see. It is not easy to discover what to do after you, except to guard the trust until that day . . .

Finally I do not know how best to bring this speech to a conclusion. Have I come to the end? May I mention perhaps in their hearts they would say, 'I have kept the faith, after these things there has been prepared for me a righteous crown, which the Lord, the righteous judge shall give me on that day, and not only to me but to all people who love His appearing'.

Glory Alleluia.

It was not easy for Alf or me to leave Africa. It had been our only home for more than thirty years. We loved the people and they loved us sincerely, and now there was the feeling that we may never see them again. Alf gave the final blessing after this gathering and more photographs were taken. He left the next day to complete business matters in Dar-es-Salaam and I followed after I had seen our goods off on their way. Alf then left me in Dar-es-Salaam waiting for the Royal Interocean Straat cargo ship to come into port, as he had to return for many local farewells in the different Diocesan centres.

I embarked on 6th July sailing north to Mombasa. As we were loading and unloading I was able to go out to our first mission station at Kaloleni and stay with Dr David and Bea Milton-Thompson and meet a few older Africans who still remembered us. We left Mombasa at night and I went on deck to see the lights over the land and say goodbye to this special place where I had first landed thirty-two years before. It was a sad uprooting feeling, very hard to describe.

We sailed south to Tanga, loaded up a full cargo of coffee-beans destined for the Nescafé factory at Port Fairy and which would be unloaded at Portland in Victoria. This was the very last part of Africa I saw as we sailed for weeks without a break before reaching Adelaide.

In the meantime Alf, back in Dodoma, was staying with Andrew and Julia Farrer. He visited all our near Diocesan centres for more farewells, speeches and presents of hens, eggs and ground nuts. He wrote to me at Adelaide about some of the farewells; I here include what he wrote of the official opening of the Mazengo School.

The official opening of the Mazengo Secondary school took place over the weekend of 17th–18th July. I was to have gone to Iringa for a farewell visit there, but on Saturday morning I was told that the President would be coming to Mazengo School on Sunday especially for the opening of the new buildings, which he wanted to have done before I left. So I had to phone Iringa and now we plan to go there next weekend.

The 'do' at the School was quite first-class despite the speed at which it was put on. Various people were quite determined that it should be opened before I left and that they get the President to do it — and they succeeded! The Headmaster was in Dar-es-Salaam and they flew him up in a special plane. John Malecela and another minister from the East African Community came, as well as the Secretary of the Common Market. Job Lusinde came up from Dar-es-Salaam as well as the Principal Secretary of Education.

We met in the Hall. The Headmaster (Richard Juma) gave the welcoming speech and then I spoke. I told how the Government had wanted to use the money for the hall on something else, but that I was determined that we should have the hall, and that finally I went to the President and personally got him to overrule. At this there was a **great** cheer that went up from the boys and teachers.

Opening of the completed buildings at Mazengo School, Dodoma by the President of Tanzania, Julius Nyerere, pictured (3rd from L.) with Alfred, Bp Yohana Madinda and government officials, 1971. (Photograph: Photo Unit, Mazengo School)

After that we inspected the school. It was quite a triumph in some ways because all the things the President liked most about the school were things the Department did not want and I insisted on having. The poor Minister of Education had to keep pointing out that he was not the Minister of Education then! I had already said goodbye to the President at Chamwino, but he took leave of me again very graciously in front of everybody.

He was quite helpful about photographs. I wanted to take a photograph of Job Lusinde and John Malecela, as two old boys of the school, and the President. Nyerere asked that I be in the photo and get somebody else to take it. All these changes of plan meant that I had an easy Sunday and I enjoyed being free. It has made me fit for this last week or two which are so very full.

Alf continued to write of farewells in the West at Manyoni and Kilimatinde, with a Hospital service and a staff Bible Study, then of the journey south to Iringa the next weekend and east to Kongwa after that. He added, 'For the rest of the time I should be here in the office. At the moment I owe no personal letters, and I have only a couple of official ones to do. I can't do much else until the mail comes in and some of the problems get cleared up. I have left everything in writing that I can think of for Bishop Madinda and also for Andrew Farrer (the accountant).' During his last month in Dodoma, Alf used another office and Bishop Madinda was installed in the Diocesan's office. By this time the election had taken place and a date late in August fixed for Yohana's enthronement as the Fourth Bishop of Central Tanganyika.

MPWAPWA WEEKEND 24TH–25TH JULY

Alf looked forward to his last visit to Mpwapwa, the first place in his Diocese where the Gospel was preached in 1876, and he wrote of this moving experience.

A Revival Fellowship Convention was planned to start on Friday, 23rd July. Bishop Gresford Chitemo was there, and there seemed to be very much blessing by the time I arrived there on the Saturday. Roger Bowen took the Bible Readings on Christ as Prophet, Priest and King, and it was really first class.

I spoke at the early Sunday morning service on the Gospel for the day, 'With what measure you mete, it shall be meted out to you again.' You have heard me speak on that before so you will know what I said. I spoke in particular in connection with judging and giving. For the morning Convention meeting we had the Bible reading and then I preached on, 'By grace are ye saved through faith and that not of yourselves. It is the gift of God.' I felt very great liberty and thought the Gospel was crystal clear, and certainly I had the attention of the great multitude that was gathered outside to hear the message. There were many hundreds present.

The afternoon farewell was conducted by the Reverend Yona Mwendi. Daniel (the Reverend Daniel Lungwa, a faithful pastor since

Alf's first arrival in the Diocese) was present but did not want to speak. He was still feeling too emotionally moved by the death of his son. Geoffrey, who was twenty-two, had been declared out of danger and then suddenly collapsed at four o'clock that morning and died in hospital. The funeral service was to be held immediately after my farewell but Daniel did not expect me to wait for it as Bishop Chitemo was going to take it. I could not but feel how difficult it was for them all, we could hear the carpenters making the coffin as the day went on. The funeral could not be earlier as they had to wait for the coffin and the digging of the grave in that stony ground. Life is hard for Africans.

The farewell was very moving. Many of the Africans asked to make personal gifts. It would have broken your heart to see people coming up bringing money, 20 cents, fifty cents, 2/-, 5/-. I knew how little some of them had, and I had to ask for grace to keep the tears away. It was hard to have to take their money, and yet not to take it would have been worse still. I cannot despise their gifts. I will put it all together and buy something for my table (in the study) when I go home, but I shall never forget this occasion.

Mrs. Chiwanga brought me a paw-paw and peanuts all nicely wrapped up. There were numerous eggs of course, and one dear old lady gave me two. I divided them up among the various households here, and then different people came up to talk to me. Petro Kutoka and his wife came. That pair, as you know, are remarkable examples of the grace of God. They were very nice. They said they had done their crying. Now they just wanted to wish God's blessing on me. I prayed for them and blessed them . . . They both seemed to shine for the Lord. I felt parting from them very much. Petro told me that it was your teaching at the Bible School that caused him to hear the call of God for ministry. He did not know whether you knew this, but it was a great seal on that ministry as he is outstanding in so many ways.

Even if one discounts a great deal of what was said to me by different people that weekend, some telling me of messages long ago that had helped them and actually quoting the text on which I preached that had brought blessing, it still leaves a great deal for which one must be grateful. It is also another indication of how powerful is the Word of God, that can stay in the heart for fifteen or twenty years and keep being a blessing. I was terribly tired when I came home, more I think from emotional exhaustion than the actual work.

Alf also wrote to me about his last weekend in Dodoma. He spoke of going to Mvumi on the Friday evening and staying with Dr Peter and Mrs Robyn Bolliger. On the Saturday morning he went to Handali, just a few miles away for a confirmation safari. Some confirmees came from Ikowa in another direction and they had a very fine service. Alf preached on, 'My peace I give unto you.' He then travelled to Idifu of which he wrote:

Alf with Matron of Mvumi Hospital, Miss Milka Kongola, during his last visit, 1971.

This was an enormous service and I preached on, 'It is for your good that I go away'. It was a very wonderful service indeed. I felt a great liberty and everybody was listening very carefully. We then had to eat more rice and chicken, but by this time I was hungry. We were back at Mvumi after lunch and I managed an hour's sleep before the farewell at the Nurses' Training School. This was arranged by Milka Kongola (the Matron). All was done with great dignity. She made a fine speech, speaking entirely without notes. The nurses gave me the plaque which I now know you had seen but left for me to receive. It is being posted today. It is really very beautiful indeed and I know why you would love it. The baobab tree is a first-class piece of artistry. There is another piece of James' work, a gift from Gideon Masimba which is again very beautiful. It is a scroll about 12″ long and 4″ high carved with the words *Mungu ni pendo* (God is love) and at the bottom two ears of millet which are beautifully executed. In the same material James carved a Gogo head specially for me as his own personal gift. It is not very large and I don't think I would commit it to the post but take it with me. I gave him my green coat which I was wearing at the time and he was tremendously thrilled. It fitted him quite well and in one sense I was glad to have one less thing to look after.

That evening I spoke to the missionary staff on Psalm 116. It is a beautiful psalm in the New English Bible. Then a prayer meeting followed. Sunday was the big farewell at the Mvumi Church. They said there would be a feast, so experience taught me not to wait but to ask to be told when they were ready. There were too many people for the church so we met outside and I preached on 'Jesus of Nazareth passes by'. Even the children listened and I had the advantage that it was an old sermon as indeed were all the others I used that weekend. There was no time for new ones. It is easier to have old material when you are tired. I really enjoyed preaching that sermon and felt the grip of the crowd.

I finished the sermon about 11.30 a.m. and was called at 1.00 p.m.. They were ready ten minutes later. With chaos and what have-you and a general air of inefficiency I was able to get away by 2.15 p.m. but only by a little organisation and speeding up of things here and there. I was given another bow and a quiver of arrows. The latter now belongs to Andrew Farrer and the bow to Ernest (our cook), but a little carved Gogo man looking after his sheep, which was the sign of a Shepherd and given to me by the Mvumi Church, I have kept.

I arrived back in Dodoma very tired, had a sleep then a hot bath, tea with the M's (Margaret McKechnie and Mary Punt) then later a meal with the usual Sunday evening boiled egg, after this off to church (Cathedral Evensong) where I gave a sermon on 'Wisdom'. I had some good material but was really too tired to make an effective job of it. I was glad to find it helped one or two, though I probably will prepare it better for another occasion. I used Luke 7:35 (NEB) as my text. Next I went to the Alliance School (Mazengo) where I preached on 'A man came running', the same sermon I broadcast from Nairobi although, of course, I altered material to suit the school. I had a very good hearing indeed. I suppose as there was nothing more that day I was able to put into it the energy it required. There is no satisfaction like the satisfaction of preaching what you know to be one hundred per cent true, about which you have no doubts at all and to feel God's Spirit upon you. I came home to a cup of coffee with the M's and so to bed.

This means that Alf preached six times over the Saturday and Sunday — all different addresses — to large congregations with the feasting and the emotion of goodbyes to missionaries and African friends. Next morning he set out for the 272 mile journey to Arusha where the 9th Annual Tanzania Keswick Convention was about to begin. He chaired it and had been its only Chairman since its inception in 1962. It had a special significance for him as it was his last engagement in Tanzania prior to leaving for Australia. He led the Bible Studies from 1 Peter. Other speakers were the Reverend Tom Houston of the Nairobi Baptist Church, the Reverend Festo Kivengere of Uganda and the Reverend Eliewaha Mshana, Principal of the Lutheran Theological College and the Reverend Canon Alan Neech, General Secretary of the Bible Churchmen's Missionary Society, England. The next day Alf was driven to Nairobi from where he was to fly to Singapore en route to Australia.

I cannot finish writing of our years in Africa without speaking of some of the beauty of the Africa we knew and its joyful effect on our spirits. We had vivid memories of white and golden sands and beautiful clean beaches where the water always seemed to be the right temperature for bathing. On my first night in Africa there was a beautiful full moon shining over the sea and lighting up the tall coconut palms whispering in the gentle breeze and the air was balmy. It was so quiet and peaceful at Kaloleni, the mornings were fresh after heavy dews, and at night there was the calling of myriads of frogs and the distant throb of drums. The air was rarely still.

One lovely morning which I specially remember was at Embu, near Mt Kenya where we shared breakfast with our friends on their verandah facing the beautiful snowy crests of the mountain (over 17,000 ft high). As was usual with those high mountains, one welcomed every clear view because before long it was swathed in clouds so that it was hard to imagine there was a mountain there at all!

I shall never forget our first view of Mt Kilimanjaro. We were travelling to Nairobi from Mombasa. In those days there was no direct road through Kenya and one had to travel west to Moshi then to Arusha and north to Nairobi. We rounded a bend in the road near Moshi just at sunset, and suddenly, without warning there in front of us was this huge beautiful mountain, its snowy glaciers tinted pink by the setting sun. As we stopped in awe to contemplate it, three giraffe stepped out on to the road and were silhouetted against the mountain. This was an unforgettable experience of joy in God's creation.

Another memorable sight was that which met our eyes when we travelled high up on the escarpment overlooking the Rift Valley in Kenya. Down in the rift lay a chain of large lakes and on one of them, Lake Elementaita, there seemed to be a wide swathe of salmon pink ribbon which was actually the massed effect of thousands of flamingos standing in the lake.

Living at Bishopsbourne provided us with 'food for the eyes' as the Africans call it. We lived on a slope of Imagi hill and from our bedroom window, on another hill we could see the road to Mvumi winding up and away. The sky was clear and the horizon wide. At night we saw the Southern Cross very low in the south and the great Comet of the sixties flashed across the sky in the early hours of the morning and was very clear to our view.

Above our bedroom, in the eaves, lived a colony of yellow-collared African love birds. They were little bright green parrots with yellow collars, white ringed black eyes in a black head and bright red beaks. They often sat on our open window and could move at a great speed when disturbed. They seemed a little unreal to me, rather like Walt Disney creations.

I loved opening the front door before breakfast and breathing in the freshness of the morning and listening to the familiar bird calls. Each morning they greeted us in chorus. Archbishop Beecher's wife was a keen naturalist and once when they were staying with us, she sat out in the garden each day, and over a week recorded more than fifty species of birds which visited the garden. There were bulbuls and hoopoes, lilac-breasted rollers, bee-eaters, superb oriental starlings, sunbirds, coucals, shrikes, barbets and many others. In the rainy season the red-chested cuckoo sang, 'It will rain' and the honey-guide sang, 'Richard, Richard, Richard'.

Alf and I shared a common enjoyment of nature — its birds, animals, scenery, etc. He became quite expert in photographing birds. There was a beautiful weaver-bird called the bishop bird which had brilliant red and black plumage. Frequently Alf would tell me, 'I had a luxury prayer today', which meant he had prayed that a bird would stay still long enough for him to capture it in his telephoto lens. Guy Timmis took a very good photograph of Alf crouched with his camera ready. He was wearing a purple shirt and white clerical collar so we called it the 'white-collared bishop bird.'

Many of our holidays were spent in game parks with friends — the Kirkaldy-Willises, the Scotchmers, Uptons and once with Robert Loane. There were very many species of deer and gazelle, from the tiny dik-dik to the huge eland to be seen, as well as lion, cheetah, elephant, rhino, hippo, monkeys and baboons. Even the insect life was varied and colourful. There were many beautiful varieties of praying mantises usually coloured like the flowers where they preyed, and there were tiny beetles like thumb-nail sized pieces of scarlet plush hurrying over the grass.

There were of course many species of snakes which we did not want to see. Two deadly black mambas and two likewise deadly puff-adders were found and killed in our garden. We were able, when water was plentiful, to have a lovely garden and even in dry Dodoma I grew roses, dahlias and chrysanthemums as well as the tropical flowers like red and cream-coloured poinsettias, white, gold and pink frangipani and many coloured bougainvillea bushes. Flowering trees such as jacaranda, erythrina, nandi flame, flamboyants, cassias and crepe myrtle filled the garden with colour. We had fruit trees too, mangos, pawpaws, (called, 'holy paw-paws' by the M's, as they grew at Bishopsbourne!) guavas, lemons, oranges and limes. When I was careful and despatched the slugs, I produced a few strawberries and mulberries as well as rhubarb.

I often experienced in later years a deep nostalgia for Africa. I think it took me two years to adjust to the Western materialistic life-style which was forced on us in Melbourne, though I found a good antidote to nostalgia was to linger over photographs and read books which evoked the memories of days past.

We thanked God for His goodness and the years He gave us in Africa and for the deep satisfaction we found in fellowship with the people, for the work He gave us and for the joy in the land itself.

CHAPTER 15

THE RIDLEY YEARS — AUGUST 1971 TO SEPTEMBER 1975

Early in August, I disembarked at Portland in Victoria, and was met and taken to Melbourne by my family, and stayed with my sister. Alf flew to Singapore from Nairobi and then to Darwin where — I was told some years later — he flew in like a fresh breeze! He phoned my sister's home from Darwin to ask news of me and was surprised when I answered the phone. He told me that he intended to fly first to Sydney to tender his resignation to the Federal Executive of the Church Missionary Society before coming home to Melbourne.

During his stay in Sydney, he conferred with Kevin Engel about the founding of a Christian Literature Society for Australia, which would extend the World Association for Christian Communication on this continent and have a special concern for South East Asian and Pacific countries.

On the evening of Alf's arrival in Melbourne, we visited Ridley College where we were warmly welcomed by Dr Leon Morris and his wife Mildred. A service was held in the Ridley Chapel, when the Archbishop of Melbourne, Sir Frank Woods, commissioned Alf as Deputy Principal of Ridley College. During this service Alf preached the sermon. He mentioned three statements of the Apostle Paul: 'I am not ashamed of the Gospel', 'I have a desire to preach Christ where Christ is not yet named', and 'I make it my ambition to please Christ in all things'. In speaking about Alf's return to his home diocese, during his Charge to Synod in 1971, the Archbishop said[1]:

> We have received additional episcopal strength in the person of Bishop Alfred Stanway who has resigned from the Diocese of Central Tanganyika in order to make room for an African, and has accepted the appointment as Deputy Principal of Ridley College. For Bishop

Stanway to come back to Victoria is to come home and there have been many here who, knowing him well, welcome him as a friend. But we welcome him too as one of the senior statesmen of the Missionary Church who has done, in collaboration with Bishop Beecher, as much and more than any other Bishop to make the two new provinces of Kenya and Tanzania viable propositions. I had the great pleasure and privilege of spending a week with him before his retirement and I can testify that I came away from his diocese not only wondering how his people could ever bear to part with him but also quite sure that he could teach us as a diocese more than we could ever teach him. About his outstanding achievements I have written in our diocesan paper. Suffice it to say here that we welcome him most heartily as a member of this Synod and we look forward to him making his contribution not only to Ridley College but also to the whole Diocese. It would be neither possible nor desirable that such a dynamic person could be bottled up within the walls of a College!

Alf started at once to gather up the threads of this new venture and he attended the All-Australia NEAC Conference which was held at Monash University in late August. This proved an excellent introduction to old and new friends, and to note the thrust of the evangelical movement in the church.

The Morrises kindly accommodated us until the staff wing of the Bearham Flats was completed and we then moved into Flat No. 8 on the campus. The whole of Ridley College complex looked small with our not-yet-oriented-to-Australia eyes! We were used to the wide expanses of Africa. We both suffered from culture shock. The evident materialism of the Western life-style, the lowered moral standards and the fast pace of life shocked us. Alf recovered quickly from this, but I took the best part of two years to adjust to life at home.

Alf set about investigating the administrative patterns of the day-to-day running of the College, which was to be his main sphere of service, and soon began to reorganise this and financial matters. Dr Morris had been engaged in an extensive building programme at the College for some years. The Aicken Hall of Residence, the Babbage lecture room, the Chapel and the Bearham flats for married students had all come into being during his Principalship of the College. Further building projects, the dining hall and both senior and junior common rooms were to be commissioned soon.

Alf enjoyed meeting with the members of the Ridley College Council and participating in their meetings. He did some lecturing in

[1]See page 10 of the Archbishop's Report and Charge to Synod delivered by the Most Reverend Frank Woods, MA, DD, Archbishop for Melbourne, in the Town Hall, South Melbourne, on Monday, 4th October, 1971.

pastoral theology and greatly enjoyed the day-to-day contact with students. Several of them in later years referred to his taking of them down the 'Dodoma Trail' and our flat was also known as the 'East Africa Travel Bureau'! He spent time in the small College bookshop, then housed in an old army hut in the grounds (called 'Stanway' during its useful life there!).

Regular Sunday morning worship services were held in the Chapel and were attended by members of the general public as well as Ridley residents. These became part of Alf's life and gave him regular opportunities for preaching — he confirmed a few adults there during our residence.

Members of the College staff met mid-morning between lectures for a brief get-together, a good time for keeping in touch with one another. Ridley, in 1972, was one of the first of the University Colleges to admit women students into residence, with other Colleges soon following this lead. As well as male tutors, two women were introduced, Audrey Grant and Heather Ferguson, the former eventually becoming Dean of Students.

The function which stimulated Alf most, and which probably proved the most beneficial for him, was the regular Heads of Colleges meetings; Dr Morris asked him to represent Ridley on his behalf. Heads of the Residential Colleges of the Melbourne University formed a review committee to discuss problems and opportunities common to all colleges. Finance and administrative matters were constantly under review and Alf became acquainted with the way in which each College dealt with its particular needs and projects. Their manner of budgeting was helpful to him, both at Ridley and later Trinity in the USA. Indeed, if he had not had the experience of these meetings, he may have hesitated to accept the later call to America.

During the first long summer vacation, Alf attended the Belgrave Heights Convention. He went back on to their Council and took part in the meetings on many future occasions. He also did deputation for the CMS in Hobart, Tasmania, and in August 1972 he and I went to the CMS Spring School in Auckland, New Zealand, then went to Christchurch for other meetings.

The Australian Christian Literature Society (ACLS) was launched by an Open Letter to Friends, signed by both Kevin Engel and Alf. In it they mentioned, among other things, the following needs:

> By conferences and surveys conducted in the Pacific and by membership of various international Christian Literature organisations, we have widened our concern for this work. You will be glad to know that we are continuing to act on these bodies and that now we have associated with others in this country.

We have decided to found the ACLS because we see the following needs. Publishing and book distribution are highly technical operations. Because this is so, many have come to grief in these fields in the past. It is possible that those seeking to meet the needs of the growing literate populations of the Pacific and South East Asia could avoid these pitfalls by having made available to them the kind of technical help which we needed when we commenced our work in Africa.

We could also ensure that these literature workers are kept in touch with those who are doing similar work in other areas as there is often relevant material which could be adapted and translated for use in more than one place.

There are nationals who should be brought to this country so that they may have the kind of technical training for publishing and distribution which is unobtainable in their own countries.

Organisations such as Africa Christian Press and Central Tanganyika Press are happy for us to act as their agents in Australia for the receipt of funds, as they have no organisation here although there are friends who are interested in supporting their programmes . . .

In seeking to meet these needs we know that some of you will want to become members of ACLS. We have fixed a membership fee of $10.00 per year. Members will receive information and material about the Society's activities because of their support and prayers.

Experience has taught us that if you wish to have a worthwhile organisation, then it must be set up with a minimum of expense and administration. A friend has offered to meet the initial cost of registration, circulars, stationery, account books, etc. We are glad to have associated with us in this work Miss Rewa Bland, who at this stage will act as honorary secretary and treasurer to the Society. We embark on this new venture assured that God has called us to begin.

A constitution was drawn up, the Society was registered and Rewa began her tasks as Secretary-Treasurer. Alf negotiated with the Federal Council of CMS to second the Reverend K.F. Engel as a Christian Literature Consultant with ACLS, and terms and conditions were agreed upon. Kevin then divided his time between CMS and ACLS.

By early 1973, the Society was launched and Alf left for Geneva and England, where he attended the working committee of the Agency for Christian Literature Development. This statement appeared in the minutes: 'Although Melbourne is further away from England than Dodoma, the committee still asked Bishop Stanway to attend their meetings.' From England, Alf then attended literacy meetings in Nairobi and was able to pack in a quick visit to his old Diocese in Tanzania before the next meeting in Johannesburg.

In 1972, Kevin carried out a literature survey in the Pacific. By Easter 1973 he undertook a literature distribution scheme for the Kristen Press in Papua New Guinea, and later he visited publishing concerns in India. From this time on the Society grew, and Kevin became more and more busy in many different countries. A large Annual Meeting of the Society was launched in 1974 at the Camberwell Civic Centre and Alf and Kevin both spoke to the meeting.

From there the work of ACLS has gone on from strength to strength. Kevin's consultancy work is in great demand and young nationals from Hong Kong and Argentina have done training periods under him. This work was close to Alf's heart and he followed it with interest and prayer to the end of his life, rejoicing in its expansion and value. In Melbourne he was a director of Church Press Ltd, publisher of *Church Scene*, from 1973-75 and from 1979-88.

In April 1973 Alf went to Papua New Guinea to give Bible Readings for the Missionary Aviation Fellowship's Annual Conference in Wewak. Afterwards he visited his godson Robert Loane, and his wife Joan at Mt Hagen where Robert was doing medical work. The MAF flew Alf to Banz to the Christian Leaders' Centre. It is a fine centre for training in leadership and in radio, cassette and literature ministries. Alf gave an address to the Evangelical Alliance Conference which dealt with adjusting to changes in a newly independent country and this was especially appreciated. Afterwards he was flown to Lae to visit ex-Tanzanian colleagues, Sue and George Emmeleus, at Port Moresby where George was on the staff of the University. He also visited Sogeri School, where Marjorie Walker was teaching. She had taught at Msalato for a few years in the sixties.

On his return to Ridley, Alf stepped back into the routine. In 1972, he had approached Mary Punt (who had come to the end of her contract with DCT) about the possibility of coming to Australia for a three year period as the House Manager for Ridley. She arrived in March 1972 and took on the House Management duties until December 1974, then in 1975 she returned to Tanzania to work with the BCMS.

Nineteen seventy-four brought several family bereavements to Alf and me. In March, Alf's younger brother, Gordon, died suddenly, which was a great shock to him. Alf took the funeral service and gave the address. From mid-May to the end of the month, Alf was in London for Literature Consultancy meetings and during this time my twin brother died after a long illness involving heart surgery.

Soon after Alf's return to Australia, his brother-in-law died. Alf took this funeral at Paynesville in Gippsland, gave the address and helped his sister Grace with her affairs. During these months he was supported by the caring community at Ridley, and continued to derive stimulation from his day by day contact with the students.

I have asked two of the students in the 1973-75 intake to write something of their memories of Alf.

John Temby, then a single student, has written:

One of the first and lasting impressions of the Bishop was a man who was always in a hurry to get things done. Yet he was not necessarily driven by the urgent, but more by an overarching desire to do God's will as he understood it. As a first year student his busyness might at first have seemed a little off-putting. Yet, as time went on, not only was his zeal contagious but there were many times for talking, yet not for wasting time.

I learned many things from the Bishop which only served to deepen my respect and love for him as with a spiritual father. Perhaps the deepest impression from his lecturing and his preaching was that God's word could not be studied without being applied. Over and over we heard 'When I was in Africa . . .'. The Bishop was unable to open the Scriptures without showing how they applied in daily life. This was not only a great lesson, but a great privilege to have this balance in Theological College.

It has helped me from that time till today (1989) in my own preaching and sharing of God's Word. As students we benefited from many pithy sayings that helped encapsulate the message, e.g. in the practising a daily devotional time in the busyness of ministry it had first to succeed in College, and so the Bishop would say, 'As now . . . so then'! His preaching was a great model for us as we learned how to share relevantly God's Word then to illustrate its truth and how to apply its truth brought his message alive.

As a man of faith, vision and prayer, we had the privilege of being exposed not only to 'how' God had worked in his life in the past, but also right up into the future. The Bishop was a learner and sought to use past and present learnings in making college administration and life more simple and straight forward. The simplicity in his prayers and the experience of God's faithfulness in answering these prayers was both a challenge and an inspiration.

One of the great loves of the Bishop's life was to see people respond to Christ and become Christians. This was both a stimulus and encouragement to the theologs in general and to me personally. In my last year in College as Senior Student it was a joy to be able to spend time with the Bishop to share what was happening in the lives of many of the secular students at Ridley. His interest was always keen, his joy obvious and his encouragement in evangelism constant.

I look back over my years at Ridley with great affection and thanks to God for the opportunity of being there. As I look back I can see the increasingly important role the Bishop had in my own life and which continued after I left College. His counsel during those years and for the next ten or twelve years afterwards played an important part in making decisions, especially in two major ones, to be ordained and to get married.

One of the married students of the years 1973-75 has written:

Bishop Alf was the grandfather figure at Ridley during his time there. His lectures in 'Introduction to the New Testament' were always stimulating and generously illustrated from his own experience on the 'Dodoma Trail'. These illustrations have stayed with me over many years and I occasionally quote them in my sermons.

As soon as we moved into our married's flat in Bearham wing, the Bishop arrived to pray with us for God's blessing in our new home. His contribution to the vision for the future of Ridley resulted in the College being on a firmer financial footing and also saw a new phase in the building programme.

The Bishop's sermons were memorable, direct and challenging and could leave one wondering why he had preached that sermon just to you in front of all those people.

When the 'freshers' started College, the initiation rites included the performance of 'tasks'. One of the favourites was to set one student the goal of sitting at high table opposite the Bishop and beat him at eating dinner. Little did the unsuspecting student know that the Bishop could eat a baked dinner in one minute and fifty seconds, and to make matters worse the student had to repeat the performance until he succeeded. Many failed this test.

Three incidents which evoked our African experience, happened during these Ridley years. In 1974, President Julius Nyerere paid a State Visit to Australia. The first we heard of this was a phone call from Canberra inviting us to a State Dinner given in Dr Nyerere's honour by Sir Paul and Lady Hasluck at Government House, Yarralumla. It was obvious to us that the President had asked for Alf's presence. After dinner with the other men, he and Alf managed a little conversation but all else was strictly formal according to the protocol of the day.

In December 1974, the Reverend Simon Chiwanga, who at this time was Minister of Education in Nyerere's cabinet, visited Australia with the Director of Education, who was a Muslim. Both visited us in our Ridley flat with a Canberra 'minder' in tow. We arranged an evening meal, buffet-style, at St Andrew's Hall and invited ex-Tanzanian missionaries and other interested CMS friends to attend. After dinner we all joined in a fact-finding session about Tanzania. Many of us had known Simon for many years and the atmosphere was friendly and informal. Next morning, Simon and his Muslim colleague attended the worship service in the Ridley Chapel, where Alf was preaching.

Our third African visitor — in March, 1975 — was the Archbishop of Uganda, Ruanda-Burundi and Boga-Zaire, Janani Luwum. He was greatly disturbed by what was going on in Uganda at that time under Idi Amin. Several of Luwum's immediate family had been killed or had disappeared at Amin's orders. He spoke in secrecy at this time and did not alert the Australian press to the enormity of what was happening. Alf drove him up to Belgrave Heights to visit a CMS Easter Conference in residence on their property, for the Annual Belgrave Heights Easter Convention.

It was with great sorrow that we heard of Archbishop Luwum's murder by Amin's orders, some time after his return to Kampala. He was a commanding figure and a brave but quietly outspoken man. The Reverend (later Bishop) Alpha Mohamed from Tanzania was also at Ridley during 1972, as a CMS bursar. He studied for a Diploma in Ministry, and often visited our flat in the late afternoon, especially when he was feeling homesick.

For a short time, Alf was Acting Principal at St Andrew's Hall — the CMS Training College — while a new Principal was being chosen. Meeting with the new recruits for CMS, and having a brief involvement in their training, appealed to him very much.

In October 1974, Alf received a letter which came as a bolt from the blue. It was written by the Reverend John Guest, an Englishman ministering in the USA, and who represented a body of evangelically-minded clergy of the Episcopal Church of the USA and some concerned laymen. Their movement was called the Fellowship of Witness and it was to be affiliated with the EFAC Movement (Evangelical Fellowship in the Anglican Communion). They had been meeting together since 1965, and John had had a vision of a place where men could be trained in the USA in an evangelically-oriented seminary, with good Biblical teaching. He and his friends wanted such a seminary to be founded and began to search for a Dean/President to head it up. Two or three people were approached but were unable to accept the invitation, but the Reverend John Stott had given them Alf's name. So this letter came, inviting him to accept the role of Dean/President of the new seminary, to be called the Trinity Episcopal School for Ministry.

Alf read the letter carefully and at lunch time brought it home. He left it for me to read adding, 'tell me your thoughts on the matter'. After he had gone I read it with great surprise. Alf was now 66 years of age and one could not envisage him taking on a task of that magnitude at that age! I hardly knew what to think. I had never wanted even to visit America! All I heard of it suggested too much speed, and while Alf was speedy enough, I was sure I wasn't! However, I felt in fairness I should say, 'I think you ought to consider it'.

Without knowing that John Stott had suggested his name, Alf wrote for his advice and likewise he wrote to Marcus Loane saying:

> I want to consult you about the enclosed letter and I would be glad of any comment you would care to make. Feel free, absolutely free to be quite devastating concerning the suggestion if you feel that is right.
>
> Normally I can shrug off most offers of service I receive on the basis that I am in the place where I ought to be and doing what I ought to be doing. This has been the case for so long that I am rather

surprised when something comes along that I cannot handle in quite the same way, and to add to my surprise Marjory thinks it might well be something I should consider. I would have expected her to be against the USA where she has never wanted to go at any time.

Until now it would have been wrong to leave Ridley College, but I am now not doing anything that somebody else could not do, and I wonder whether I am being used here to full capacity? Many of the things that give me the deepest satisfaction are not strictly related to College life, although to some extent they arise from the position I occupy. Anyway I know you will speak freely. I am surprised that I am not able to say 'No' at once ...

To John Stott he wrote:

I enclose a photostat of a letter I received today. I realise you may not have been correctly quoted but you will know enough about the position to tell me what you think.

I have no academic qualifications of any significance, but I get on well with Americans and I wonder whether what I am now doing at Ridley couldn't be done by somebody else.

Normally I can shrug off offers of service with great ease on the grounds that I am in the place where I ought to be and doing what I ought to be doing. I haven't quite got that feeling at the moment, so I have written to you and to Marcus for any comment you feel free to make, and please be as free as you like.

Both Marcus and John answered, encouraging him to accept the call. So he replied to John Guest showing interest in their invitation and asking for more information. A strong board of future trustees was being formed in the USA, and they discussed the matter with the Bishop of Pittsburgh, Bishop George Appleyard, as they wished the new school to be sited in the Pittsburgh area of Pennsylvania. Bishop Appleyard was naturally apprehensive about the thought of a new Episcopal Seminary coming into being in his Diocese, but he did not forbid it.

Dr Morris was loath to lose Alf, and needed any resignation to be tendered well ahead, in order to fill the vacancy his leaving would present. The embryo Board of the 'Trinity to be' now wanted Alf to fly to the States to meet them. The name chosen for the new seminary was to be Trinity Episcopal School for Ministry (TESM). This was to be incorporated on 1st May and the new body could not offer Alf the post until after that date, but the members of the *pro-tem* Committee, who would become the members of the Trinity Board, unanimously invited him to become Dean/President of the School and wanted him by September 1975.

The United Church of Papua New Guinea and the Solomon Islands, had written to Alf in February 1974 about his speaking to their leaders on the implications of a church adjusting to a newly independent country. Like Tanzania, Papua New Guinea had been a mandated territory, but administered by the Australian Government. Their letter said:

> Many of us who have responsibility in the United Church in this country are deeply conscious of the significant time in which we live. Self-government is here and Independence soon to come. We are aware that we must minister in a new world.
>
> Some of us have had the privilege of reading a paper you presented to the Evangelical Alliance Conference at Banz and through it were awakened to some of the issues which confront us. We are realising how sensitive we must be both to the new world around us and to the Holy Spirit who would teach us. We also realise how deeply entrenched are our inherited and acquired attitudes. We therefore feel the need, throughout our ranks of ministers and workers, for a conference where issues could be studied and where we could meet to be renewed together in the Lord.
>
> I write to ask if you would consider coming to this country for a week or so, sometime in the foreseeable future to lead us in such a conference. The time and details of such a visit would be dependent entirely upon your availability and subsequent negotiations.
>
> This invitation comes from the New Guinea Island region of the United Church, based in Rabaul. It is possible that the leaders of the Church in Port Moresby may also be pleased to have you lead a conference there on your way through.
>
> We trust you may be in a position to be with us in this way.
>
> Yours sincerely,
> I. TO KUNAI
> (Acting Bishop)

Alf replied saying that it would be possible to come in late November of this year (College lectures would be over).

They replied:

> ... But the General Assembly of the United Church is meeting near Rabaul in late November this year, and the Moderator may wish to invite you to address the Assembly or lead the Assembly members in a weekend retreat, as well. This would make up to five days meeting with people here; and with a day's travel each way would keep you away from home for a week.
>
> We have not yet heard from Port Moresby whether they would like you to break your journey and address a gathering there too . . .
>
> ... Our Chief Minister has proposed 1st December 1974 as the date for full independence for Papua New Guinea. There is opposition to it coming so early, but if the proposal is carried then your visit will be very timely and relevant indeed this November.
>
> With kind regards,
> Yours sincerely,
> IOSIA TO KUNAI
> Acting Bishop

Alf replied that he had heard from Port Moresby and said he was keeping in touch with Bishop Kunai. He also said, 'I see Independence may be delayed, the best dates would be after 19th November'.

On 25th July he received a letter from Bishop Saimon Gaius of the United Church of Papua New Guinea and the Solomon Islands, acknowledging that Alf would arrive on 19th November. The letter said:

> ... This will fit in very well with our arrangement. At the same time we will be having the Assembly of the United Church here in Rabaul area so this will be a good opportunity for delegates from all over Papua New Guinea and the Solomons to attend the meetings. ...
>
> SAIMON GAIUS
> Bishop

In August therefore, Alf made provisional bookings for this visit, and in due course he went as planned. I never did hear much about this trip as he arrived in Sydney on his return journey en route to Melbourne, and went down to a nasty attack of malaria. He arrived home quite weakened by this attack and was in bed for some days.

However, the programme for his visit was as follows. An initial evening address on the day of his arrival with the chief messages being for a two-day conference of overseas mission staff on the general theme of 'The position of the expatriate in a country getting independence'.

The following day Alf was asked to address indigenous ministers and pastors with time for questions and discussion when interpreters would be provided as the vernacular or Pidgin would be spoken by the people.

The Moderator of the United Church who sent the Port Moresby programme wrote:

> What we are interested to hear and discuss with you will be the place of the Church in an independent country and the role of expatriates in their partnership with local church leaders and communities. Whether it is good for the local church to keep the experienced expatriate workers. Or is it better to have only short term workers for special appointments when a country is already independent? ...
>
> There will be about 40 of us attending and we are looking forward to seeing and hearing you. I am sure our church leaders coming to the Assembly will benefit a lot from experience in African churches ...
>
> L. BOZETO
> Moderator

Alf left for Pittsburgh to meet members of the Board of the Trinity Episcopal School for Ministry on 13th May, 1975. He stopped off at California en route to meet one member who was unable to get to Pittsburgh for the first meeting. He met with Bishop Appleyard during this visit and the whole matter of the new school was discussed openly.

On Alf's return to Melbourne he assured Ridley Council that he contemplated resignation from the College only under the deep sense that this was what God was calling him to do.

In June, his sister Grace suffered a stroke and was in Bairnsdale Hospital, but before we could visit her she died. Alf felt her death deeply. She was the last remaining member of his family and he had always felt specially close to her. We went to Paynesville for her funeral service which he conducted and paid tribute to her, and was able to make arrangements about her estate. Grace's illness had been one factor disturbing him as he knew he would be leaving for the USA in September.

Margaret McKechnie arrived back in Melbourne from Africa at the end of May 1975 and started to help at Ridley on the clerical-financial front immediately. This was an enormous relief for Alf as he knew she would be able to carry on the financial management during any interim period.

Alf decided to have an exhaustive medical checkup at the Shepherd Foundation in Melbourne. It was certainly exhaustive and a great deal of checking was done by a computer. He was highly amused after pressing all the buttons and answering the computer enquiries when 'have you cheated anywhere?' came up on the screen. By pressing the final button he was able to say 'not at all'. The overall report was excellent and he was assured that his health was good.

There was a farewell dinner at the College and this was followed by a service in the Chapel, when Archbishop Woods gave both of us his blessing. The College Council presented Alf with a copy of the *Dictionary of the Christian Church*, edited by J.D. Douglas, at a farewell party.

It was quite a wrench for Alf to say goodbye to the many caring Ridley friends. He was specially to miss his quick visits to the flat above us where he enjoyed many a game of *Acquire* with John (later Bishop) and Jill Wilson and their two daughters, Susan and Jenny.

I set about packing up the home, selling off our electrical goods (which were no of use in the USA) and some furniture, and storing the rest. An amusing sequel to this was that Alf had carefully placed his traveller's cheques in his filing cabinet which went off to the store — but he was able to redeem these at a later date!

The day before we flew out of Melbourne, Alf acted as proxy father to Jeanne Keeble on her marriage to Alan James. Jeanne had been a nursing sister in Tanzania.

The Ridley experience fitted us for the USA. We did not feel culture shock on this inter-continental transfer. We moved from one Western life-style to another, and that made adjustment much easier.

CHAPTER 16

TRINITY EPISCOPAL SCHOOL FOR MINISTRY — SEPTEMBER 1975 TO NOVEMBER 1978

We flew from Melbourne to London on Alf's sixty-seventh birthday. There had been a hitch over our visas for the USA but we were assured they could be completed in London. However, this delayed us further in England and Alf was forced to put off his departure by several days. As I was to travel a week later he agreed that we should meet in New York, where there was to be a nation-wide Renewal Conference of the American Episcopal Church.

On the evening of my arrival, the members of the Board of Trustees for the new School met together and we were introduced to them. The Reverend Dr John Stott from London was to give several addresses at the Conference. Festo Kivengere, then Bishop of Kigezi in Uganda, was also present and Alf gave his introductory talk to a keen and supportive body of people.

The Fellowship of Witness members had an enquiry desk and literature about the new School, so that they could meet with interested folk. The Reverend Peter Moore was the first Chairman of the Trinity Board of Trustees. Alf had met him as far back as 1962 and on subsequent visits to the States, and had put him on his prayer-list back in those days. Many who were to become strong supporters of the School were at this Conference and Alf began arranging visits to their churches in the near future.

We were flown to Pittsburgh in a private plane and driven from there to Sewickley by the Reverend John and Susan Yates. John was Associate Rector of St Stephen's, Sewickley and the Reverend John Guest was the Rector. The Reverend (later Bishop) John Howe was also an Associate Rector of St Stephen's. Alf called them 'the three Johns'. The warmth of the welcome we received was quite overwhelming. The Yates drove us past our 'Home-to-be' where a large white banner stretched across the building said

'Welcome home Marjory'. We were given gracious hospitality by Henry and Nancy Chalfant, while we waited for our household goods to arrive from Australia. Everywhere we were welcomed with genuine love and kindness which characterised the support given us through the entire length of our stay in America. I had steeled myself not to put down any roots in America, since uprooting was always painful.

It is a curious fact that Alf had played a part in that very town of Sewickley back in the sixties, when he visited America. He had dedicated the refurbishment of St Stephen's Church in a special service. He had met with several of the local families, never suspecting that he would one day live in Sewickley and worship in that church. The town was situated a few miles out from Pittsburgh along the Ohio River. A very comfortable, convenient and attractive home had been purchased for us to live in, and this became 'Trinity' for the months preceding the opening of the School. During these months, Alf was seeking students, faculty and financial support.

The pre-requisite qualification for an enquiring student was that he or she be a graduate. The degrees which would be granted from Trinity — once the college was chartered — would be Masters' Degrees in Divinity, after the successful conclusion of the three year course. Students would be required to take the GOE (General Ordination Examination). The Government of Pennsylvania also had their own requirements for the School and its progress would be noted and reported on at regular intervals. A library consisting of a stated number of volumes would need to be set up and approved, as well as an Endowment Fund of half-a-million dollars set aside in reserve.

A bedroom of our home was set up with second-hand office equipment to start with, and Miss Betty Buckingham, who had worked for John Guest, became the first staff member. Enquiries from hopeful students-to-be came in steadily from all over the States and they came to Alf to be interviewed. At that stage there was no bishop willing to send anyone to the proposed TESM, so that meant they were to come without any backing. They had to trust that if they gave their lives to Christ, He would open up the ministry for them and this in fact did happen. All of these students found ministries in the future.

On 15th April, 1976 the following announcement was made:

FACULTY APPOINTMENTS LAUNCH
TRINITY EPISCOPAL SCHOOL FOR MINISTRY

The Trustees of a new School for educating men and women for ministry in the Protestant Episcopal Church have disclosed major appointments to their faculty. The School, operating under the name of TRINITY EPISCOPAL SCHOOL FOR MINISTRY, was incorporated in 1975 and is headquartered in suburban Pittsburgh.

Selected to be the President (or Dean, the traditional title for the head of an Episcopal seminary) is Bishop Alfred Stanway, a seminary leader of international reputation and wide experience. Bishop Stanway, an Australian, was formerly the Deputy Principal of Ridley College of the University of Melbourne and was also a missionary Bishop in Africa for over twenty years.

On 8th March, Bishop Stanway announced the first faculty appointments: the Reverend Dr John H. Rodgers, Jr, to be Senior Professor, and the Reverend Peter H. Davids as Assistant Professor of Biblical Studies. Dr Rodgers is at present Associate Dean and Chaplain of Virginia Theological Seminary and is a graduate of the US Naval Academy and Virginia Seminary. Dr Davids is currently on the faculty of Bibleschule Wiedenest in Germany.

Bishop Stanway also revealed that a panel of noted visiting professor-lecturers will be employed: the Reverend Dr John R.W. Stott, All Souls Church, London, England; the Reverend Dr J.I. Packer, and the Reverend Michael Green of St Aldate's, Oxford.

One of the prospective students who came for an interview was Leslie Fairfield. He had a doctorate in philosophy from Harvard and was lecturing in History in the University of Indiana. He was a member of the FOW (Fellowship of Witness) and was to become a lecturer (in Church History)-cum-student. He wrote an editorial for the FOW magazine *Kerygma* under the title of 'Why Trinity Episcopal School for Ministry?'. This was published following the actual official opening of the School and sets forth clearly the answer to this question:

This edition of *Kerygma* intends especially to introduce Trinity Episcopal School for Ministry to the wider church. Trinity was founded in 1975 through the auspices of the Fellowship of Witness, and opened its doors to the initial class in September 1976. What is Trinity's 'raison d'etre' then, its contribution within the Episcopal Church? What are Trinity's specific goals?

First of all, Trinity is dedicated to voicing the EVANGELICAL HERITAGE of the Anglican Church. The School believes firmly in the authority of Scripture: not in a literalist or 'fundamentalist' sense, but with a deep conviction that in the Bible God spoke to man and speaks to us today. Trinity believes, too, that the theology of the great 16th century reformers offers a pathway into the Scriptures that is particularly biblical and authoritative. Having a high view of the Bible, then, Trinity stands committed to a thorough study of the Holy Scripture. For the same reason, Trinity aims to train students as evangelists, in obedience to the great commission of our Lord Jesus Christ, 'Go ye into the world and make disciples of all nations'.

Second, Trinity acknowledges the central work of the **Holy Spirit**, converting, enlightening and empowering Christians for service. The School believes that God calls us, through the Word and the

Holy Spirit, then we confess Jesus as our Saviour and our Lord. Trinity, therefore, believes the importance of helping students deepen their walk with Christ: through the corporate worship of the School community, by disciplines of daily prayer and Bible study, and through mutual encouragement for holiness of Christian living. In all of this, Trinity would hope to be a faithful instrument of the renewal which the Holy Spirit is effecting in the Episcopal Church to-day. Trinity, likewise, feels called to pray and work for righteousness and justice in society at large. We remember that Jesus 'saw a great multitude, and was moved with compassion toward them'. And we believe that the Holy Spirit, Who spoke by the prophets, still rebukes corporate and social evil in our time.

Third, Trinity believes in the MINISTRY OF ALL GOD'S PEOPLE. The School offers a one-year course to prepare Christians for effective service to God, in whatever their particular calling. Affirming the centrality of the parish community in the Christian life, Trinity seeks to find new ways of encouraging and stimulating the ministries of all members of the Body. The School likewise aims to train parish clergy who share this vision of corporate ministry.

Finally, Trinity is deeply and thankfully ANGLICAN. There are other evangelical divinity schools in the United States, some of the highest quality. But Trinity Episcopal School for Ministry senses a call to express this biblical and evangelical Christian witness in and through the riches of the Anglican tradition. Liturgical worship, celebration of both Word and Sacrament, forms the core of the School's Christian living. The classical creeds and the thirty-nine Articles of Religion ground the School's teaching. Episcopal order supplies the framework in which Trinity works and ministers. The faithful exercise of human reason enables the School community to worship God with their minds, and to rejoice in the knowledge that all truth is God's. All these emphases of the Anglican heritage are joyfully affirmed and expressed at Trinity.

These four commitments then, answer the question: 'Why Trinity?'. Please pray with us that Trinity Episcopal School for Ministry may remain faithful to the calling from Our Lord which brought it into being.

Alf was quietly confident that God's hand was over the whole venture and that He would bring together all the resources for getting the School started. In seeking for the first faculty members, Dr Peter Davids was invited to join us. He had done a BA at Wheaton College, an MDivinity at Trinity Evangelical Divinity School and a PhD at Manchester University (UK). Alf had heard of Dr John Rodgers who, at this time, was Professor of Systematic Theology, Chaplain and Associate Dean for Student Affairs at the Virginia Theological Seminary. After prayer, Alf felt it right to invite John to join the TESM Faculty, so we went to Washington and then to the Seminary. Alf was very much to the point about his visit and simply said 'If God calls you, will you join us?'. John visited

Sewickley, bringing with him the Reverend Yona Mwendi, a Tanzanian pastor at that time studying in the Virginia Seminary. John Rodgers had done a BS at the United States Naval Academy, an MDiv at the Virginia Theological Seminary and a ThD at the University of Basle, Switzerland.

When it seemed a suitable house could be available, large enough for a growing family, John decided to come. Suitable housing for the Davids and Fairfield families was also found. It sounds easy to write it but each need for housing was resolved with prayer at the very time it was needed.

Many of the original seventeen students were married and some had small children. They had to find their own accommodation. As the months passed, it was decided to open the School at the beginning of the 1976 academic year. Funds were gradually coming in and many of Alf's weekends were spent travelling throughout the States, wherever he was invited to preach and speak about Trinity.

A venue for the School became possible. We were able to rent classroom, office and dormitory space (for single students) at the Robert Morris College in Coraopolis, on the other side of the Ohio River. It was an ideal temporary location and a date was set for the opening of the School — 25th September, 1976.

However, before that date, Alf received a letter early in August from his successor in Central Tanganyika, Bishop Yohana Madinda, saying that Mr Kahama of the Tanzanian Cabinet had been speaking with him on behalf of President Nyerere. The President wanted to invite Alf to visit the country, but unofficially, to visit the Diocese of Central Tanganyika, and to arrange talks with him — the Tanzanian Government would pay Alf's fare. They were aware that Alf would be visiting Tanzania in November 1977 for the Golden Jubilee of the Diocese, but they did not want to wait that long. In the same letter, Yohana explained that he was to have an Assistant Bishop, the Reverend Alpha Mohamed, and that the Archbishop had suggested 15th August as the Consecration date.

Some frantic telephoning ensued between America and Africa. Yohana suggested that Alf be there for the Consecration and meet with the Government officials afterwards. These meetings concerned the change-over of the Andrea Mwaka Primary School in Dodoma to be an International English-medium School for children of expatriates working in the country. It would eventually teach up to matriculation standard and Alf was able to give advice regarding the school to President Nyerere.

Alf only had a few days in which to obtain a visa, book air-tickets etc. When he went to Pittsburgh to the Immigration Department, he was met by the same 'hitch' that dogged our entrance into the States. It transpired that an official document which had purportedly been sent to us, was missing. Betty Buckingham found it filed in the office of St Stephen's Church and thankfully the problem was solved. Alf really felt this was a loving touch from God enabling him to be present at Alpha's consecration and to assist in laying hands on him. He greatly enjoyed meeting up with all his former clergy and missionary staff.

Faculty and Visiting Lecturers at the opening of TESM, September 1976. L.-R. The Rev. Paul Zahl, Dr Leslie Fairfield, Alfred Stanway, Dr John Rodgers, Dr Peter Davids, Dr Fitzsimons Allison.

On Saturday, 25th September, 1976 two hundred and fifty people were present from all over the USA, as Trinity Episcopal School for Ministry formally opened with an academic convocation, in the Hale Hall on the Campus of the Robert Morris College. The convocation was presided over by the Chairman of the Board of Trustees, the Reverend Peter Moore, who at that time was the Executive Director of FOCUS (Fellowship of Christians in Universities and Schools). Peter gave an opening address, the principal academic address was given by Dr John Rodgers and the closing remarks by Alf. Some of the statements made on that day are quoted below.

From Peter's talk:

We thought it might be important for you to hear a few words from a representative of the Board of Trustees — those of us coming from different parts of the country, not involved in the day to day operations of the School, but having it very high on our list of priorities .... It is our vision as members of the Board and Faculty to see Trinity Episcopal School for Ministry make a unique contribution to the life of the Church in the years to come .... As Episcopalians we need the vitality and vision of evangelism. When Anglicans have that they are often at the very best. Worship comes alive; churches grow; people give; the Bible becomes a living book with great personal authority for the believer; people begin to love each other in the Spirit and long to share their faith with others .... As Evangelicals we need the Episcopal Church. Without it we feel rootless, cut off from centuries of devotion, theology and practical wisdom. We need the Church's corporate concern for the needy and downtrodden. We need the Church's seriousness over liturgical worship, the Church's witness to the sacraments as means of grace, the episcopate as a God-given blessing for the guidance and oversight of His Church. When Evangelicals have embodied these qualities they have often been at their best — saved from narrow parochialism, sectarianism and a myopic concern for their own special emphasis to the neglect of the broader and deeper dimensions of Christian experience ...

Today I am deeply conscious of three things:

FIRST, our weakness and imperfection .... Now that we will no longer call ourselves 'miserable offenders' we need special reminders that all that we do partakes of the fall — as well, we trust, of grace ... secularism, materialism and humanism are never totally outside of us. They are always within us as well. We stand always under the cross, where Jesus' blood was shed to keep us from being as bad as we might be.

SECOND, I am, as we all on the Board and faculty are, conscious of God's guiding hand on this venture. This has been quite staggering to those of us closest to the formation of this School. Consider these facts. The first serious candidate we considered for President and Dean was Bishop Alfred Stanway! After thirty-four years on the mission field and retirement with its own new challenges in the church in Australia, he accepted our call ... Friends were given for the establishment of the School. Board members from across the country were drawn together, faculty — the very ones we most wanted were called, and themselves felt a call to be a part of the new School: housing for faculty and students was provided just when needed and for remarkably reasonable amounts, a campus more than adequate to our needs was made available ...

THIRD, I am conscious of the great balance needed between love and truth — a balance I hope will be characteristic of this School. We must speak the truth in love ... The life of Christians living, studying, working together should be and can be characterised by supernatural love. If we speak the truth in love, the Church and the world will listen. May it be so, and may God be glorified for ever and ever.

Dr Rodger's address was entitled 'Education for Ministry in the Anglican Evangelical Perspective'.

He made four points, one general and three more specific.

FIRST, the more general one:

Trinity Episcopal School for Ministry stands deeply, thankfully, and loyally in the Anglican tradition. Because Anglican Evangelicals do not make church tradition normative and do not place it on the level of Holy Scripture, it is sometimes thought that we are lacking in appreciation for tradition. This is not so . . . there is first the blessing of the teaching and practice of the early Church Fathers . . . Then there is God's gift to the Church through the great sixteenth century Reformers . . . Luther, Calvin, Bullinger, Cranmer, Latimer, Ridley, and later the judicious Hooker . . . They are one of God's richest gifts to His Church. It would be true to say that in matters of central theological significance we have not excelled the Reformers on a single point and in much we have fallen sadly behind them.

It seems to me that among Anglicans it is the Anglican Evangelicals who have appreciated and rejoiced most deeply in the benefits which God has given to the Church through these great men. There is also, flowing from this period, the classic Anglican tradition of common worship, embodied in the theology and cadences of the Book of Common Prayer, the wondrous balance in practice of Word and Sacrament, the enjoyment of the pastoral office of Episcopacy, and all this in the context of Reformed truth . . . what more could a person ask?

There is the rich understanding of the work of the Holy Spirit and the inner devotional life which arises from the work of the Puritans and the Evangelical Revivals of the eighteenth and subsequent centuries, personal conversion to Christ, commitment to walk in holiness, mutual conversation to build one another up in Christ, a desire to be useful in personal evangelism . . . this, too, is part of the Anglican Evangelical tradition in which this School stands.

Lastly, there is the tradition of the love of truth, the utter conviction that God's word in Christ is compatible with His truth wherever it may be found, and that all truth needs to be put to Christian use . . . no nervous hiding, no obscurantism, but a relaxed confidence that Christ alone is the proper interpreter of any discoveries of any age rightly and humbly held.

This then is the general point: Anglican Evangelical theological education stands in a wise and blessed inheritance and is thereby delivered from both undue narrowness and the whims of the moment . . . and released into a joyous and confident ministry. For this we, at Trinity, are deeply grateful and we pledge ourselves to bring our students into a true appreciation of this tradition in which they stand. Here is a tradition which is at one and the same time and in the best sense **conserving**, **radical**, and **liberating**.

Three specific contributions which I believe the Anglican Evangelical perspective brings to theological education for ministry (ordained and lay).

FIRST, a deep confidence in the Holy Scriptures as the Word of God written . . . God's Word in Christ has been lost and obscured by the manner in which we approach God's Word written . . . When the authority, sufficiency, clarity and efficacy of the Holy Scriptures are lost, then we are left with human speculation, tentative gropings and finally SILENCE. To paraphrase Amos, '. . . if the lion does not roar, who will bother to jump?'. Christian faith is not a leap into the dark, but a step into the light — the light of God's Word.

There is nothing in Scripture nor in modern critical studies which endanger this claim, and we hope at Trinity so to search the Scriptures together that from this time of study will come persons into the life of the church who can share this confidence, humbly, lovingly, intelligently and persuasively. There can be little doubt that the church needs more profoundly this contribution of confidence in, and wise sane interpretation of, the Holy Scriptures as the Word of God written, 'Man lives not by bread alone, but by every word which proceedeth forth from the mouth of God'.

SECOND, the centrality, finality and sufficiency of the cross of Christ . . . Lose that and you have lost the very quintessence of the Gospel. Anglican Evangelicals have placed, and place at the forefront of their message, piety and education, the finished work of Christ. Why have we done this? Simply because there is, for us, no faithfulness to Scripture and no Good News without this. We know that the Gospel of the Cross is 'the power of God unto salvation' and we desire very much to share this conviction with those within and without the Church. Here, too, we have a contribution. We believe we are divinely called to share with the Church. 'Woe is me if I preach not the Gospel'.

The matter of Christian living . . . the personal and social consequences of being made new in Christ: Christian Holiness.

There is one point I must, in all honesty make clear. For Anglican Evangelicals, with all-out desire to bring all things into captivity to Christ, there can be no replacing the Gospel and personal fellowship with God by social action, for the simple reason that we don't get lasting social renewal and fruits without getting to the heart of the problem, at the root. And the root is the heart of man to which God speaks through the Word and the Spirit. Why not both personal as well as social holiness? Isn't that the biblical way? Why not a rediscovery of personal quiet time, of fellowship with the Lord, of daily guidance and answered prayer . . . practices which gladden the heart of man and lend an incredible depth and significance to daily life and make us faithful in little things, preparing us for the bigger things as well. We are excited that God has called us to this great task . . . in fact could anything be more exciting? We think not . . . Thanks be to God!

Alf's address closed the convocation, and it is difficult to get the effect of what he said on paper but it did appear to have a profound effect on his audience. I have quoted it rather fully:

'I trust thee O Lord, to help me'.

Against these words from this Psalm I have written the date 15th October, 1975, the date I was thinking about this School. It is only by trusting to God that we have come to this hour, as the psalmist says, 'I trust thee O Lord, to help me'. We were without a place to meet, without faculty, without students, and it was a long, long haul from there to the opening to-day. As I read the verse again the other day,

I thought — it's all come to pass, and I am grateful to God, grateful to those whose gifts have made it possible . . .

I want to say at the beginning, what are we looking for as the end product of a seminary like this? That is what I want to speak about this morning. For forty-eight years, I have been a member of the Church Missionary Society, the largest Anglican Missionary Society in the world, one that has done so much under God to spread the Anglican Communion across the world. Well, they have four great principles which their founders laid out at their first little meeting when they were smaller than we are now, and they have stuck to those principles all through the years, and I have adopted them for my life as well, because they are so good.

First	Begin in a small way
Second	Follow God's leading
Third	Put money in a subsidiary place, that is, it is not important.
Fourth	Under God, everything will depend on the quality of the men chosen for the task.

So, what do we want in this place? We want men and women of God. There are many things that we could say on an occasion like this: the scholarship that we hope to engender, the skills we hope to develop, the techniques we hope to impart — and they'll all be there. There will be no shortcuts in this seminary. The students have been warned by me when they were interviewed.

It's a good hard-working institution. They'll have to adapt themselves to that kind of a life, if they are going to be members of Trinity Episcopal School for Ministry. What governs any organisation are the goals they have set. And the goal we had is the kind of man we want.

I want to tell you what I think the kind of man ought to be.

FIRST of all, somebody who is unashamed of the Gospel of Christ.

Paul says he is unashamed of it because it is the power of God unto salvation for everyone that believes, unashamed of it because of its content, the content of the Gospel that speaks of our glorious Lord and Saviour, Jesus Christ. It raises Him up as the great name above all names in Heaven and on earth. It is the one real hope that will meet the needs of all mankind.

Second, because of its truth — for if the Gospel is not true, we have no message to proclaim, we have no right to be in the Church of God at all. Thirdly, because of its power. God has the power to change lives. We want the men to know that power in their own lives, how greatly we can change their lives and set them free, and then to see it in the lives of others and in those to whom they minister.

SECOND. And certainly **I want them to be men and women of prayer**. It's not enough to be able to teach about prayer or to talk about prayer, but they must need to be able to go into the secret place and know that they will be heard. They go there so their ministries may be enriched after leaving this School; so that their sermons may be alive; so that their counselling may do what it is meant to do — to draw people back to God; and so that their pastoral care may be gracious and loving; and so that they, themselves, because they have been men and women of prayer, will be free of anxiety, and therefore able to be set free to do the work of the Lord.

THIRD. Then they should be liberated persons. That word has so many connotations, but I always speak of it in the Biblical sense. Jesus said 'You shall know the truth, and the truth shall set you free'. 'If the Son shall set you free, you shall be free indeed'. The freedom that Christ gives, the real freedom from the bondage of sin, the freedom from those habits which keep a man from being the kind of man God meant him to be. Then the freedom from the deadness of self-interest. You can feel the sadness in Paul's life when he is writing to the Philippian Church and says 'I have no man whom I can send, for they all seek their own, not the things of Jesus Christ'. And then he spoke of Timothy — Timothy, the different one: Timothy the one who first of all sought the things of Jesus Christ. The sad thing is that men can be in the ministry and not seek first the Kingdom of God. We hope that those who go to this School will be delivered from the deadness of self-interest. Then, the men need to be set free from the love of money and possessions.

Americans are very rich people indeed, and have a very large share of the world's goods. And some people feel that somehow or other, that when you give up a great deal to become a minister of the Gospel of Christ and serve the Lord, that you won't have a temptation for the love of things or the love of money. Paul wrote to Timothy to beware of the love of money because some, having loved it, pierced themselves through with many sorrows. It doesn't matter whether you have a lot or whether you have a little — you can still be possessed by the love of money. And because you have been without, you may desire it more than some who have it, and it's always a dead path for the minister of the Gospel of Christ. There are only two ways for the minister of the Gospel of Christ. He can look after his own interests, and God will let him. Or he can look after the interests of the Kingdom of God, and God will look after his interests. So I have found it.

And then he needs to be delivered from **the tyranny of the love of the world**. John puts it very strongly when he says, 'If any man love the world, the love of the Father is not in him'. What is the love of the world? Well, some people break it down to definitions of little, small things. I like the definition that Archbishop Fisher, of Canterbury, gave when he visited us in East Africa. He said that 'the world is all that section of society that is organised outside of three great principles: the sovereign rule of God, the redemption that is in Christ Jesus, and the life of the world to come'. He went on to say that a great deal of society is organised outside of those principles. That is, society where this world is their horizon, where there is nothing up and over and beyond this world. But if a man is going to be delivered from those things, he's going to be bound by other things. He's going to be bound as the slave of Christ. In the old slave laws, when a man was due to go out after his seven years, if he wanted to, he could go to his master and say: 'I love my master, I will not go out free'.

If we love our Master, we will not go out free. We are committed, and bound by that commitment to our Lord Jesus Christ, bound by our baptismal promises, some of us bound by ordination, bound by the secret moment when you told the Lord you would give him all there is of your life, and that commitment is there. That is what integrates personality, that's what establishes purpose in life. The Christian has found purpose in his committal to his Lord and Master Jesus Christ. He is also bound by his indebtedness to preach the Gospel.

How can a man be a recipient of the grace of God and not want to take it to others? I want to say that if a man is unconcerned with the spread of the Gospel of Christ, it must be a very weak kind of grace that he's got hold of. There is nothing plainer than this, that if a man really loves the Lord and depends on Him for the whole of his salvation, he wants to make that claim known to others. Then he is indebted to preach God's word. I needn't say much more than that because that has already been covered by Dr Rodgers. But it's from the word of God that we get our instruction. It's not just that God has spoken long ago and that that has been recorded in the word of God — it's not that God **HAS** SPOKEN, BUT God speaks **TODAY** through his word. That quotation that Dr Rodgers gave you, 'We have devised a method of studying the word of God out of which no word from God ever comes', shows that if God has not spoken, then we have no message to proclaim; if God has spoken we have a message to preach. Woe be to us if we preach some other message.

Then the **FOURTH** mark of the men we want is that **they shall be seekers after holiness**. I didn't know that word was so bad in the States! (Laughter). The writer of the Hebrews says, 'Holiness without which no man will see the Lord'. 'Be ye holy' says the Scripture, because God is saying, 'I am holy'. It is a mark of Christian people. When a Christian and minister of God gives up the battle for holiness, he is already a back-slider at heart. Whenever he reaches a stage where he is satisfied with his progress in the Christian life and thinks 'now I have reached it', he is a back-slider. Always in the Christian life there is more beyond and always the more he walks with God, the more he will be discontented with the quality of life he has. For there are riches, better things beyond, and he should be marked by that desire for holiness. Paul, the apostle said, 'I make it my ambition to please Christ in all things'. One single sentence can change the life and pattern of a man.

That is his aim, in his home life, in his study, in his work, in his witness, in his reading, in his giving, in his day-by-day conversations — in his ambition to please Christ. What are you aiming at? Are you like Paul, who said, 'I make it my ambition to please Christ in all things?'.

FIFTH. Then a man needs to have compassion for the poor and needy. The most needy are those without the Gospel of Christ. It is a mark of the Christian man that he has compassion. Jesus looked at that 'great crowd of people' and he had compassion on them. The disciples said, 'Let us send them away', and Jesus said, 'There is no need to send them away. Give ye them to eat'.

Then **SIXTH, they should be men who are alive with the life of the Spirit of God.** What is the good of being able to speak well, to be sound in doctrine, and know the way you ought to live if the whole of your life is not made alive with the Spirit of God. There is one mark which the Spirit of God can give to a man when he is called a minister that will make people know that he is God's man and it is this: when he speaks men and women will hear God's voice speaking to them through him. Then they will know. That is our 'imprimatur'. It is greater than any degree you can get from Trinity School. It is greater than any qualification you can get in the United States or elsewhere. It is better than any praise men can give you. That imprimatur of the Spirit of God himself ... if you speak then men hear God speaking to them. Then they know you are a man of God.

Then **FINALLY, he needs to be a man who is gripped with a deep sense of gratitude for the privilege of being called to be Christ's servant.** For if ever a man begins to think of what he is putting into the ministry, or what great favour he is performing for the people he is ministering to, or the organisation he has joined, he's half dead. There is nothing quite like the privilege of being God's servant. I want to put this kind of question to all of you today: if other people knew you like God knows you, all your faults and all your thoughts, all your sins, all the things in your heart that have been in there, all the wrong thoughts that you have ever had, would they trust you with the kind of work that God trusts you with? Here is the supreme confidence that God has in His own grace. He will take people like you and me and give you the privilege of being His servant. He has to take people like you and me. That is the only kind He possesses. People who are at best weak men, weak women, made strong. The Christian life is not a case of girding up your loins and saying, 'I will be strong'. It is a case of acknowledging your weakness. Paul said: 'When I am weak, then am I strong, for God's strength is made perfect in weakness'. When a man loses the sense of gratitude for being called to God's service, then there is something very wrong with his work in ministry.

So, to reiterate these seven principles:
1. A man who is not ashamed of the Gospel of Christ.
2. A man of prayer.
3. A liberated person.
4. A seeker after holiness.
5. One with compassion for the poor and needy.
6. One alive in the Spirit of God.
7. One gripped with the sense of privilege.

To this end we dedicate ourselves. Our hope is that from this class every single one will go out and be effective in God's service. And my dream is that from this first batch of students, there will come such a development of God's Spirit on some of them that they will be those who will go out and make Christ's name known and ring across the United States of America.

God help us.

After the official opening of the School, lectures commenced in earnest. Each day covered the four elements of worship, learning and study, fellowship and service. The students led the worship sessions each morning by rota. They were required to prepare personal time-tables of how each day was to be spent, and Alf inspected these and discussed them with each individual student. The School was entirely dependent on their financial needs being met from outside sources. Rent for the site, salaries and other such recurring expenditure depended on the free-will giving of Trinity supporters. Each day a list of needs and donations was posted on the chapel door. Janet Leighton, a student wife commented, 'we learned to pray faithfully for God to provide what was necessary. Sometimes the resources trickled in, sometimes they came in larger donations, but God was continually meeting the School's needs, simultaneously creating in us the confidence that He would keep on taking care of us'. Alf never lacked trust and confidence in God's supply.

Alf lectured in Pastoral Theology, Dr Fairfield in Church History, Dr Davids in New Testament and Dr Rodgers in Systematic Theology. Special times were set aside before the full time-table began for an introductory study of New Testament Greek. The library began to grow and collected needed volumes from many sources. As the resources grew there were requests for Alf to travel to many parts of the USA where interest in Trinity was growing.

On Thursday evenings the entire School community, students, faculty, staff, wives and children gathered together for a shared fellowship meal of soup and bread — very superior home-made soups and delicious home-cooked breads produced by their wives! A service of Holy Communion followed. This became a fine time of fellowship and of getting to know one another, singing together and fostering mutual care.

Service took the form of students going out weekly to help in surrounding churches and communities and in door-to-door evangelism. Visiting lecturers spoke of specialist needs in areas where help was needed.

Mrs Nancy Chalfant from Sewickley spoke to the School about the problems of caring for retarded children and about places where students could visit to see the problem at first-hand and see how it was being tackled. She spoke out of her own experience of rearing and caring for a severely handicapped child for many years. On another occasion, Dr Ruth Sandland came to visit us. She was a long-time friend from Melbourne (at that time engaged in the radio-therapy programme at St Bartholomew's and Great Ormond Street

Hospitals in London). She spoke to the students on the subject of terminal illness.

Ruth was a member of the Church of All Souls' Langham Place in London and had been there when Alf visited on several occasions, notably when he spoke at the launching of their large stewardship appeal. It was said that Alf's address on the subject was held to be a turning-point in the giving.

At times God's faithfulness was demonstrated to us at the School at the point of immediate need. One day, John Rodgers came to see Alf. It was the day for paying the monthly salaries and the School was short of US$2150. Alf said, 'It may come in the post'. 'Well', said John, 'the mail is here and it hasn't come'. 'It will come by hand', said Alf. They prayed about this and before long a student came who paid a backlog of fees, US$650. A little later another student came with a cheque for US$1,000 he had received in the mail, a sum given to Trinity in memory of a relative. That afternoon John had a business appointment in Pittsburgh and, when leaving, was given an envelope containing US$500. John was deeply grateful and Alf said, 'This has happened to strengthen your faith; I had no doubt that God would supply our need'.

Robert Crock was the respected Treasurer of the School who came to consult Alf about Guidance. Alf proceeded to give him six points to follow. He enunciated one and two and was about to state the third when Robert said, 'Don't go on Bishop, I'm stuck on the second!'. Before long, Robert died and Alf asked George Oliver to accept the post of Treasurer. George gladly agreed. He was a Vice-President of a Pittsburgh Bank and decided to take early retirement. Although the task grew more arduous as time went on, George is still at the post today. He and Eleanor, his wife, were very kind to us and we loved them very much.

During 1976, Alf had early symptoms of Parkinson's disease though these were not diagnosed then as such. One morning he was preaching in a church in Pittsburgh and stopped in the middle of a sentence. He did not go on for some time but then continued normally. Afterwards, I asked him why he had stopped and he said, 'I couldn't speak!'. We wondered if it had been a slight stroke. Some weeks later he had a type of virus affecting the gastric system and spent a few days in bed. After that whenever he spoke the words came rushing out very rapidly; then his voice settled down again.

Alf preached occasionally at our parish Church of St Stephen's and arranged to take a 'team' of members to a 'Sharing of our Faith' Mission at St Christopher's, Springfield, Virginia, where the Reverend Alden (later Bishop) Hathaway was the rector. I was included in the team and none of us was told what he or she was expected to do or say! Each of us was called on spontaneously by Alf to give our thoughts on a question or problem advanced by a St Christopher's parishioner. This proved a stimulating and encouraging time and a friendship deepened between Alden and Alf. Several students from Trinity were to work under Alden in the future when he became the Bishop of Pittsburgh.

We arranged to take our annual leave at year's end in Australia. We were due to arrive just before Christmas and to return to the USA late in January. Alf had agreed to give one of the morning addresses at Belgrave Heights at the annual Convention (his voice was to prove a little unreliable).

During this visit Alf saw his solicitor about the estate of his sister, Grace. This had been finalised and he decided to sell Grace's home in Paynesville and purchase a home for us for our retirement in Melbourne, which we estimated to begin in late 1978. While Alf was busy doing this, I sought advice from friends in the real estate business regarding a suitable purchase. We decided that a house with even a moderate-sized garden attached might prove a burden, so we looked for a home unit with three bedrooms, or two bedrooms and a study. Just a week before we were to return to the USA, such a unit was advertised in Mount Waverley. We inspected it, realised it met our basic requirements and Alf decided to negotiate for it.

A friend drove him to Paynesville where there was a prospective buyer for that estate. He arranged for its sale and there was enough time for negotiations with the solicitor and the bank in Melbourne. He was able to sign the required documents on the morning of our departure for the USA. It was comforting to know there was somewhere for us to go in our retirement.

Nineteen seventy-seven proved a busy and fruitful year. Regular meetings were held with the Trinity Board of Trustees — the question of a property for Trinity was in the forefront of our needs. Several good properties came on the market but negotiations were fruitless. Some supporters were disappointed with these fruitless efforts but Alf was wont to say 'God must have something better for us!'. We had several prayer meetings at our home for a property.

During this year I began to notice facial changes in Alf. There seemed to be a rigidity in his cheeks. In my mind 'Parkinson's Disease??' popped up, but I swept this thought aside as, in my ignorance, I believed a tremor always accompanied this complaint.

In late October of 1977, we travelled to Tanzania via England for the special celebrations of the Golden Jubilee of the Diocese of Central Tanganyika. We were met at Dar-es-Salaam by Bishop

Gresford Chitemo who drove us to Morogoro to stay with Mary Punt. It was a great joy to be back in Africa. Gresford drove us and Mary to Dodoma and some of his clergy and parishioners met us by the roadside as we journeyed through his diocese.

A little way out from Dodoma, some of our African women friends waited by the roadside with songs and flower leis they had made to welcome us. It was wonderful to be greeting so many African friends and missionaries as they came in for the Celebration. Among close missionary friends was Dr Joe Taylor who had not seen us for some time. He was stationed at Moshi near the Kilimanjaro Christian Medical Centre and engaged in ophthalmic practice which took him to many parts of Africa, chiefly by a plane called 'Wings for Sight'. On seeing Alf again after a long period he said 'Have you seen a neurologist lately?'. 'No' said Alf, 'Why?' He replied, 'You have Parkinson's disease', and to me he said, 'Haven't you noticed his face?'. I said I had, but thought it must be the ageing process. It is hard to describe the effect this encounter had on Alf and me. Within myself, I felt very down-hearted as I knew there was no cure and that a long physical decline lay ahead. I do not know what Alf thought at the time — he said nothing. We could not bring ourselves to discuss it for a long time.

The celebrations were wonderful. There were processions through the streets of several choirs, Mothers' Union members and youth groups with African musical instruments and drums. Large artistic bill-boards outside the Cathedral showed the progress of the diocese over 50 years. The Cathedral was packed. Many important people were there including President Nyerere, the Regional Commissioner and other Government officials, and all the clergy of the diocese and visiting clergy and bishops.

Alf had been asked to preach and by God's grace his voice was normal. He outlined the growth of the work and cited Bishop Chambers' constant reference to 'the best for God'. When the time came for the Jubilee offering, the livestock had to be received outside, so the dignitaries and local Government officials moved to the close to bless the sheep, goats, hens and cattle. George Hart, from the Hombolo Leprosy Settlement had brought their offering of a magnificent Charolais bull which he had bred. Afterwards there was a feast and speech-making. Yohana Madinda presented President Nyerere with a Swahili Bible, and the day concluded with a dinner at the home of the Regional Commissioner.

Alf and I visited diocesan centres at Mvumi and Msalato and then flew north in a Missionary Aviation Fellowship Cessna to Moshi getting some wonderful views of Kilimanjaro. Dr and Mrs Hannah were now back in Africa serving at Moshi where Wellesley was in psychiatric practice. We stayed with the Taylors, who arranged tests for Alf at the Kilimanjaro Christian Medical Centre, which confirmed the diagnosis of Parkinson's disease. Joe Taylor then phoned London and arranged for Alf to see a Harley Street neurologist on our way home who started him on the drug 'Artane'.

When we returned to Sewickley, Alf was not at all well — very 'nervous', 'confused', and his voice was most unreliable. He saw a neurologist in Pittsburgh who took him off 'Artane' and put him on the L-dopa drug 'Sinemet'. This helped Alf very much and he was able to cope with the work-load.

During the 1977-78 academic year, student numbers had increased, more staff and faculty were added and the library grew. Courses were extended and some lectures were open to the public at night; student wives were welcomed to the daily lectures. Financial support increased as did expenses. A Kenyan, Charles Gaikia, had joined the School as a bursar and we had a phone call from a homesick Tanzanian, Philemon Sudayi, at the Virginia Seminary. He wanted to speak in Swahili! He came to stay with us for a week and he and Charles cooked African food.

During the summer vacation, we visited England in the pre-Lambeth 1978 period, and met Bishop Yohana and Mwendwa Madinda at a CTDA meeting in London. Alf had suffered from muscle failure following the flight from New York and needed medical help. His voice failed him, too, and I had to take over the projected talk he was to give.

Time was running out for us. The Pennsylvania Government sent their representative to enquire into the School's activities and to interview the Faculty, students, staff and Alf. Every aspect of the School's life and teaching was enquired into. He asked Alf why he was not staying on! Alf replied that he was nearing 70 years of age, his voice was unreliable etc. The official report later stated that the representative had nothing negative to say about the School.

Alf was told of a church in the town of Ambridge which was for sale, preferably to a Christian organisation. Ambridge was a steel mill town of former years and immigrants from Europe settled there. Among them were people of the same Calvinistic faith but communicating in two different languages, so two churches were built. Now some generations later they all spoke English and it was agreed to worship together in the larger church and sell the smaller one. They heard of Trinity's need and contacted Alf. He and George Oliver — and subsequently other Board members and supporters — viewed the church. Its sale price was US$125,000 which was ridiculously cheap. The property was in good order and the church would make a splendid chapel, adequate for a good number of students. Attached to the church were some classrooms, a kitchen, dining-room etc., though there was no room for parking. It was agreed that it was a good proposition.

Alf wrote off to supporters, Board members and students appealing for the US$125,000 and it came in quite quickly. The property was in a good condition and the classrooms adequate, but other facilities were needed for a library and for administrative facilities and parking.

Very soon a supermarket across the street came up for sale at the same price — US$125,000. It was 15,000 square feet in size and could be converted into the library and administration block and there was a good parking space. This, too, seemed to be the way God was leading and again the money came in to buy the property.

Now a very much larger sum was required to convert the supermarket and furnish it according to requirements. But before this could be appealed for, a Presbyterian Foundation from the South wrote saying they had heard we had a 'project' which they would like to support. Because it was to be used for educational purposes, they could use their gift as tax relief. They asked Alf how much money was required for the conversion and Alf wrote back to thank them and to say we required US$300,000. This gift came to us and later, after we had gone, they sent another large gift.

The School was becoming established. The library was growing steadily and efforts were made to get some money lodged in the Endowment Fund. So now, we were ready to leave. Our three years were up. It seemed that Alf had laid a base for both the visible School and the teaching needed to launch Trinity Episcopal School for Ministry into the Episcopal Church of America. Dr John Rodgers was chosen as the Dean/President to succeed Alf after we left.

So Alf celebrated his 70th birthday on 9th September, 1978 with his usual enjoyment. All the faculty members and their wives had a meal with us. We planned to leave Sewickley on 1st November. On reviewing our three years in the USA, Alf saw that God had raised up a band of students, a fine faculty, all the necessary staff and buildings for the School and the needed finance. There was a very long way to go yet. The School had to reach the standards required by Government before being chartered to grant degrees. It had also to meet with the requirements for the next goal, the accreditation by the Theological Schools of America. We were able to praise God for what happened in our day and for the way in which Trinity became accredited and accepted as the eleventh seminary of the Episcopal Church, under Dr Rodgers in 1985.

The Board of Trustees gave a dinner in our honour with speeches and the gift of a silver salver. A farewell service was held in the Pittsburgh Cathedral at which Alf was enabled to preach. At a social gathering following that, we were presented with two beautiful 'friendship' quilts (secretly sewn by the ladies), each with forty embroidered patches of some topical reference. We were also told that a Scholarship Fund had been initiated, to be called the Alfred and Marjory Stanway Foundation Scholarship. Its purpose would be to bring African students from the Anglican Church in East Africa, rotating through Kenya, Uganda and Tanzania, to study at Trinity for two years. This news brought much joy to Alf and me.

George and Eleanor Oliver had us to stay with them while we packed up and sent off our goods to Australia and we appreciated their love and concern. On our last morning the students and wives came to say good-bye as we left for the airport. It was a sad time for us all.

We found American Christians to be very caring people, openly showing their feelings and most helpful in all kinds of situations. There is a softness in their natures which we Australians seem to lack. We seem to have a 'toughness' which prevents us from showing the degree of love and care shown by our American counterparts. We praised God for our time in the USA and looked back on it with satisfaction and heart-warming memories. Alf had prayed in 1968 that he would be granted ten more years of effective service, and he realised this had been given to him by God and he praised him for it.

CHAPTER 17

THE ULTIMATE GOALS
— 1978–89

We flew from Pittsburgh to Los Angeles on 1st November, 1978 and stayed a night in Santa Monica and visited Sadru Damji, an old friend from Dodoma. He had migrated to California and was still practising his Ismailia Muslim faith. From there we flew to Nadi in Fiji and rested for three days. Betty Durham joined us there from Suva where she was engaged in full-time Christian Literature work. Alf was very interested to hear all about this and about the progress being made in the Pacific literature field.

On the Sunday evening we flew to Sydney and were met by Marcus and went to stay at Bishopscourt until the following Wednesday. Marcus had been knighted by the Queen in 1976 and was now the first Australian-born Primate of the Anglican Church in Australia. In spite of his extremely busy life, he was still writing study, devotional and biographical books, as he had done throughout his career. Alf was delighted by Marcus's quiet achievements.

This last journey was stressful for Alf and he arrived in Sydney in a nervous state but was able to unwind while we were there. It was good to meet up with Patricia again and enjoy her gracious hospitality.

On arrival in Melbourne we stayed for two days at St Andrew's Hall where Dr David (later Archbishop) Penman was Principal. This gave us time to organise our goods out of storage, and to have the telephone connected in our home unit. At that time there was nothing at all in the house except newly installed electrical equipment. CMS had arranged a small function for our many friends to welcome us back and we met at St Andrew's Hall when the Reverend Kevin Curnow gave a lively address about Alf 'advancing in Africa, pioneering in Pittsburgh and vacillating in Victoria'.

We moved into our new home on a Friday morning. At noon the vicar of St Andrew's, Glen Waverley, the Reverend Phillip Saunders, with a warden and his wife, arrived bearing casseroles, scones and other goodies for us. They offered to arrange transport to take us to St Andrew's for the morning service on the following Sunday and we appreciated these caring acts very much. Philip had written to Alf while we were still in USA saying that he had heard we were moving to the Waverley area and had invited Alf to take part in ministry at St Andrew's. Alf had replied thanking him for this offer but explained the nature of his voice problems.

All our stored goods arrived and enabled us to live picnic-style until our household effects arrived from America in January. On that day, John Alder, Alf's co-boarder from the long ago St Albans days, arrived to help us unload and settle our belongings. Although the dominant symptom troubling Alf at that time was the muscular failure in his throat, he was able to cope with most other things and the purchase of a car made our travel easy. So he resumed most of the interests he had pursued prior to going to the States. These included CMS of which he became a Vice-President, the Belgrave Heights Convention Council, Ridley functions, ACLS and directors' meetings of the *Church Scene*.

Alf assisted at the regular services at St Andrew's where we became members. In addition, from 1979 he led one of the elective study courses in adult Christian Education which were held in private homes between the 8 a.m. and 11 a.m. services. Alf chose his own subjects and over the years, these included a 14 weeks study on Great Chapters of the Bible, 12 weeks on the Epistle to the Ephesians, 12 weeks on 'Towards Christian Maturity' and 14 weeks on 'I believe in Prayer'. I was present at these teaching sessions and recognised that Alf was using all his experience of God's leading over many years and all his understanding of God's Word in seeking to open people's minds to Christian truth. The attendances were good.

During the latter years his speech was often very rapid and he used an electronic device sent by Charles Kalt in USA. Called a Personal Speech Delay (or PSD), this device has an ear-plug and a microphone, thus slowing his voice down — it was a good aid for some time. Alf began speech therapy regularly at the Alfred Hospital. This also was helpful although the therapist and Alf realised it could only assist for a limited time. For a while at St Andrew's, a feature of Sunday Evening services was interviewing Christians who were foremost in their professions or occupations. Two friends whom Alf interviewed were Bruce Teele, a stockbroker from the firm of J.B. Were & Son, and Dr W.H. Kirkaldy-

Willis, our old friend, then Professor of Orthopaedics in Saskatoon University.

From 1978-83, Alf had a reasonable life-style. We were able to attend most of the functions which interested him and he was still able to drive the car. We paid regular visits to his neurologist who tried various drugs in differing doses until he felt he had found those most suited to Alf's needs. In late 1983, Alf came to the decision, with which I agreed, to give up driving — the medicines he took bore warnings about driving after dosages. Then came a period when he had falls down steps at railway stations, on trams and down the steps at the Cathedral. It became necessary to give up using public transport and from this time forward he was driven by friends or used taxis, and was safer with someone accompanying him.

Alf put the proceeds from the sale of the car into debenture stock which, with other shares, some inherited, brought us an income which helped to keep pace with inflation. In fact, we were more secure financially during these last years of Alf's life than ever before. His response was — 'We must give more away!' and, of course, he did. Most days he read the *Age* newspaper at breakfast, the world news, the business news and the daily stock-market report while I did the crossword. Afterwards we had our family prayers using prayer-cycles from CMS, DCT etc.

God blessed us with the visits of many overseas friends. Bishop Madinda's wife, Mwendwa and Bishop Chiterno's wife, Violet, had come to Australia for an International Mothers' Union Conference in Brisbane in July 1979. They insisted on coming to Melbourne to see their parents (us!). They felt at home and cooked their *ugali* (the stiff maize-meal porridge — their staple food at home) which was missing from Australian menus.

Early in 1980 friends from England came — Bishop Oliver Allison, former Bishop in the Sudan, Dr Denis Burkitt, of world fame for his research into the necessity of fibre in our diet, and his wife Olive . We had known each other from East Africa days. Paul Fueter, a Swiss Moravian colleague from Tanganyika also came. He now worked with the United Bible Societies in London. In July, John Rodgers arrived after attending an International Christian Conference in Thailand and was followed by Yohana Madinda who, likewise, had been in Thailand. These visits were stimulating and exciting for Alf.

From the beginning of October 1980 to the end of January 1981, Alf accepted a chaplaincy in Lord Howe Island. He knew he could lead the regular services with a little care and give short, carefully prepared, sermons. What he did not realise was that the Island radio broadcast daily morning periods of Christian worship, and that he was expected to take regular religious education in the Island school. However, I took on these assignments for him and the holiday aspect of our stay was delightful. The climate was ideal and swimming very beneficial. When we returned to Melbourne Alf celebrated the 30th anniversary of his consecration on 2nd February, 1951 with a special service at St Andrew's. The Reverend Dr John Wilson gave the bidding prayer and preached.

John Rodgers had invited Alf back to Pittsburgh for Trinity's Commencement ceremony in May 1981 when it was hoped the School would be chartered. Alf was invited to present the degrees and give the commencement address. Both our air-fares were paid, and by adding a little extra we were able to take a round-the-world ticket, travelling first to Vancouver where we stayed with Rita and Jim Houston of Regent College.

Alf was hoping to confer degrees on the first three graduating classes of students but there was still some doubt about this. It was unlikely that the State's chartering process would be finished in time for the Commencement ceremony. Dr Leslie Fairfield heard just before the commencement that the authority to grant degrees had been retroactively awarded. He said, 'I called Alf and told him he would be able to confer the degrees. In typical Alf fashion he said "Thank you very much" and hung up! But his host came upon him at the telephone in tears!'. The ceremony was held in St Stephen's Church, Sewickley. The Reverend Everett (Terry) Fullam of Connecticut preached and Alf gave the Commencement Address with no noticeable voice faults, and conferred the degrees on the three classes which had graduated since TESM's opening. It was in this address that I heard him refer to his prayer in 1968 that God would grant him a further ten years of effective ministry. Those years at TESM from 1975-78, he said, were the last of that decade.

We left Pittsburgh for Washington to stay with Susan and John Yates and their five children. Their middle child, Christopher, was Alf's godson. John was Rector of the famous historic Falls Church where George Washington had worshipped, and they had been our close friends and neighbours in Sewickley. Writing about Alf later, John had this to say:

> Everything he did was quick — he walked, talked, ate, thought and even prayed more rapidly than any person I have ever known. Alf broke up all my stereotypes of a Christian leader.
>   Although he was a fast-moving man and a do-er, he **never** tried to rush God. He knew that man's efforts were only worthwhile if they were led and blessed by the Holy Spirit. He knew that all necessary resources belong to God — he trusted the Lord would indeed provide.

Alf with godson, Christopher Stanway Yates at Falls Church, Virginia, 1981.

During September the Commonwealth Heads of Government Meetings (CHOGM) were held in Melbourne. The Queen and Prince Philip came for the opening ceremonies and lived aboard their yacht *Britannia* in Port Melbourne. Alf had asked permission to lead a deputation of CMS personnel for an interview with President Nyerere who, with his wife Maria, occupied a suite in the Hilton Hotel. Permission was granted, and Dr Alan Cole, then Federal Secretary, with the Reverend Peter Dawson, Missionary Personnel Secretary of CMS Australia, and the Reverend John Stewart, General Secretary of CMS Victoria, also Messrs Alan Kerr, Alan Truett and ourselves, were thoroughly 'vetted' and then taken up to the Nyerere suite. It was a very friendly visit with impromptu questions and answers. Nyerere expressed his concern over the inability of countries trading in primary produce to compete with those trading in manufactured goods. It took seven times the amount of cotton to buy a truck this year as it had taken a few years previously. The economy of poor countries was decreasing while that of Western countries was increasing. Nyerere was as friendly as always.

To us an even more exciting visitor was George Nhigula. He worked in the Ministry of Foreign Affairs in Dar-es-Salaam and was a member of the Tanzanian delegation. He phoned Alf to ask if he might come and visit us. We discovered that the only time he had available was between 5.00–7.00 p.m. so it was arranged that he come for dinner. He arrived from the city by taxi and we spent a stimulating two hours with him. Very many years ago, as a young graduate and a committed Christian, he and Alf had spent a long train journey in Tanganyika in the same compartment. He belonged to the African Inland Church at Mwanza and was concerned about marriage. He knew whom he wished to marry but the girl's parents were being difficult. He and Alf sat and prayed and talked and Alf gave him the best advice he could in the circumstances. George's actions ended happily and he had a very blessed marriage. Since those days he had gone ahead in government and had filled diplomatic posts in Japan and India. In India he had met Bishop Jack Dain who gave him Alf's Melbourne address, and he started to correspond with us — it was a loving acquaintanceship again.

During 1982 Alf had reasonable health apart from the voice problems. John Temby came to St Andrew's Church as our curate and we enjoyed his ministry. Recently he sent me this comment about those days:

> It was a source of real encouragement and joy when I learned that I had been appointed to the parish of St Andrew's, Glen Waverley, because it happened to be the Stanways' home church.
>
> Having kept in touch with the Bishop while he was in the United States, to now have two years where we would be close was a real plus. It was both a privilege and joy, therefore, to be asked to meet with the Bishop to prepare material for the Adult Christian Education courses. To once again share the Scriptures together reinforced those lessons learned in past years regarding the need, not only to understand God's Word, but to apply it. Because our meeting was early in the morning I used to stay for breakfast and share in the Stanways' Devotions (Family Prayers). This afforded the opportunity of seeing their relationship at close quarters and to learn from that. This weekly time was very special as again and again I was able to see the Bishop modelling the Christian life as he taught it.
>
> During these years and those that were to follow I never once heard the Bishop complain about having Parkinson's Disease or the toll it had taken on his speech. His acceptance of the disease as being under God's control and his willingness to patiently endure it, was both a great lesson and inspiration.
>
> The highlight of my time in Glen Waverley came in August 1982 when, with failing speech, the Bishop was willing to speak at our wedding. This was the last time the Bishop spoke publicly so had extra meaning for Kate and me, showing once again his selflessness and his love and care for us personally. To me Paul's words in

Philippians 4:9 exemplified the Bishop's life, 'What you have learned
and received and heard and seen in me, do'.

Indeed, this was Alf's very last sermon and it proceeded smoothly
with no voice failure. I remember him giving advice to John about
parish ministry, and one sentence has remained with me: 'John,
listen to your wife, she won't always be right but she will be worth
listening to!'

In this year of 1982 Bishop David Gitari of Mt Kenya East visited
us. As a young graduate in Nairobi he had been a fellow missioner
with Alf in the Colleges then preparing to be the University.

Luis Palau, the internationally known evangelist, was conducting
a mission in Newcastle and John and Kathie Guest, from Sewickley,
USA — accompanied by David and Elsie Mackenzie — came to
Australia to assist. They visited us in Melbourne for a few days —
David was one of the graduating students from TESM in 1981.

In 1983 Alf, having given up driving, was experiencing muscle
failure in other parts of his body. He kept up a large correspondence and, although he used a portable typewriter, he found that his
fingers did not have enough pressure on the keys for the letters to
print properly. He bemoaned the loss of a secretary. One day I was
having coffee in Melbourne with Margaret McKechnie and I happened casually to mention this fact to her. Margaret took up the
point at once and said, 'Would he like me to come and help him?'
Would he! He was absolutely thrilled at the suggestion so Margaret
arranged to come each Tuesday and help with the correspondence
(at this time Alf could still dictate a little). She took home the
dictated letters to type for him and when these were ready she
posted them back to him to sign and send off. This was a
tremendous help and blessing to Alf. No-one could have been
better as Margaret had been his personal secretary for fourteen
years. She knew the people to whom he wrote and was used to his
methods.

From that time on Margaret came on Tuesdays to the end of
Alf's life. This was also a great help to me as it allowed me to go off
to various engagements knowing that Alf was not alone. This was
very important in view of his proneness to falling. He also purchased an electric typewriter which responded to the lightest touch
of his fingers.

Amon Nsekela was another African friend who came to visit us.
He had been on the staff of Mazengo School in our time. Now he
was head of the Reserve Bank of Tanzania and was in Melbourne
on business. From America this year came Steve and Harriette
Smith, from the first batch of TESM students. They had been
working in the Seychelles Islands; and the Reverend Daniel Serwanga

of African Enterprise stopped by one day. He had been a schoolboy at Maseno during 1944-47 and remembered us well.

Soon after we moved to Mt Waverley Alf formed a small 'growth group' of men from St Andrew's who met in our home. These men who were in executive or managerial posts stayed with Alf faithfully year by year until he could no longer converse with them. They studied the Bible during these gatherings and became close and supportive of Alf which he appreciated very much.

During March 1984 a large team of African Enterprise speakers visited Australia and held meetings in many centres in Melbourne. We were delighted to have Gresford Chitemo for two quick visits and a friend drove Alf to St Hilary's, Kew to meet with Bishop Festo Kivengere. This was the last time they were to see each other. From America came Tom and Hazle Houston, old friends from Nairobi. Tom was the General Secretary of World Vision International and they were in Australia in connection with his work. He and Alf had often shared platforms at conventions in East Africa.

Alf in retirement. (Photograph: Audrey Grant)

In July a special function was held at Ridley College to open the Leon Morris Library, the Alfred Stanway Lecture Rooms and the Bookshop. This was a very happy occasion and all these buildings were splendid in design and function and much needed facilities for the College. Members of the College Council, friends and students attended the Opening Ceremony. It was a great blessing to have a good adequate library with study facilities and the lecture rooms, like the library, are in constant use. They are called Stanway (Alpha) and Stanway (Beta). The Bookshop, as well as serving the students' needs, is a great resource centre. Both Dr Morris and Alf were proud to be so honoured.

Soon after this, Alf had a bad fall. There was no obvious injury, but from this time his condition deteriorated steadily. He now suffered restrictions in chewing and swallowing. He was in hospital for a week and a CAT scan was taken which showed the affected area at the base of the brain. The neurologist arranged for a speech therapist to visit him in hospital and get his voice moving again. From now on it became unwise for him to walk about alone outside the house.

The 21st December saw Alf's first goal reached — the fiftieth anniversary of his ordination to the diaconate. A Thanksgiving Service and luncheon party was organised at Holy Trinity Oakleigh for John Romanis, Alf and Lindsay Amey, all of whom were ordained together. John had been vicar for some years at Holy Trinity. Lindsay and Ruth had been parishioners there after their return from the Mission field. Alf and I were its 'own missionaries' and the Reverend Dr John Wilson — our preacher for the day — had been a reader and deacon there himself.

In his address, John Wilson mentioned that Lindsay Amey and Ruth **retired** from Uganda in 1965 after more than 30 years of service and were accepted by CMS for Oenpelli in Northern Australia for some years following. Alf **retired** from Tanzania to Ridley College and further **retired** to America! John and Gwen **retired** from Holy Trinity to a busy ministry at St Stephen's Greythorn! Although they had not themselves served on the mission field, they were in the front rank of those who prayed for, supported and kept contact with CMS missionaries through all these fifty years and onwards.

In his address, John Wilson said:

You have had good companions along the way, many rich experiences, many opportunities to serve, and already there has been good reward for your labours. But not from the first day until now have you been allowed to believe that all was over. Through good times and sometimes very difficult ones, the Lord moves us on. You have seen much — but not all, you have done much — but not all and this challenge to be as those who are waiting which you had at the beginning of your ministries remains until today. To be looking ahead filled with expectancy, to what the Lord will yet do, to His Coming as the New Age is revealed in its fullness, that is your calling.

From the Gospel reading John said he noticed something very striking regarding **Service**.

The remarkable thing is that although the servants — the deacons — are to be like those who are waiting for their master to come, the Master, when He comes, does all the serving! The Master will take off His coat, have the servant sit down, and He will wait on them (Luke 12:37). This is one of the parables of Jesus which turns normal life upside down. The Master comes to serve the servants! It seems odd but this apparent absurdity is deeply characteristic of the whole earthly ministry of our Lord.

The Son of man came not to be served
but to give His life a ransom for many.

It is the ministry of our Lord which is the pattern for those who are deacons in the Church of God. We can never leave this behind, as though we can outgrow it, and as though it has no more relevance. The message then is this, continue to be as those who are waiting for their Master. The Gospel tells us that you will be blessed if you do so. **He** will make you very happy.

And we are all so happy and thankful that we are able to share this time of rejoicing with you.

Thanks be to God.

Nineteen eighty-five started sadly for us, as my sister and brother-in-law died within a fortnight of each other, so Alf and I made two trips to Stawell for their funeral services. We both missed them very much for they had made a home for us and cared for us on many of our leaves from Africa. John and Blanche Rodgers of TESM, with their son Paul, spent three months of their sabbatical leave at Ridley College and were able to visit us several times. John was interviewed by the *New Life* weekly and a splendid article about TESM appeared in their Newsheet of 18th July. By this time, John had been Dean/President of TESM for seven years, and under his leadership the School became the 11th Seminary of the Episcopal Church of the USA. They had received, just that year, accreditation from the theological schools. John said, 'There is nothing higher by way of official accreditation, so we now take our place as a fully recognised seminary of the Episcopal Church'. This goal, achieved by his successor, had been much anticipated by Alf and it gave him deep satisfaction.

John Rodgers said:

In 1976, the year the doors opened, we did not know how many students we would have. We had a long discussion and decided that we needed at least one student to start. We did not see how we could start without any, and we were not sure that we had to have more than one! However, we actually began with 17 students which was most encouraging, because at that point there was not one bishop who was willing to send anyone to us. That meant they came without any support. The students had to trust that if they gave their lives to Christ, He would open up the ministry for them. Actually, all 17 were ordained, which indicated that, without seeming to be iconoclastic, it is really the Lord who is Head of the Church and not the bishops. Now, a number of bishops support the school, several of them are on our Board. This is encouraging.

Bishop Maxwell Wiggins spent a few days with us in 1985 on his return to New Zealand from East Africa where he had attended the celebrations for the division of his former Diocese of Victoria Nyanza into three, the new dioceses being Kagera and Mara. Max was quite upset by Alf's physical appearance as he had not seen him for some years. However after a few days he could see how Alf was coping with his disabilities which now included problems of balance and gait and muscular failure from time to time in different parts of his body. Other New Zealand friends who called on us were George and Joan Hart on their way home for retirement from Tanzania.

Nineteen eighty-six brought a quick and much appreciated visit from John Stott, who was speaking at conferences and conventions in Australia over the summer vacation period. Then Sheila and Arthur Scotchmer came to Melbourne for ten days. They had wanted to see the Stanway lecture rooms at Ridley College and the Morris library, and during their visit they were able to join with other friends in a celebratory service for the 50th anniversary of the priesting of John, Lindsay and Alf. This was another goal Alf had looked forward to.

Among the things which made Alf happy in this retirement period was to note how God provided for His missionary servants. After many years in overseas missionary service, not one of those whom we knew personally lacked the provision of a home and an income. We had been, personally, convinced that God would provide for us — and He did. It was good to see the principle, 'God is no man's debtor', working out for those faithful in ministry.

During this year two Africans whom we had known for many years attended an International Conference connected with the Anglican Church's Partnership in Mission Programme. It was called MISAG, meaning Missionary Issues and Strategy Advisory Group and was held in Brisbane. The first to come was the Reverend Martin Mbwana. For some years he had been the Provincial Secretary of the Province of Tanzania, but was now in London working in conjunction with the Anglican Consultative Council. He belonged to the UMCA (now USPG) tradition in Tanzania, and was succeeded by the Reverend Canon Simon Chiwanga. Simon also spent a few profitable days in Melbourne before proceeding to the Brisbane meetings.

In August 1987, Marcus Loane's book *Men to Remember* was published as a follow-up to a previous volume of biographical sketches called *Mark These Men*. *Men to Remember* starts with the early Anglican torch-bearers such as Columba and the Lindisfarne Mission through to Wycliffe, Whitefield and the Wesleys. Then the book directs us to the three early bishops of Sydney followed by three Sydney Archbishops. The final chapter is about three missionaries, Alfred Stanway, Paul White and Jack Dain. Alf was deeply moved by Marcus's appraisal of his work as there was no one whom he considered knew him as well as Marcus.

Also in 1987 another work of Marcus' was published called *The Voice of the Psalms*. It consisted of 'studies in one hundred of the Psalms of David'. The dedication read:

to

Alfred Stanway

of whom it may be said

That in the service of God,

Whatsoever his hand found to do

He did with all his might.

(Ecclesiastes 9:10)

Alf was again humbled to be so honoured. He was very fond of this book and we read one of the studies each day after lunch for the last months of his life.

The big event for Alf in 1987 was the dinner given in his honour by the Australian Christian Literature Society. It was held at Ridley College on 18th August. Marcus was invited to be the guest speaker and came to Melbourne specially for this function. Members of the Society and old friends attended and there were no spare seats!

Jeanette Boyd, of St Andrew's Hall, had put together a series of 70 slides showing selected photographs from Alf's earliest journey to Africa and throughout his East African career. These were shown with a racy commentary by Kevin Engel who also had made a special trip from Sydney for the occasion accompanied by Dorothy his wife.

On each table was a piece of stationery on which guests were asked to write their messages to Alf for this special day. By the end of the evening all of these were collated and presented to Alf in an album. Marcus followed the slide viewing with his address which paid tribute to Alf's career as a missionary and his work in Christian literature. It was a happy mixture of the serious and humorous stories from the past. Alf had prepared a reply which I read for him and as I had the 'last word' I was able to respond to Marcus's stories with a final anti-Marcus punch-line! Following these sessions the Christian Book of the Year award was presented by Alf to Jim Houston for *The Cultured Pearl* published by the Victorian Council of Churches. Other awards in differing categories were also made and Alf was presented with a copy of *The Cultured Pearl*.

The next goal Alf wished to reach was his 80th birthday — 9th September, 1988. Margaret McKechnie had organized a celebration for Saturday, 10th September at St Thomas's Moonee Ponds where CMS was holding a family fair that day. The Vicar, the Reverend Tom Morgan and his wife, Doreen, opened their home for the lunch and get-together which followed a service in the church. Bishop John and Mrs Stewart were present with us. They had just returned from Lambeth 1988 and he brought messages from many of the overseas bishops whom they met.

John (now Bishop) Wilson preached. That very morning Bishop Donald Mtetemela (then assistant to Bishop Madinda, with responsibility for the Southern area of the Diocese of Central Tanganyika and based at Iringa) had arrived in Melbourne and reached St Thomas's in time for lunch. Alf was delighted because Donald, as a schoolboy, had sought his help for his further education and was encouraged to do the pre-theology course at Kongwa College. Donald's career went on from there.

After lunch an informal gathering was addressed by old friends of long-standing, Madge Prentice, George Pearson, John Alder, Dulcie McLeish, Jean Meyer, John Temby, and Ron Gleeson. Eric Stockton, as Chairman, mentioned a few extra items particularly regarding Alf's contribution to CMS at home. I also spoke of our life together more in a light-hearted way and read Alf's message which said:

As I ponder in my mind what I should say in these few minutes, I thought I should say something about gratitude, as that is uppermost in my mind. It behoves me, first, to express my gratitude to God for bringing Bishop Donald in our midst today, reminding me of those memorable days in Africa. To Donald I say (this was in Swahili) 'I am very happy to welcome you here to our homeland today. May God bless you greatly'.

There are a few to whom I should express my thanks publicly. Margaret McKechnie for all she has done to make this occasion possible but more so, for a life-time of service to God and to me. She makes it possible for me to keep up a modest correspondence these days. Thank you, Margaret. You are the best backstop I know! Thanks are also due to Tom and Doreen Morgan and Bishop John Wilson for their contribution to this function.

Now to turn my mind to gratitude to God. First of all I am grateful to God for these 80 years. Since I turned to Christ at my conversion I have never had any sense of doubt that I was one who found mercy and had become one of His children.

Secondly, I have never doubted that my call to Africa was valid, and with the passing of the years this became more insistent. Next I am grateful for friendship and fellowship, the fellowship in the furtherance of the Gospel that which nothing can surpass. When I told CMS of my call to Africa they welcomed me and that began my association with the CMS of which I am proud to be a member still.

When we were on the mission field we were made aware that we were prayed for very much. So many blessings came on the work that one was forced to the conclusion that we were being upheld by fellow members of the Society. God's personal dealings with me encouraged me to believe that if He called you to a task He would be delighted to supply what was needed, and in my book on prayer (which is in the making) I have set out examples that show His faithfulness.

I am grateful for Marjory, not only as a wife, but one who was an effective missionary and has been my prayer partner for over 50 years. The sum total of answered prayer is overwhelming in its effect and binds you in friendship with those who participate with you in praying; and you, my friends, are amongst my thanksgivings. Thank you for your prayers. I close with these verses:

Psalm 116: 14 (NEB)

'How can I repay the Lord
For all His gifts to me?
I will take in my hands the cup of salvation
And invoke the Lord by name.
A precious thing in the Lord's sight
Is the death of those who die faithful to Him.
I will pay my vows to the Lord
In the presence of all His people.
Praise the Lord'.

This was the most extended of Alf's birthdays I had ever experienced, perhaps because it was his last and it was a most desired goal to reach! The real birthday fell on the day before, Friday, when my ladies' Bible Class met in our home and they shared a cake I had made and decorated with a few token candles. I had held back all the mail that looked like birthday cards for him to open after breakfast.

A great surprise awaited us both at church on Sunday. We noticed people going into the service with individually carried flowers. At the conclusion of the service they came up and mounted the flowers in an 80-shaped base and this was then set up on an easel and a large cake with 80 lighted candles was wheeled in. It was a work of art with a central coloured plaque which portrayed a robed bishop. Alf duly blew out as many candles as he could and I had to assist him. Afterwards the whole congregation joined in coffee with THE cake. This was all very entertaining for Alf and we felt it was the end of the celebrations, but two more cakes were to follow! One was made for him by Mary Milford (nee Loane) and the other came with a former curate and his wife and children.

Bishop Donald Mtetemela had left an afternoon free to come to spend a little time with us. He was distressed that Alf had been unable to speak at their previous meeting and, unknown to us, before he came on this visit, he prayed that Alf would be able to say something he would understand. Alf was discussing various Africans with Donald by pencil on paper but, at one stage, he said quite clearly, 'he's a very good man'. Donald's face lit up and he told me afterwards that this was an answer to his prayer. It seemed to confirm to him that Alf's thinking was clear.

Just a fortnight later something seemed wrong. Alf was unable to tell me what he felt but he was falling often, and sometimes I had to phone a nephew to help me to pick him up. We hired a wheel chair but I felt I should call the doctor. She came and diagnosed pneumonia and he was admitted to Waverley Hospital for a fort-night. I had developed some viral infection myself and was not well so welcomed Alf's introduction into Respite care. He spent three weeks at the Peter James Centre at Burwood. This is a beautiful new hospital with everything necessary for comfort and help. Physio, occupational and speech therapists worked with him and he came home reasonably well.

The 1988 Melbourne Synod, which met the following month, passed this Motion:

> That this Synod congratulates Bishop Alfred Stanway on his 80th birthday, and records its gratitude for his notable ministry as CMS Missionary, Bishop, and Theological Educator in East Africa, Aus-tralia and America'.

Notice of this was communicated to Alf by the Registrar, R.F.S. Crosbie.

Church Scene printed an editorial on 2nd September, 1988 which was written by John Denton, the Secretary of the General Synod of Australia, from which are following extracts:

CONGRATULATIONS, BISHOP ALFRED!

We salute Bishop Alfred Stanway, a great son of the Australian Church who is eighty on September 9th.

When intelligence, entrepreneurial skills and high motivation come together, one expects the possessor of such gifts to be a mercurial magnate and not a clergyman. Why did Alfred choose the latter course? The answer is that a twenty year old, full of ambition, was confronted with the claims of Jesus Christ upon his life and his conversion was a total restructuring of goals and priorities. And another gift was added — the gift of faith. The proclamation of the Gospel and the strengthening of the faith of new Christians became his transforming passion. Throughout his life he reached many face to face but he was also a statesman for the Kingdom of God, many thousands whom he never saw finding faith through the enterprises to which he set his hand.

Very early his soul was branded with the word 'Africa', and during the years of preparation, Ridley College and a curacy, he became an outstanding leader of youth work, the fruits of which abide to this day ... Kenya was very much a white colony but Alfred became General Secretary of the African Council and Archdeacon for African work which immersed him in the concerns and aspirations of African people at a time when independence was approaching on the Indian sub-continent. The message was travelling through the Colonial world. The ebb and flow of the independence movements on the continent all fitted into the projected patterns of this brilliant chess-player's imagination. Alfred was never surprised politically.

He became Bishop of Central Tanganyika in 1951 and with prodigious energy set about the production of a strong autonomous African Church. Seven dioceses now occupy the territory of the old Central Tanganyika. Alf had many tussles with mission support boards in sending countries. He believed that if the church was to be a part of the fibre of the future, national indigenous leadership had to come before politicised pressure demanded it. Bishop Stanway has always seen the vital link between evangelism and Christian literature. From the simplest expository text given to villagers who passed through adult literacy schemes to feeding the minds of students or making available imported texts constituted a wide-ranging strategy in Christian literature.

Alfred's financial and investment skills are legendary. He set high standards of accountability for himself and required them in others. This gave confidence. He geared evangelistic outreach to stewardship teaching for the new Christians and gave his trust to local responsibility, sometimes quite green .... aphorisms are part of the man and many have a financial twist, for example: 'Never be concerned about anything that can be resolved by money'.

Prayer is the breath of life for Alfred and in all his relationships and enterprises prayer was the discipline most exercised. This frequent encounter at the Throne of Grace is, without doubt, his abiding priority and prayer was often the subject of his pastoral teaching. To be absent from the mission prayer meeting was akin to fraud! The triangle formed by Alfred, prayer and God's answers, is a study in itself.

After twenty years as 'Alfred Central Tanganyika' he gave the first fruits of his retirement to his old college, Ridley, but at a time when contemporaries may be looking after a few old clients, Alfred was off to another continent. Witnesses say that the exuberance and expectancy of 1975 matched that of 1937 as he responded to the invitation to set up the Trinity Episcopal School for Ministry, an evangelical college near Pittsburgh. For three years he applied all his gifts and experience not only to the foundation of the institution, but to the spiritual formation of staff and students. This was the keystone of his phenomenal career.

Alf's frailty increased. He had lost a great deal of weight and he had just one more goal he wished to reach — our Golden Wedding in June, 1989. He tranquilly followed his routine, a 6 a.m. rising for prayer, and after breakfast he gave time to his correspondence and stamp collection. He enjoyed his weekly chess games with Phillip Saunders who was now coping with a greater disability which occurred some months after successful heart surgery. He came when he could to play chess with Alf.

Throughout 1989 Alf was prone to say to friends (in writing or on an alphabet board) quite happily 'Next stop Heaven'. He never missed Sunday morning attendances at church. After 13 weeks from the last respite care, he was due to go back for a fortnight in the middle of February. I had arranged to have our home painted and some repairs done and gas central heating installed while Alf was away from the chaos. During this period, our new Vicar, the Reverend Gordon Hargreaves was installed and his wife Ann and two children Elizabeth and Bradley were all welcomed at the Special Service. We arranged to bring Alf to this service as Gordon was one of those reading for ordination while we were at Ridley.

At the end of that month, Bishop Yohana Madinda died, suddenly, at home in Dodoma from a heart attack. He was 63 years of age. By African custom the mourning time is divided into two periods, the first immediately following the death when people come in great numbers to convey sympathy to the bereaved. During the first week hundreds of people visited Bishopsbourne to pay their respects to the family, including the President, Ali Hassan Mwinyi, and past President Julius Nyerere with other Government officials. We heard that the funeral was attended by 'thousands and thousands of people'. Bishop Rusibamayila, the senior Bishop gave the address and all the other bishops of the Province were present. Yohana was buried in the grounds of the Cathedral and the assistant Bishop, Donald Mtetemela, was asked to lead the Diocese for the next ninety days. The Selection Committee for DCT met to prepare a list of candidates to send to the Archbishop and the other bishops of the Province.

The second part of the mourning was set for three months ahead, at the end of May, when memorial services would be held and a Revival Fellowship Convention would take place. Yohana's death saddened us, as it was so unexpected. A small committee of ex-Tanzanian missionaries met in Melbourne to plan a Memorial Service for him and another was planned for Sydney, each to be on the last Sunday in May.

After respite care Alf came home with his last set goal in view ... 3rd June, our Golden Wedding. Godfrey Mdimi Mhogolo was chosen to be the Fifth Bishop of Central Tanganyika and the Consecration was arranged for 25th June. Bishop John and Mrs Wilson were to go to Tanzania for this ceremony representing the Diocese of Melbourne. But before this Mdimi Mhogolo and Irene, his wife, came to Australia and were able to come to see Alf. We had known Mdimi as a young man in Dodoma and he had completed a BTh in Melbourne at Ridley College where John Wilson had been his Old Testament lecturer. He brought photographs of Bishop Madinda's funeral, copies of the last Synod resolutions, and much information about which Alf was keen to hear.

While Alf was in the new respite care period the Memorial Service for Yohana was held at our Church of St Andrew's, Glen Waverley. Alf came home for that service which was led by the Reverend George Pearson with Archbishop Penman preaching and I, on Alf's behalf, giving the address of tribute to Yohana. We had known him for 38 years and he and Alf had worked very closely in Dodoma during the last eight years of Alf's service there. Bishop John and Jill Wilson and a good crowd of CMS members and former Tanzanian missionaries were present at the service and, to our delight, the Reverend Francis Foulkes from New Zealand, a former Principal of St Andrew's Hall, was briefly in Melbourne and came to the service with his wife, Marjorie. Their daughter and her husband and children were CMS candidates in training at St Andrew's Hall. At the conclusion of the service the Tanzanian missionaries sang 'Utukufu Aleluia' (Glory, Alleluia), the Revival Fellowship chorus, for Yohana.

While Alf completed his time in respite at the Peter James Centre, Margaret and I planned all the details for the celebration on the following Saturday. Over 80 invitations went out and nearly everyone accepted. I made the celebration cake — the largest I had ever made — and other friends prepared the afternoon tea and decorated the hall with golden balloons, gold candles and circlets of golden chrysanthemums for the tables.

Among those present was my bridesmaid Grace Camm who served in Kenya for over 30 years and Callon Moore who was at our wedding in Mombasa. Bishops Stewart and Butterss and their wives joined us with Bishop John and Jill Wilson. John had agreed to compere the afternoon.

A very happy feature was the arrival from Sydney of Kevin and Dorothy Engel who drove down from Sydney with Val and Max Corbett. Two other visitors from Sydney — who worked with us in Tanzania — Joan Eatch and Bessie Parker were also present. Chris Bakewell had come up from Lakes Entrance, the Tembys from

Geelong and the Rechners from Romsey and Winchelsea. Alf sported a buttonhole of deep gold chrysanthemums. He had worked hard with me and his alphabet board preparing what he wanted to say for the occasion, and John Wilson was to read this for him. This is really **Alf's last word** — he never prepared another:

ST HILARY'S KEW, SATURDAY 3RD JUNE, 1989.

I would like to start with thanksgiving that so many of you who are such busy people are joining with us today in our celebration. The only other Golden Wedding Anniversary celebration I have attended was that of Charles and Muriel Sandland and that turned out to be a very happy family gathering — using family in the wider sense — which I feel is being repeated today. It is good to have Charles and Muriel here with us.

My thoughts have turned to gratitude to God. His blessings never come singly and always with joy. My Diocesan staff used constantly to ask me 'Bishop, what was the sequel to such and such a blessing?' because there always was a sequel, and it is only as one looks back one sees the sequel was preceded by an initiative. Looking back on my life I found that *prayer* had been the big factor, and progress in the Christian life was not by large leaps and bounds forward but by following the leading of the Spirit which opened up our outlook; as Jabez of old realised when he prayed, 'Lord, enlarge my coast'. When we perceived that there was no way forward we would decide to put it in the hands of God without recourse to man, as Hudson Taylor taught, 'Move man through God by prayer alone'.

Ours has been a committed Christian home marked by daily family prayers, tithing plus the left handed giving and this has enriched our lives. The provision for our retirement and the uniting of our lives to many godly friends has meant that God not only blessed His work, but we also have shared in that blessing.

Many would ask, could one who so believed in prayer not be healed? I can say in response, my trust in God is undiminished and what He allows I accept. I would like to close with these words which I rejoice in:

Psalm 16: 5 & 6:

'The Lord is my chosen portion and my cup: thou holdest my lot. The lines have fallen for me in pleasant places; yea I have a goodly heritage.'

I was able to give a short talk as did Grace Camm and Margaret McKechnie. Bishop Wilson read Alf's address and Kevin Engel and Max Corbett related humorous incidents from the past — with a little exaggerated embroidery on Max's part! These made Alf laugh spontaneously. Others who added remarks were Val Corbett and Genevieve Cutler, and John Temby brought the proceedings to a close with prayer and the doxology.

Quite a number of those present sensed that Alf was making his last public appearance and saying a last happy farewell to friends, and this proved to be true.

Early the next week he worked out personal thanks to three of his friends from the business world who had been present, Harold McCracken, Charles Sandland and Len Buck. He seemed not to have any goals ahead now so settled down to his usual routine.

Alf had spoken to a friend some years previously about confidence in God saying,

> If I were asked the thing that I would like to lose least in life, I'd say it is confidence in God. It has meant more to me than anything I know, that is the fact that one can have confidence in the character of God, because it is revealed to us in the person of Jesus Christ. All my philosophy is based on that'.

Regarding the American project he said,

> We have never really sought the will of God and found God to fail us. And I couldn't believe that God who was saying to us now, 'Get up and go' was leading us astray. Confidence in God is what it was. Looking back across all the 50 odd years of the Christian life, you realise that there couldn't be any possibility that He'd lead you astray at the end of the road when He had been with you all the time.

CHAPTER 18

'This God is our God for ever and ever,
He will be our Guide even unto death'

Psalm 48:14 (AV)

Before our marriage Alf and I chose this text for our life together and how true it has proved! Alf daily sought God's guidance and it was a constant feature in our family prayers.

Following the golden wedding celebration Alf settled once again to his correspondence, stamps and an occasional game of chess. He did not indicate that he had any other earthly goal in view. He played his last chess game with Philip Saunders on the afternoon of 21st June. I had been monitoring his blood pressure daily for his neurologist. It was often very low, caused by the large doses of drugs he needed to keep him mobile. On the morning of 22nd June I noticed the pressure reading was many degrees above his average and asked if he felt all right. He indicated that he did but about an hour later complained of a pain from armpit to armpit across his chest.

I contacted our doctor who sent a trained worker to take a cardiograph and blood test. Alf had lunch and tried to rest but was very uncomfortable when lying down. I was making a cup of tea for him when the phone rang. The Dr said it appeared that Alf was in the early stages of a heart attack. She had reserved a bed for him in the Cardiac Care Unit at Epworth Hospital and an ambulance was on the way. He was admitted to Cardiac Care by 3.30 p.m., put on a monitoring device and given helpful medication until the specialist was able to see him — and me — at 6.00 p.m.

For the next three days Alf made good progress, was off the monitoring machine. The Dr discussed an after-care programme with me but on the night of Monday 26th, he lost ground. Gordon, our vicar, took me to see him on Tuesday afternoon, but it was obvious that he was completely disoriented; his eyes were closed and he did not know us or respond to our voices. Also he was very restless. At 9.30 p.m. that night of 27th June, he slipped quietly away to be with his Lord and Saviour to his 'next stop Heaven' which he had been anticipating for so long.

That night we informed friends in England, Africa and America, as they were still in the daylight hours. Gordon Hargreaves advised Archbishop David Penman who, with great kindness, contacted the Tanzanian Provincial Office and Archbishop John Ramadhani who was in Dodoma at the time. In fact, all the bishops from the whole Province of Tanzania were in Dodoma. Just two days previously the Reverend Mdimi Mhogolo had been consecrated as the Fifth Bishop of Central Tanganyika, and the following Sunday the Reverend Francis Ntiruka was to be consecrated as the First Bishop of Tabora, an area cut off from the Diocese of Western Tanganyika. I cannot think of any other time when all those bishops — thirteen in all — would have been together in the one place for a week. Bishop John Wilson from Melbourne was also there — God's timing was perfect.

During this week of waiting in Dodoma, Bishop Alpha Mohamed was speaking to Betty Durham at Msalato about Alf's death. He said, 'It was as though he handed over the torch and passed on'.

Alf had discussed with me the details of his funeral and Thanksgiving Service. He very much wished Marcus Loane to speak at the latter and Marcus had graciously agreed to do so if he were still here! Alf had wanted John Wilson to take part too, but John did this in Africa instead! Alf's last fully conscious day — the Sunday — was when Mdimi was consecrated as one of his successors as Bishop of Central Tanganyika.

According to Alf's wishes, the funeral service was at Paynesville. On Friday 30th June, Tony Hickson, a member of Alf's men's group and a dear friend, drove Gordon Hargreaves, Margaret McKechnie and me the four-hour journey to Paynesville. Archbishop Penman, still suffering the after effects of influenza, had come off the Adelaide express at Melbourne that morning on his return from a consecration in the Diocese of the Murray. He flew to Bairnsdale with the Victorian Secretary of the CMS, the Reverend Edwin Lang and arrived in Paynesville for lunch with us. It was arranged for John Temby from Geelong to lead the prayers, for Gordon to read Psalm 145 and Tony to read the New Testament lesson — 1 Corinthians 1:18-2:10 — and Archbishop Penman to give the address.

The setting in the little church of St Peter's by the Lake at

Paynesville was very tranquil and comforting to me. The Holy Table was under a large clear glass picture window which overlooked a wooded approach to Lake Victoria. The pulpit resembled the prow of a fishing boat with the dual impression of our Lord preaching from a boat and the fishing industry in Paynesville. My nephew Max and Evelyn, with some elderly cousins of Alf's, supported me. Marcus' daughter Mary came from Melbourne and his son Robert (Alf's godson) and Joan Loane left Wollongong in New South Wales very early that morning to be at the service. Colleagues who had worked with us in Tanzania and were present were Chris Bakewell from Lakes Entrance, Enid Stahl of Sydney (but visiting Victoria), Jeanette Boyd, Margaret McKechnie and Marjorie Walker and other friends from Melbourne.

In his address the Archbishop gave as his text, 1 Corinthians 15:57-58 (NIV), 'Thanks be to God! He gave us the victory through our Lord Jesus Christ. Therefore my dear brothers and sisters stand firm. Let nothing move you. Always give yourselves fully to the work of the Lord, because you know that your labour in the Lord is not in vain'.

These are some of Archbishop Penman's remarks:

If ever a Christian lived those words, Alfred Stanway did. He spent the final twenty years of his missionary service in Africa as Bishop of Central Tanganyika. Bishop Stephen Neill describes how when Alfred Stanway came to Tanganyika (as it was then), he determined to find the African leaders and 'bring them on', as the phrase was. He would not allow European missionaries to take places of leadership for which there were good African candidates. He planned the outreach and extension of the church in his diocese, and because his way of doing things was ahead of his time, he often had to go quietly out on a limb to do what he was convinced was right to extend the Kingdom.

Regarding Ridley he said he had no claim to being an academic theologian, but Leon Morris rightly thought that a godly man with administrative flair and considerable pastoral and evangelistic gifts would have both a contribution of note to make to the formation of future pastors and help the college on a more mundane but no less vital level.

In an age when most are enjoying retirement, *The Herald* (a Melbourne evening newspaper) featured Alf in a series of 'Golden Oldies', people of the older generation who were still contributing notably to community life.

He went to the USA to help in the establishment of Trinity Episcopal School for Ministry in Pittsburgh, Pennsylvania. His vigorous imaginative approach, his ready grasping of the initiative, his whole-hearted giving of himself to a work to which he believed the Lord had called him, were both a glowing example to the foundation members of that institution which have borne rich fruit today. So much, and so much more, time does not allow us to rehearse what under God, Alf Stanway achieved.

The ways of God are, indeed, marvellous. How Alf must be enjoying it all. Thanks be to God! He has given Alf the victory through our Lord Jesus Christ.

The Archbishop went on to speak of a facsimile message he had received on 28th June from the newly consecrated Mdimi Mhogolo, which said:

We have received with sorrow and thanksgiving to God the news of the death of our Father, our dear Bishop Alfred Stanway. We are grieving because we no longer have a spiritual Father with us. We give thanks to the Lord for His grace in giving him rest from the mortal body and welcoming him to be with his Saviour for ever and ever. The God of all comfort will continue to comfort you and all of us. The Lord be with you.

Archbishop Penman concluded his address with the emphasis on **confidence**:

It is in that sure and certain hope of the Resurrection to eternal life that we lay his body to rest to-day, **confident** that he now rejoices in the victory of our Lord Jesus Christ as never before; **confident** that his prodigious labour in the Lord is in no way frustrated or cut short but continues, and continues fruitfully and is finding its fulfilment in the over-arching will and purpose of the Lord he loved and served so well; **confident** that he now enjoys to the full the life of the Spirit which he, as we, enjoy but in part in this life; and **confident** that in God's good time we, with him, will be with the Lord for ever. 1 Thessalonians 4:17.

Alf's body was laid to rest next to that of his sister, Grace, and her husband John, surrounded by other Stanways of their generation.

At 2.30 p.m. on the afternoon of Monday 3rd July, a Thanksgiving Service was held in St Paul's Cathedral Melbourne. Alf had asked for the service to be held here, as it was here he was deaconed (and later priested) fifty-five years ago by the late Archbishop Frederick Head. The end of his ministry was to be as his beginning and a large congregation was present.

Bishop James Grant, the Dean of the Cathedral, commenced the service with the opening sentences of comfort and the psalm and lesson were read. After the singing of the hymn 'Beneath the Cross of Jesus', the Reverend Canon Maurice Betteridge, the present Principal of Ridley College and a former Federal Secretary of CMS Australia, led the prayers.

'In Heavenly love abiding' was then sung and the Most Reverend Marcus Loane, KBE rose to give the address. It was a most stirring address, very clearly articulated and lucid, and to me especially, very, very moving.

He said that if he had to choose the text for the day it might have been like David's lament for Abner, 'Know ye not that a prince and a great man is fallen this day in Israel?' (2 Samuel 3:38). Alf would not have agreed, said Marcus: the verse he chose was from the New Testament — 'You are in Christ Jesus by God's act, for He has made Him our wisdom; He is our righteousness; in Him we are consecrated and set free' (Corinthians 1:30, NEB).

Marcus gave a resume of Alf's career through the last 60 years, 34 of them in East Africa, emphasising the various posts he occupied, and particularly, the last 20 years as Bishop of Central Tanganyika. He spoke also of Alf's four years as Deputy Principal of Ridley College, Melbourne, followed by three years spent in founding the Trinity Episcopal School for Ministry.

Marcus told of Alf's long battle with the worsening affects of Parkinson's Disease, his work in conjunction with Christian literature and his other interests. He gave facets of Alf's personality:

> He was very human, with a great zest for life and an endless fund of stories. He was, himself, the subject of all sorts of stories — some true, some legendary. He was always so alive and vital; he filled the house where he was. Warm-hearted and generous, he had a great gift for friendship, was always on the watch for souls and was a personal evangelist par excellence. He was a man in whose life the reality of prayer was often seen in overwhelming clarity, and he was a man of faith out of the ordinary. He dared to believe in the God of the impossible. His love of Africa; his total dedication as a missionary; his gift for personal evangelism marked him out as one of the two or three most remarkable of all my Australian-born contemporaries.

Marcus concluded with David's words, 'Know ye not that a prince and a great man is fallen this day in Israel?'. 'As a prince he had power with God and prevailed, and his greatness was seen as one who was totally surrendered to God. Wherein did the secret lie? He was in Christ Jesus by the direct intervention of God's grace: for He alone was his wisdom and righteousness, for sanctification for redemption.'

After the singing of 'Praise to the Holiest in the Height', Archbishop Penman spoke of the facsimile messages of 28th June which he had received from Dodoma. The Archbishop and Primate of Tanzania, the Most Reverend John Ramadhani spoke of the shock and grief with which the news was received in Dodoma, and how deeply they would feel the loss. Bishop Alpha Mohamed sent a message from himself, Marion and the children asking the comfort of the Lord Jesus for the bereaved, and as well as the message from Mdimi Mhogolo, quoted at the funeral service. All the bishops of the seven dioceses formed out of the original DCT of Alf's episcopate, sent a combined message of comfort and condolence. They said:

> We praise the Lord for the foundation he laid down on which we

continue to build God's Church. We will miss him, but we are sure he is now with the Lord, and one day we will join him.

Archbishop Penman concluded with a prayer for the Church of the Province of Tanzania and dismissed us with his blessing.

(It is with great sadness that I reflect on the fact that this service was one of the very last to have David Penman's voice and presence in Melbourne. At that time no one could foresee that in three months' time he, himself, would be with the Lord. Almost at once after Alf's memorial service, he left for overseas and reached Manila for the World Conference on Evangelism in which he played a leading role. On his return to Melbourne he had only one Sunday when he ministered and then was stricken with the heart-attack which was to take him from us.

I am deeply grateful for his loving and unstinting efforts to inform Tanzania of Alf's death, then to fit in the funeral, so far away in Paynesville, into a week crammed full of appointments. One other gracious act was to arrange to have photographs taken at the church and cemetery on the previous Friday. Jean Penman handed these to me in person, already printed, at the Thanksgiving Service on Monday.)

After the Cathedral service friends gathered in the Chapter House for a cup of tea. Alf would have been delighted to note those who had flown down from Sydney. Sir Marcus and Lady Loane, Bishop John Reid, Bishop Kenneth Short (the Dean of St Andrew's Cathedral, Sydney), also John Denton and Kevin Engel. Many many Victorian friends were present. The memory of this service will bring fresh blessing to me as I contemplate it from time to time.

On the 30th June, the day of Alf's funeral, Marcus, John Reid and Ken Short were robing to take part in a service in St Andrew's Cathedral, Sydney, in commemoration of Archbishop Cranmer. Prior to the service Marcus suggested that there should be a Thanksgiving or Memorial Service for Alf in Sydney, that John Reid should preach and that Ken — as Dean of St Andrew's — arrange the Service.

So it was arranged for me to come up to Sydney for a special service on 10th August, as many former CMS missionaries from Tanzania who were now living in Sydney would like to share in it. Marcus invited me to come and stay in their home at that time.

The service in Sydney was in the form of Evensong and was led by the Dean, Jack Shellard, an educational missionary in Tanzania during our time there, read the lesson from the Epistle to the Hebrews 12:22-13:7. Enid Stahl, a nursing sister who became the Mothers' Union organiser in Tanzania later on, gave a Reflection on Alf. She had worked in Mackay House for some time and had met with him daily. The Reverend Kevin Engel also gave a Reflection;

both Enid's and Kevin's messages were appreciative and helpful. The Reverend Max Corbett led the prayers and the address was given by Bishop John Reid who had known Alf for many years.

Bishop Reid's text was from Psalm 126:6 — 'He that goes forth weeping, bearing the seed for sowing, shall come home with shouts of joy, bringing his sheaves with him.'

He spoke of Alf's early days and call to ministry, how he learned early in life to live by faith, and appeared to have a gift of faith by which he took on big projects when only slender resources were apparent.

Bishop Reid spoke of Alf's prayer life and how God answered those prayers. He spoke of his extraordinary achievements and the enthusiasm which motivated him — as it would an undergraduate — even in middle life. So much was achieved and so many prayers answered, it was tempting to think it was all so easy. But there were periods when the need for capital, for all the many projects being developed, was so urgent that it was a daily cause of concern and Alf was driven to earnest prayer for God's supply. Alf often said that if it were not for his past experience of God's faithfulness, he would be afraid. He learned to trust implicitly when times were difficult.

In speaking of Alf's many achievements in his so-called 'retirement', Bishop Reid referred to what he regarded as his most remarkable achievement: what he accomplished for God in America. The very thought of Alf Stanway heading up a new seminary was a most unlikely suggestion but it turned out in performance to be really brilliant. Bishop Reid then referred to Alf's illness and decline into silence, which on entering God's Kingdom turned to shouts of joy in the presence of his Lord.

Marcus and Patricia arranged for a morning coffee gathering when the Reverend Denis and Elizabeth Wann who had served in Morogoro many years ago were able to spend time with me. An afternoon function was held at their home for quite a few of our former colleagues in Tanzania — a happy occasion for us all.

There was one more notable memorial service to be held and that took place in USA at Ambridge in the Chapel of the Trinity Episcopal School for Ministry. Alf's death had occurred during the long vacation of the seminary. Dr John Rodgers arranged for a Service on 12th October and advertised it widely. Members of the Board of Trustees met that day and, at night, there was an informal gathering when many people gave personal testimonies of their knowledge of Alf. Some were past graduates who came from afar, one from California. The next morning there was a service of Holy Communion when the Reverend Peter Moore preached, whose association with Alf went back to 1962. He came down from

Toronto, where he was then ministering, to be the special speaker for this Thanksgiving Service. He had been a foundation member of the FOW and the first Chairman of Trinity's Board of Trustees and is still a great protagonist for the School.

Peter preached from Isaiah Chapter 61, with special reference to verse 4: 'They shall build up the ancient ruins, they raise up the former devastations, they shall repair the ruined cities, the devastations of many generations'.

He spoke of Alf coming as the chosen servant of the Lord, modelling for them what a true servant was really like, to build up new hope and life and vigour for the Episcopal Church.

The Societies in Australia which Alf had supported sent appreciative tributes. From CMS came messages from the Reverend David Claydon, Federal Secretary for Australia, and from the Victorian Branch Secretary, the Reverend Edwin Lang. ACLS inserted a beautiful tribute in the Obituary Notices of the daily newspapers, and Gerald Davis, Editor of *Church Scene* gave his own personal tribute:

> I am one of many who will miss Alf Stanway. He was a director of our company from its foundation, apart from his three years in the USA, until eight months ago. His commitment to our work, his ability to take long views and his steadiness when we were under stress made him our human anchor.

New Life, an inter-denominational Christian weekly printed a very full article about the Melbourne Thanksgiving Service, and Margaret McKechnie wrote an article for the Ridley Report on Alf's days there as a student and later as Deputy Principal. The October editions of the CMS family magazine *Checkpoint* published an article about eight former CMS missionaries who had died in 1989. The following is the section about Alf from page 7 of the magazine:

> Bishop Alfred Stanway, the third Bishop of the Diocese of Central Tanganyika (DCT) died on Tuesday 27th June, two days after the consecration in Dodoma of the Reverend Godfrey Mdimi Mhogolo as the fifth Bishop of Central Tanganyika. During his episcopacy from 1951 to 1971, Alf Stanway sought to develop national leadership combined with spiritual insight and Christian character. He was convinced that no church remains alive when its individual members have no knowledge of Christ as Saviour.
>
> Bishop Stanway, a Victorian, was born in 1908. From the time of his conversion he dedicated his outstanding gifts to the service of his Saviour. After training at Ridley College and a curacy, he was accepted as a missionary of the Church Missionary Society of Australia in 1936. After some years in the Diocese of Mombasa, he was transferred to Nyanza where he was Rural Dean from 1945 to 1947. From 1948 to 1951 he was Secretary for the African Council and Archdeacon for the African work of the Diocese.

On 2nd February, 1951 he was consecrated in Westminster Abbey as Bishop of DCT. He was enthroned in the Cathedral of the Holy Spirit, Dodoma, on 11th March, 1951. As bishop he used his considerable gifts of leadership, spiritual insight, forward planning and financial acumen with great effect.

He recognised the needs of the European and Asian populations in Tanganyika as well as those of the African church. He saw the need for Christian literature, bookshops, adult literacy and more and better theological education for clergy, catechists and other lay people. The Bible School movement owes its birth to his vision. He encouraged initiative in others and helped others find and use their talents. There were no hidden agendas in his dealings with people.

Without any bias he singled out those needing special attention, whether in Africa or elsewhere on his travels throughout the world. He and his wife, Marjory, were 'parents' to many missionaries in their time on the field (they celebrated their Golden Wedding Anniversary on 3rd June this year). Without children themselves, they nevertheless had many 'children', who have kept in contact over the years and who remember him with great love, affection and respect.

Alfred Stanway was not afraid of change. In 1955 the Reverend Yohana Omari was consecrated as the first African Assistant Bishop of DCT. In 1963 the Diocese of Victoria Nyanza was created out of DCT, then in 1965 the Diocese of Morogoro and in 1966 the Diocese of Western Tanganyika. In this time CMS continued to send missionaries who were mainly involved in Diocesan institutions. He was bishop when the Church of the Province of Tanzania was created in 1970. He encouraged national leadership in word and deed.

When he resigned from the Diocese in 1971, his place was taken by Bishop Yohana Madinda, a man of great spirituality and vision whose episcopacy, until his death in February this year, was marked by a great desire for people to know Jesus as Saviour.

From August 1971 to September 1975 Bishop Stanway was Deputy Principal of Ridley College. During this time he and Kevin Engel founded the Australian Christian Literature Society (ACLS).

From September 1975 to November 1978 he was in America setting up Trinity Episcopal School for Ministry in Pittsburgh. So in retirement he still encouraged Christian outreach and growth by literature and theological training of all Christians. He is still remembered in America with awe and affection.

On the Stanways' return to Australia, they worshipped at St Andrew's, Glen Waverley. He took Bible Studies until ill-health stopped this. He encouraged and supported the work of many Christian activities in prayer and giving and never stopped encouraging the African church. Despite failing health, he continued to give his support and counsel to all who came to him. In a letter this year he said, 'I have no axes to grind now and can give an unbiased ear and opinion'. To the end he served his Saviour and was always suggesting or encouraging new ventures for building up the church and for evangelism.

A memorial service was held in St Paul's Cathedral, Melbourne on Monday, 3rd July. The Most Reverend Marcus Loane, a long-standing

friend and former Primate of Australia, gave the address. He started
with David's lament for Abner 'Know ye not that there is a prince and
a great man fallen this day in Israel?' (2 Samuel 3:38). However, Alf
would rather have had 'You are in Christ Jesus by God's Act: for He
has made Him our wisdom, He is our righteousness; in Him we are
consecrated and set free' (1 Corinthians 1:30). As freed people let us
consecrate ourselves to Jesus Christ, our righteousness.

Other tributes came from many parts of the world. In the September Newsletter of TESM — called *Seed and Harvest* — a profile of
Alf was printed with comments and tributes from many who knew
him. They spoke of his faith and his prayer life, his careful
stewardship, his pastoral care and his vision for renewal. Dr
Rodgers concluded, in his letter, with his own assessment of Alf as
a man with a gift of faith and trust:

> through Alf we found God teaching us to rely on Him more and more.
> Alf had one of the quickest minds I have ever met. What was
> wonderful was that all of his mental ability was deeply surrendered to
> Christ as Saviour and Lord, as indeed was all his life ... Supremely
> Alf was a man of prayer. His lectures on prayer, even though they are
> difficult to understand because of the effect of his Parkinson's
> Disease, are worth every bit of effort to hear.

Edward Abell, a trustee since the School's founding, remarked that
Alf always used 'his excellent business judgement and practical
mind in approaching even spiritual problems'. The Council of the
Belgrave Heights Convention recorded an article about Alf in the
Minutes of its Annual Meeting at Belgrave in December. It spoke
of his long association with the Council and the contribution he
made throughout the 55 years following his joining the Council in
1934. It said, among other things:

> He was among the most notable Council members in the Conven-
> tion's history, and when he was able to attend meetings, our Council
> was strengthened by his wisdom and enriched by his unswerving
> devotion to his Lord. We thank God upon every remembrance of him.

I want to close this long story with my own tribute to Alf. My
honest assessment, which I hope is unprejudiced, is that he was
the most practical Christian I knew, though I admit I knew no
others to the same degree as I knew him.

As a child his mother had him commit to memory these words
(I do not know their origin):

> Sow a thought
> and you reap an action
> Sow an action
> and you reap a habit.
> Sow a habit
> and you reap a character.
> Sow a character
> and you reap a destiny.

These words must have taken deep root in his life for as long as I knew him he was always 'forming habits', based on his understanding of Scripture. As others have said elsewhere in these pages, 'he applied Scripture to life'.

Between ourselves we often quoted principles which arose in this way as the occasion demanded, such as:

> 'Don't vindicate yourself'.
> 'You win by losing'.
> 'The stronger character gives in first' — this arose out of the teaching in Romans Chapter 14 about those who are weak in faith.
> 'Move man through God by prayer alone'.
> 'Be quick to forgive'.

These and many other such sayings were sprinkled through our days. From the very beginning of our life together I was exhorted to form good habits too, the habit of a siesta at the tropical coast, the habit of having language books always under my eyes to attract me to study and, in our very last communication on the Sunday before he died, he exhorted me to 'form a habit' of always leaving coins for him to buy newspapers! (I had forgotten to do this.)

I do thank God for the fifty years He gave us together. There is no relationship which can compare with that which is possible between a husband and his wife when both are committed to Christ and to each other, 'each for the other, and both for the Lord'.

I knew Alf as kind, generous, loving and caring. He was also warm-hearted, cheerful and optimistic. In counselling a young couple about to be married in Dodoma, I learned from them that Alf advised the groom to try, whenever it was possible, to do what his wife asked him to do. He told them that he had made up his mind very early in our marriage that, when I asked him to do something for me, he would get up and do it at once. On reflection I realised this was so, though he had never told me of this resolve.

He was never secretive and was not afraid of his whole life being open before others. He was not interested in self-advancement or ambitious for himself. He believed God ordered our lives. He trusted me utterly and accepted my management of our home.

He enjoyed beauty and order but was never wedded to possessions, and at all times was willing to 'hang loosely' to material things. He loved our home-life, and when far away — although he always went off joyously — he would write often, sometimes every day, and say how much he was looking forward to being back at home, and counting the days to that time.

I also proved him wise in decision-making which was a tremendous relief to me, and I miss this aspect of our partnership very much indeed. There is peace in my heart in knowing that there is no regret for anything in the years given us to spend together, and that memory brings only happiness of past joys and the anticipation of meeting again in the new life to come.

I will always be grateful that I took the opportunity on the anniversary of our fifty years together to thank him for what I had learned from him of Christian principles and priorities. I am sure there will be many others who, with me, can say:

'He died, but through his faith he is still speaking'.
Hebrews 11:4 (RSV)